# ENCYCLOPAEDIA OF INDIAN GOVERNMENT: PROGRAMMES AND POLICIES

# ENCYCLOPAEDIA
# OF
# INDIAN GOVERNMENT: PROGRAMMES AND POLICIES

Vol. 3

Rural Development

*Edited by*

**Satish Tiwari**

**ANMOL PUBLICATIONS PVT. LTD.**

**NEW DELHI - 110 002 (INDIA)**

**ANMOL PUBLICATIONS PVT. LTD.**
4374/4B, Ansari Road, Daryaganj
New Delhi - 110 002

*Encyclopaedia of Indian Government: Programmes and Policies*



First Edition, 2000
ISBN 81-261-0515-1 (Set)



PRINTED IN INDIA

Published by J.L. Kumar for Anmol Publications Pvt. Ltd., New Delhi - 110 002 and Printed at Mehra Offset Press, Delhi

# Contents


*Preface* *vii*

1. Employment and Poverty Alleviation 1

2. India's Population: Issues and Options 66

3. Rural Development 181

4. Special Component Plan and Tribal Development Planning 262

5. Wastelands Development 287

# Preface

Encyclopaedia of Indian Government: Programmes and Policies contains authoritative information on about fifty departmental policies and their future developmental programmes.

Organised to be completed in 40 volumes, this gigantic work covers Agriculture; Atomic Energy; Chemicals and Fertilizers; Coal; Commerce; Communication; Culture; Defence; Education; Environment and Forests; External Affairs; Finance; Food & Consumer Affairs; Food Processing Industries; Health and Family Welfare; Home Affairs and Internal Security; Human Resources; Industry; Information and Broadcasting; Labour; Law, Justice and Company Affairs; Non-conventional Energy Sources; Ocean Development; Parliamentary Affairs; Personnel, Public Grievances and Pensions; Petroleum and Natural Gas; Planning and Programme Implementation; Planning and Statistics; Posts and Telegraphs; Power; Rural Development; Science and Technology; Social Justice and Empowerment; Space; States Affairs; Steel; Steel and Mines; Sugar and Edible Oils; Surface Transport; Textiles; Tourism; Urban Development; Water Resources; Women and Child development etc.

Based on the information derived from authoritative sources, this work contains authentic facts and figures. I am deeply beholden to all the scholars whose writings are cited or substantially made use of in the present work. I am also thankful to Anmol Publications Pvt. Ltd. for undertaking publication of this encyclopaedia. I am solely responsible for shortcomings in presentation of matter.

Encyclopaedic in nature, this will prove a dependable reference work for scholars and academics besides those appearing for different competitive examinations.

**—Satish Tiwari**

# 1

# Employment and Poverty Alleviation

**Wage employment programmes**

The high incidence of poverty in rural India is directly related to prevalence of unemployment and underemployment on a large scale. Majority of the rural population is landless and sustains entirely on wage employment. While the self-employment programmes are intended to remove poverty on a sustainable basis, there is need to take care of the wage employment needs of the rural poor. The rural workforce continues to suffer due to excessive seasonality of employment, lack of wage employment opportunities and low wage rates. Migration of labour, discrimination between wages paid to men and women, distressed child labour etc. are therefore, common features of rural areas.

Efforts to provide wage employment, as a short-run strategy for alleviation of rural poverty has been a major component of development planning in India. The major programmes under implementation in this direction are the Jawahar Rozgar Yojana (JRY), Employment Assurance Scheme (EAS). The Million Wells Scheme (MWS) is also one such programme which helps the beneficiary to acquire an asset for his/her sustained self-employment on land-based activities.

### Jawahar Rozgar Yojana

The Jawahar Rozgar Yojana (JRY) was started in April i 1989 by merging the on-going National Rural Employment Programme (NREP) and Rural Landless Employment Guarantee Programme (RLEGP) into a single rural employment programme.

#### Objectives

The main objective of JRY is generation of additional gainful employment for the unemployed and underemployed persons, both men and women, in rural areas. The secondary objective of the Yojana is creation of durable community and social assets. The Yojana has been designed to arrest the seasonality of wage employment and provide a positive impact on the prevailing wage rates in rural areas. It also contributes to improvement in the quality of life of the rural poor by providing supplementary source of income through wage employment and by creating community and social assets.

#### Target group and special safeguards for certain sections

The JRY is targeted to benefit people living below the poverty line in rural areas. Preference, however, is given to the Scheduled Castes, the Scheduled Tribes and freed bonded labourers. At least 30 % of employment is to be provided to women under the Yojana. 22.5% of funds have to be to spent on individual beneficiary schemes for the direct benefit of SCs/STs.

#### Allocation procedure

JRY is a Centrally Sponsored Scheme. The expenditure under the programme is shared between the Centre and the States in the ratio of 80:20. Central assistance is provided to the States on the basis of proportion of rural poor in a State/UT to the total rural poor in the country. From the States to the districts, the allocation is made on the index of backwardness formulated on the basis of equal weightage to the proportion of rural Scheduled Caste/Scheduled Tribes population in a district to total rural SC/ST population in the State and the inverse of per capital production of agricultural workers in that district.

**Implementing agencies**

JRY is implemented in a decentralised fashion by the Panchayati Raj Institutions. The major share of funds are utilized at the village level by the Gram Panchayats. At the district level the responsibility of co-ordination, guidance and monitoring is vested with the DRDA/Zilla Parishad (ZP). Funds under JRY are distributed among DRDAs/ZPs, Intermediate Panchayats / Village Panchayats in a district in the ratio of 15:15:70.

The resources allocated to DRDA/ZP, intermediate panchayats and gram panchayats are to be spent within the geographical boundaries of each unit. These funds cannot be diverted under any circumstances except where two or more intermediate level panchayats / Gram Panchayats decide to pool the resources together to take up a work for their common benefit.

**Financial and physical performance under JRY**

Since inception in 1989-90 upto 1997-98, the Yojana has been able to generate a total of 70003.32 lakh mandays, of employment. The expenditure during this period was Rs. 27649.00 crores. The year-wise financial and physical performance under JRY since 1989-90 is given in Table- 1. 1 and 1.2 respectively.

**Performance during 1998-99**

In 1998-99, the Central allocation for the Yojana was Rs. 2078.44 crores. Against this, releases made to the States/ UTs are Rs. 1398.19 crores upto November, 1998. The total availability of funds with the States/ UTs, however, is Rs. 2222.16 crores which included States, UTs, matching share of Rs. 347.67 crores and opening balance of Rs. 476.30 crores. Against this the expenditure reported is Rs. 1243.71 crores upto November, 1998. The employment generated is 1902.80 lakh mandays during this period against the target of 3966.57 lakh mandays for 1998-99. The State-wise details are given in Annexures - III & IV.

**Monitoring of JRY**

The performance of JRY is monitored regularly by the Centre and the State Governments. To facilitate proper monitoring, emphasis is laid on building a strong data base and periodical feedback through monthly and annual progress reports. The physical and financial achievement under the programme is monitored at the Central level through monthly and annual progress reports received from the States. The Department of Rural Employment and Poverty Alleviation has evolved a system to ensure that the guidelines are followed strictly. The utilisation certificates, audit reports and other parameters such as matching grants from the States, minimum expenditure etc. are examined before the release of second instalment. Periodical reviews are carried out by the Central Government in the meeting of Secretaries of the State Governments. Senior officials of the Ministry also see operation of various Rural Development programmes during their visits to the States under the Area Officers Scheme. The scheme is supervised by officials of DRDA/ZP at the district level. The State Level Coordination Committee (SLCC) for the rural development programmes monitors the programmes at the State level. State Government officials also inspect the programmes.

For better monitoring and to check diversion, embezzlement and misappropriation of rural development funds including JRY, Government of India has issued instructions to all the State Governments for constitution of Vigilance and Monitoring Committees at State/district and block level. In many States these committees have been constituted and have started functioning.

**Concurrent evaluation of JRY**

The Ministry of Rural Areas and Employment had undertaken concurrent evaluation of JRY from June, 1993 to May, 1994 covering 470 districts, 933 blocks and 4700 Village Panchayats. The findings of the Report in brief are as follows:

Among the positive aspects highlighted in the Evaluation Report are that nearly 82.16% of available funds were spent on community development projects; construction of rural link roads received the highest priority; average wages paid per manday of the unskilled workers were more or less on the lines of minimum wages prescribed under the Act; the wage and non-wage component of the expenditure was 52.84:47.16; by and large, payment of wages to workers was made either on a daily basis or weekly basis; muster rolls were maintained; of the total assets created, 76.11 % were found to be in good/satisfactory condition; the share of SCs/STs in generation of employment was satisfactory; roughly, 11 mandays of employment were created during the reference period; family members of the workers also received employment during the last 30 days preceding the date of survey and 76.96% of the assets were created by village panchayat.

The evaluation, however, has highlighted some inadequacies. More than 50 % of elected panchayat heads were not imparted training for implementation of JRY works. The share of women in employment generation was less than the prescribed 30%. 49.97% of the works could not be completed on account of shortage of funds. Some discrepancies were observed between payment of wages to male and female workers. The use of locally available material in various works undertaken by Panchayats was not appreciable.

**Recently introduced important changes in the yojana**

The Yojana is reviewed regularly. In light of the outcome of these reviews and experience gained through time in implementing the Yojana, changes are brought about in the guidelines to sharpen it's focus on the genuinely needy and deserving in tune with the social and moral commitments towards socially deprived sections of the society. Some recently introduced changes are as follows:

- preference in employment under the Yojana to the parents of child labourers withdrawn from hazardous/non-hazardous occupation;
- foodgrains to be given as a part of wages under JRY at the rate of 1 kg. per person-day at the same price fixed for the people below the poverty line under Targeted PDS. Distribution of foodgrains, however, is optional on the part of the State Governments;
- earmarking of three per cent of the funds to create barrier free infrastructures like a pucca path or a street connecting the house of the beneficiaries or a sloped entrance in the house of the beneficiaries or in public places like Panchayat Ghar, schools, hospitals, park etc. in favour of physically handicapped persons living below poverty line in rural areas;
- keeping of funds under JRY in separate saving bank accounts of ZP/DRDA.

**New initiatives and looking to the future**

JRY is implemented by the village panchayats with active participation of people. The programme, therefore, empowers the village panchayats and the people. The programme also contributes significantly in creating social and community assets and economic infrastructures at the village level. In order that the panchayats have reasonable autonomy in implementation of the programme and have freedom from bureaucratic control in approval and technical scrutiny of the works and at the same time become effective in development of the basic infrastructures at the village level, steps are being taken to restructure and entrust the implementation of JRY entirely to the Village Panchayats.

**Employment assurance scheme**

The Employment Assurance Scheme (EAS) was introduced w.e.f. 2nd October, 1993 in the rural areas of 1778 blocks of 261 districts in which the Revamped Public Distribution System (RPDS) was in operation. The blocks selected were in the drought prone areas, desert areas, tribal areas and hill areas.

**Expansion of EAS**

During 1994-95, EAS was extended to 409 blocks under DPAP/DDP and Modified Area Development Approach (MADA) blocks having larger concentration of tribal population. In March, 1995 the scheme was further extended to 256 blocks (233 flood prone blocks in the States of Uttar Pradesh, Bihar and Assam, and 23 blocks of Jammu and Kashmir in view of the special conditions prevailing there). The Intensified Jawahar Rozgar Yojana (IJRY) was merged with EAS w.e.f. 1. 1. 1996. Consequently, 722 non-EAS blocks in 120 IJRY districts were also covered under EAS. On universlisation, the remaining blocks were covered under the scheme in two phases Le 1123 blocks in 1996-97 and 1121 blocks in 1997-98. At present, the scheme is being implemented in all the 5448 rural blocks of the country.

**Objectives**

The primary objective of the Employment Assurance Scheme is to provide gainful employment during lean agricultural season in manual work to all able bodied adults in rural areas who are in need and desirous of work, but cannot find it. The secondary objective is the creation of economic infrastructure and community assets for sustained employment and development.

**Salient features**

- The scheme is operative in all the rural blocks of the country.
- It is a demand driven scheme with no fixed earmarking of annual funds for any district or block.
- Expenditure is shared between the Centre and the States on 80:20 basis.
- The Central assistance under the scheme is directly released block-wise to DRDA/ZPs based on the demand for wage employment and expenditure.
- All adult rural poor normally residing in the villages are covered.
- A maximum of 2 adults per family are *provided* the assurance of up to 100 days of employment. New works will not be opened under this scheme if employment potential is available through plan and non-plan works already in progress and the assurance could be fulfilled by utilising the same.
- Works should be labour intensive which result in the creation of durable productive assets.
- As an individual beneficiary oriented scheme, on

the lands of BPL families, horticulture development is a permitted activity.

- Implementing agencies are Block Development Officers, District Officers of various line Departments and PRIs at all three levels.
- The desirous workers have to get themselves registered with village level workers or Gram Panchayats and are issued a family card.
- When about 10 workers demand work, new projects can be started by the block level officer for providing employment.
- The State Level Coordination Committee for the Rural Development programmes is responsible for the overall supervision, guidance and monitoring of EAS.

**Block-wise entitlement of funds under EAS**

As per the present classification of blocks into 'A', '13' and 'C' categories, the central share of each instalment to the blocks is Rs. 40 lakhs, Rs. 30 lakhs and Rs. 20 lakhs respectively. The State share is Rs. 10 lakhs, Rs. 7.50 lakhs and Rs. 5 lakhs respectively. The shelf of projects for new works to be taken up in each of the categories should not exceed 150% of the funds expected by a block in two installments.

The classification of the blocks into 'A', '13' and 'C' categories was made earlier on the basis of the criteria of backwardness and size of the population. These were mostly blocks in hilly, tribal, drought prone and desert areas. These criteria were followed upto the merger of IJRY with EAS. As per this criteria blocks with population above 196287 were put in 'A' category; blocks with population between 196287 and 65585 were put in '13' category and blocks with population below 65585 were put in 'C' category. Consequent upon universalisation of EAS all the remaining blocks have been put in 'C' category for the purpose of determining the entitlement of funds by each.

**Financial and physical performance under EAS**

Since inception of EAS in 1993-94 to 1997-98, a total of 15447.33 lakh mandays of employment have been generated by utilising Rs. 8205.20 crores.

**Performance during 1998-99**

During 1998-99, the Central allocation for EAS is Rs. 1990 crores. Against this, releases made to the States/UTs are Rs. 1564.21 crores upto November 1998. The total availability of funds with the States/ UTs, however, is Rs. 2816.93 crores which includes States/UTs matching share of Rs. 391.05 crores and opening balance of Rs. 861.67 crores. Against this, the expenditure reported is Rs. 1571.97 crores (upto November, 1998). The employment generated is 2376.14 lakh mandays during the period. The State-wise details are given in Annexures - V & VI.

The year-wise financial and physical performance under EAS since 1993-94 is given below in Table- 1.3.

**Number of persons registered under EAS**

A total of 4.12 crore persons have been registered under EAS in various States/UTs since inception of the scheme upto November, 1998.

**Evaluation**

The Programme Evaluation Organisation (PEO) Wing of Planning Commission is in the process of evaluating the programme.

**Some recently Introduced changes In EAS**

- Panchayati Raj Institutions of all three levels have been included as Implementing Agencies.

- The shelf of Projects would be prepared based on suggestions of Gram Sabhas and Panchayats as well as from other sources like line departments, people's representatives etc. as per felt needs of the people.
- Registration of wage-seekers would be done in Gram Panchayats and work-site etc.
- The implementing agencies have been permitted to utilise one person from among the beneficiaries group as animator/leader/ facilitator in maintenance of muster roll, payment of wages, monitoring of quality of works etc. Such person will be eligible to receive wages applicable to unskilled labourers.
- The States have been requested to evolve and publish "Rural Standard Schedule of Rates" as has already been done by some States to eliminate the role of contractors in EAS works.
- To make the implementation of the programme more transparent instructions have been issued to all the states to exhibit prominently the details of funds received, works sanctioned, estimated cost, quantity of material used, workers engaged and wage rates etc. in the Panchayat Office/work site. The accounts of the Gram Panchayats are also open for scrutiny by the Gram Sabha.
- To avoid multiplicity of Committees and as per the recommendation of the Standing Committee of Parliament a decision has been taken to merge District and Block level EAS Committees with the existing Vigilance and Monitoring Committees.
- In case of Karbi-Anglong and North-Kachar hill districts of Assam the Principal Secretaries of the respective Autonomous Hill Councils have been declared as Implementing Agencies of EAS in place of the Deputy Commissioners.

### Million wells scheme

Million Wells Scheme (MWS) was launched as a sub-scheme of National Rural Employment Programme (NREP) and Rural Landless Employment Guarantee Programme (RLEGP) during 1988-89. It continued as a sub-scheme of Jawahar Rozgar Yojana from April 1989 to 31.12.95. From 1. 1.96, MWS is an independent scheme.

### Objectives

The objective of the scheme is to provide open irrigation wells free of cost to poor, small and marginal farmers who are below the poverty line and freed bonded labourers.

### Target group

Up to 1992-93, the target group for MWS comprised of small and marginal farmers belonging to SCs/STs and freed bonded labourers. From 1993-94 onwards, MWS has been extended to include poor small and marginal farmers belonging to non-SC/ST category as well, who are below the poverty line and are listed in the IRDP register of the village. The financial assistance provided to SC/ ST poor, small and marginal farmers under MWS, however, must not be less than two-thirds of the total funds utilised under the scheme in any year.

### Allocation of funds

The MWS is a Centrally sponsored scheme. Funds under the scheme are shared between the Centre and the States on 80:20 basis. State-wise allocation is arrived at on the basis of the proportion of rural poor in a State to the total rural poor in the country. State Governments fix the district-wise allocation and physical targets keeping in view the size of the un-irrigated land in a district, potential for well irrigation and need for improvements of land held by the rural poor.

**Works to be taken up under MWS**

MWS is primarily intended to provide open wells. Tube wells and bore wells are not to be taken up under this scheme. However, where wells are not feasible due to geological factors, funds under the scheme could be utilised for other works of minor irrigation like irrigation tanks, water harvesting structures and also for the development of lands belonging to the target group. The fund cannot be diverted for any other purpose.

Each well/irrigation source constructed under MWS has to be located in the holding of the beneficiary and an entry to that effect should be made in the revenue records.

The beneficiaries themselves undertake the construction of wells through their own labour and by hiring local labour for which they are paid. Engagement of contractors is strictly prohibited under the scheme.

**Cost/area norms**

The cost/area norms in regard to works under MWS is decided by a committee comprising of Chief Secretary/ Secretary (Rural Development), Secretary (Planning), Secretary (Irrigation) and Chief Engineer, Minor Irrigation of the State.

**Implementing/executive agency**

At the district level DRDA/ZP is the implementing agency of the scheme. But the beneficiaries themselves execute the construction of wells under MWS through their own labour for which they are paid or by hiring local labour. In no case the work should be entrusted to contractors.

**Performance under million wells scheme**

Since inception of the scheme in 1988-89 till 1997-98, a total of 12,63,090 wells have been constructed under

MWS with an expenditure of Rs. 4728.17 crores. The total number of beneficiaries is 12,63,090. The year-wise resources allocated, utilised and wells constructed since inception under MWS is given in table 1.4.

**Performance during 1998-99 (Upto November, 1998)**

The Central allocation under MWS for 1998-99 is Rs. 448.97 crores. Against this, Rs. 228.14 crores have been released to States/UTs upto November, 1998. During this period, a total of 49821 wells have been constructed with an expenditure of Rs. 225.89 crores. The State-wise details of allocation and releases, category-wise expenditure and number of wells constructed are given in Annexure VII, VIII and IX

**Monitoring and supervision**

The DRDA/ZP is also responsible for monitoring and supervision of the scheme in the district. The state level monitoring is the responsibility of the State Level Coordination Committee of the State. At the State level, Secretary, Rural Development is the nodal agency for implementation of the scheme. Apart from the above, the implementation of the scheme is also supervised by the Monitoring and Vigilance Committees set up at the State, District and Block levels for all the programmes of the Ministry.

At the Central level, the MWS is regularly monitored through monthly and annual progress reports from the districts/states. The Area Officers of the Ministry of Rural Areas and Employment also provide feedback on the implementation of MWS.

**Evaluation**

A regular Concurrent Evaluation of MWS by this Ministry is under process. However, some State specific Concurrent Evaluation (September-December, 1995) by the Lal Bahadur Shastri National Academy of Administration (LBSNAA), Mussoorie has revealed that the scheme is definitely a success as it has provided water sources for agriculture and other activities. Similarly, in an evaluation of Rural Development Programme in Andhra Pradesh conducted by the Institute of Resource Development and Social Management, it has been brought out that MWS has helped the farmers by providing an assured irrigation facility for agriculture. The farmers raise mostly commercial crops. The scheme has helped the farmers to enhance both crop production and productivity. As a result of this the beneficiary household income has gone up from Rs. 750 to Rs. 2500 per month. These findings of the evaluation studies show that MWS has been useful and effective in alleviation of poverty particularly of the rural SC/ST poor, marginal/small farmers and providing income appreciation on a long term basis.

These evaluations, however, also reveal some weaknesses of the scheme. In many cases, the land of the beneficiary continues to be single cropped area. Motivation to procure pump sets and use it for a second crop has been found to be inadequate. The beneficiaries are not able to make optimal utilisation of the wells because of lack of complementary facilities like lifting devices (pump sets) and power to energize.

**Recently introduced changes in MWS**

Some recently introduced changes in MWS are as follows:

- Strict compliance to ensure 2/3rd of MWS expenditure for the benefit of SCs/STs;
- Providing lifting device to the beneficiaries wherever needed under IRDP/SC/ST Finance Corporations etc.;

- Educating beneficiaries in improved farm practices through agricultural extension programmes;
- Active involvement of the Panchayati Raj Institutions in planning and selection of MWS beneficiaries. The village Panchayat has to select the beneficiaries which have to be then approved by the DRDA/ZPs;
- Reservation of 3% allocation for the year for disabled persons. This reservation would be horizontal reservation Le disabled persons belonging to SCs/STs and others would fall in their respective categories;
- Fixation of district-wise physical and financial targets from 1997-98 onwards which was not done earlier;
- Priority to be given to MWS beneficiaries under the horticulture development component of Employment Assurance Scheme.

## Self-employment and entrepreneurship development programmes

### Integrated rural development programme

Poverty eradication has been one of the major objectives of planned development. The strategy and policy of direct attack on poverty by way of target approach for rural poor came into being in the Fourth Five Year Plan. With the main objective of improving the asset base of the poor and to involve the poor in the production/income generation processes of the economy, Integrated Rural Development Programme (IRDP) was initiated. IRDP was taken up initially in 2300 blocks and has been extended to all the blocks of the country since 2nd October, 1980.

**Programme implementation**

*Programme*

IRDP aims at providing income generating assets and self-employment opportunities for the rural poor. Assistance under IRDP is given to a target group of rural poor belonging to families Below Poverty Line (BPL), in the form of subsidy by the Government and term credit by financial institutions.

**Criteria for allocation of funds to the states**

Allocation of funds to States is being made by the Central Government in proportion to the poverty levels in each State on the basis of official estimates of the Planning Commission. These official estimates of poverty are arrived at by the Planning Commission based on the National Sample Survey Organisation Consumer Expenditure Surveys conducted every five years.

Devolution of funds to districts is based on a formula evolved by the respective State Government. Further devolution to the Blocks is done by the Governing Body of the DRDA based on the criteria approved by it.

**Target group**

The target group consists of families of small and marginal farmers, agricultural labourers and rural artisans etc. whose per capita monthly expenditure does not exceed the poverty line (ranging between Rs. 216.65 and Rs. 327.48 for different States/UTs) as estimated by the Planning Commission. Currently, the Below Poverty Line census is being carried out in all the States and the revised poverty line will be used to categorise BPL families. Within the target group, special safeguards have been provided by reservation of

- 50% benefits for SCs/STs,

- 40% for women and
- 3% for physically handicapped persons.
- Priority is also to be given to women headed households, assignees, of surplus land, freed bonded labourers and acceptors of small family norm. However, this should not in any way adversely affect the safeguards provided for SCs/STs, women and physically handicapped persons.
- The flow of financial assistance (subsidy + credit) to the categories described above should be commensurate with the percentage of the physical coverage.

**Pattern of subsidy**

The pattern of subsidy is

- 25% for small farmers;
- 33 1/3% for marginal farmers, agricultural labourers, and rural artisans; and
- 50% for SCs/STs beneficiaries and physically handicapped persons.

The ceiling on subsidy in respect of individuals is

- Rs. 4000 in normal areas;
- Rs. 5000 in DPAP/DDP areas;
- Rs. 6000 for SC/ST families and physically handicapped persons;
- Rs. 7,500 or 50% of the project cost, whichever is less for unemployed educated youth; and
- For activities involving at least 5 persons, the ceiling has been fixed at Rs.1.25 lakhs or 50% of the project cost, whichever is less.

**Implementing agency**

District Rural Development Agency/Zilla Parishad is the implementing agency for this programme. The Governing Body at the district level provides guidance and directions to DRDAs. It includes local MPs, MLAs, and Chairman of Zilla Parishad, Heads of District Development Departments and representatives of SCs/STs, women and NGOs. At the grassroots level, the programme is carried out by Block Development Officer, and the other block staff with the help of the village level functionaries.

**Funding pattern and release of funds**

IRDP is financed on a 50:50 cost-sharing basis by the Centre as well as by the States. The funds are released directly to the DRDAs.

**BPL census and selection of beneficiaries**

In order to target assistance to poor families, a BPL census is conducted at the beginning of each Plan period by the States, at the behest of Ministry of Rural Areas and Employment. The Gram Sabha is involved in the identification and selection of beneficiaries under IRDP from the initial stage itself. After the survey/census is completed, the same is verified in the Gram Sabha and once it is approved, such a list is drawn up. The same is sent to the Panchayat Samitis/blocks and DRDAs for record.

**Identification of thrust areas and selection of projects for beneficiaries**

The project profiles to be taken up for beneficiaries, take into account the beneficiary's needs and aptitudes and the local resource endowment. The investment target for the year, the choice of the BPL family for the activity, forward and backward linkages and infrastructural support, etc. are also taken into account while making a project profile. The activities can be taken up in Primary sectors, Secondary sectors and Tertiary sectors.

**District credit plans**

The District Credit Plan and the Annual Action Plan are formulated by the Lead banks according to the guidelines issued by Reserve Bank of India (RBI) from time to time. The District Credit Plans are prepared normally for a period of three to five years. Action plans are prepared for each year. While preparing the District Credit Plans, the targets laid down by Government of India and RBI with regard to the share of lending to the priority sectors, weaker sections, small scale industries etc. are to be kept in view. It is also ensured by the DRDAs that the Annual Plans prepared by them for IRDP are integrated into the District Credit Plans and Annual Action Plan prepared by the Lead banks so that necessary credit support for IRDP is made available.

**Credit target**

At the beginning of the year target for credit for IRDP at the all-India level as well as at the State level are fixed. This is done in consultation with the RBI, NABARD and the participating banks. Credit should normally flow in the ratio 2:1 to subsidy. However, the effort is to see that credit-subsidy ratio exceed 2: 1. The ceiling limit for collateral free loans is Rs. 50,000.

**Acquisition of assets and cash disbursement scheme**

The assets procured should be of standard quality, at economic prices and to the satisfaction of the beneficiary.

Beneficiaries under IRDP are generally given assets and not the cash. However, sometimes the quality or the price is not to the satisfaction of beneficiaries. It provides greater freedom to the beneficiaries for the purchase of quality assets and to minimize the leakage in its disbursement if the assistance is given to the beneficiary in cash. Experience has shown that reliance can be placed on the good sense of the beneficiaries in purchasing of assets subject to some safeguards. Disbursement of money in cash to a beneficiary improves his/her bargaining power and has the added advantage of reducing delays and other malpractices prevalent in disbursement in kind. Hence, with effect from the year 1991-92 it was decided to permit disbursement of assistance in cash under the Cash Disbursement Scheme with a view to giving greater choice to beneficiaries in purchasing assets. Initially it was implemented in 50% of the blocks. With effect from the year 1996-97, it is extended to all the blocks of the country.

**Release of subsidy (back-end subsidy)**

Earlier, simultaneously with the disbursement of loan by the bank, the subsidy amount was debited from the DRDA account and credited to the account of the beneficiaries. Thus in effect, the beneficiary was burdened only with the bank credit portion. This adjustment of subsidy at the beginning itself was termed as Front-End subsidy. It was, however, found that the beneficiaries were repaying the loan immediately, thereby availing of amount of the subsidy. This in effect meant misuse of subsidy. To make beneficiary utilise the loan for sustainable income generation, the system of Front-End subsidy has been replaced by the Back-End subsidy. The subsidy would be adjusted only in the last few instillments. At the same time a lock-in period for subsidy has also been stipulated and the subsidy would be adjusted only in the last few installments and it will not be allowed in the event of the repayment made before the stipulated lock-in period. The loan document would be taken by the bank for the full project cost and it would be inter-alia stipulated that in case of misutilisation of the loan, the entire amount of subsidy would be forfeited. Such forfeited amount of subsidy will be available to the bank for adjustment against the borrower's dues.

**Family credit plan**

A new project of Family Credit Plan (FCP) has been launched in the year 1994-95. It is in operation in 316 selected districts. Under this scheme, more than a single member of the family can be given assistance, subject to the normal subsidy limits for the family. The banks mobilize higher credit for families selected under this scheme. The current levels of investment under FCP have crossed Rs. 26,110 at the all-India level.

**Monitoring and supervision**

IRDP is being monitored from the Central level down to grassroots level. At the State level, a State Level Coordination Committee (SLCC) monitors the programme. At the Central level, the Central Level Coordination Committee (CLCC) monitors and reviews the implementation of the scheme and lays down policy guidelines. A High Level Coordination Committee on credit support to IRDP also functions at the Central level to monitor and review all aspects relating to credit linkage for IRDP. The progress under IRDP is being monitored on a monthly, quarterly, half yearly and annual basis through reports and returns submitted by DRDAs/States. The shortfall, if any, in the performance under IRDP has been brought from time to time to the notice of all concerned States/UTs for corrective measures. Over and above, the implementation of the Programme is monitored through the annual Project Directors' Workshop and periodic meetings with the State Secretaries. At the Block/DRDA level monitoring is done through field visits and physical verification of assets for which an inspection schedule for the district and block functionaries has been laid down.

### Programme support

#### *Programme infrastructure under IRDP*

Absence of linkages has long been identified to be one of the important reasons for lack of sustainability of IRDP schemes. IRDP infrastructure funds are spent for filling critical gaps in infrastructure requirements and to enable IRDP beneficiaries full utilisation of their assets. Marketing linkages/infrastructure are given priority. Recognizing that infrastructural gaps often lead to difficulties in sustaining IRDP projects, the sanctioning powers for infrastructural projects were considerably decentralised with effect from 1994-95. Currently, projects upto Rs. 10 lakhs can be sanctioned with the approval of the Governing Body of the DRDA and upto Rs. 25 lakhs with the approval of the Divisional Commissioner or Secretary, Rural Development at the State level. Only infrastructural projects beyond Rs. 25 lakhs need to be approved by the State Level Sanctioning Committee. Similarly, the ceiling on permissible expenditure on infrastructure has been raised to 20% from the present level of 10%. For States in the North-Eastern region, including, Sikkim, this has been enhanced to 25%.

### Institutional Arrangement For Credit Financing

#### *Consultative arrangements for credit*

##### *High level committee at central level*

A High Level Committee on Credit (HLCC) for IRDP, headed by the Secretary, Department of Rural Employment and Poverty Alleviation, Government of India and including senior representatives from the Government of India, State Governments, Commercial Banks, NABARD and RBI has been constituted to consider the various problems arising from time to time in the course of implementation of the programme and review the credit arrangements to recommend changes and improvements as and when necessary. This Committee meets regularly.

*State level bankers' committee*

State Level Bankers' Committees (SLBCs) have been set up for inter-institutional coordination and joint implementation of development programmes. The meetings of this committee are convened by the designated convenor bank (which is usually the bank with substantial lead responsibility in the State). The agenda items discussed by SLBC relate mainly to branch expansion, implementation of Annual Action Plan/ District Credit Plans, support from government agencies, inter-bank differences, problems raised at District Consultative Committee which require attention at State level etc.

*District level consultative committee*

At the District Level a District Level Consultative Committee (DLCC) has been constituted under the Chairmanship of the District Collector. All the banks and the District level officers of the Government, NABARD, DRDA and DIC are represented on this Committee. This forum should be utilised for allocating share of Credit disbursement to various banks, monitoring and reviewing the overall progress in physical and financial terms, ironing out inter-agency differences and to prepare items for consideration of State Level Committee.

*Block level consultative committee*

The Block Level Consultative Committee (BLCC) has been constituted at the block level under the chairmanship of the Sub-Divisional Officer. Meetings are to be attended by Block Development Officer, Branch

Managers of all commercial banks and Chairman/ Secretary of the Primary Land Development Bank, District, Tehsildar and APO (Credit). The project officer DRDA, the Lead Bank Officer and the Lead District Officer may attend the meetings as special invitees.

*Block level bankers' committee*

Under Service Area Approach, a Block Level Bankers Committee (BLBC) is to be constituted in each block. All the banks operating in the Block including the District Central Cooperative Bank and RRB are members of the committee. The BDO and other technical officers in the Block such as Extension Officers for agriculture, industries and cooperatives will also be its members. The Chairman of the committee will be the Lead Bank Officer. Lead Bank Officer will also be the convenor.

**Risk fund for consumption credit**

To meet the small consumption needs of weaker sections of society, a scheme of Risk Fund for Consumption Credit has been in operation as a non-Plan scheme since 1977-78. The scheme is intended to enable Commercial banks, Cooperative banks and Regional Rural Banks to provide consumption loans, not exceeding Rs. 1000 per borrower to weaker sections of society.

**Insurance cover for various assets**

Insurance Cover is available for livestock assets given under the programme. The General Insurance Corporation provides this cover on certain terms and conditions.

**Performance during the eighth and ninth plan**

***Review of progress (1992-97)***

During the Eighth Five Year Plan, more than 108 lakh families have been assisted. There has been a shift of emphasis from mere coverage of families to qualitative aspects of the programme through enhancement of the average level of per family investment. Credit targets have been fixed from 1995-96 onwards. As a result of these interventions, the average level of investment per family which was Rs. 7889 at the beginning of the Eighth Plan period rose to more than Rs. 14,950 during 1996-97 and further increased to Rs. 17,771 during the current year.

**Performance during 1997-98**

During 1997-98, total allocation was Rs. 1133.51 crores against which Rs. 1109.54 crores have been utilized. The physical and financial progress may be seen at Annexure-X. The Ministry has fixed a credit target totalling Rs. 2,700 crores for the programme of which Rs. 1996.64 crores have been mobilized during the year. A total of more than 17.07 lakh families have been covered during this period of which SC/ST account for 46.40% and women 34.33% of total coverage. The lower coverage of families is due to a shift of emphasis to qualitative aspects of the programme such as enhancement of average level of investment per family.

**Performance during 1998-99**

During 1998-99, the total allocation is Rs. 1456.28 crores against which Rs. 541.87 crores have been utilized up to November, 98. The physical and financial progress may be seen at Annexure-XI. The Ministry has fixed a credit target totaling Rs. 3200 crores for the programme of which Rs. 980.72 crores have been mobilized during year (upto November, 98). A total of more than 7.82 lakh families have been covered during this period of which SC/ST account for 45% and women 34% of total coverage. The lower coverage of families is due to a shift of emphasis to qualitative aspects of the programme such as enhancement of average level of investment per family. The average level of investment per family which was Rs.7,889 at the beginning of the Eighth Plan period rose to more than Rs. 17,771 during 1998-99 (upto November, 98).

**Development of women and children in rural areas**

Development Of Women And Children In Rural Areas (DWCRA) was launched as a sub-scheme of IRDP during the year 1982-83 in 50 districts. It subsequently expanded to cover all the districts in the country by 1994-95. The flow of benefits to poor women, in spite of reservation, under various poverty alleviation programmes viz., IRDP and TRYSEM were found to be not making much impact. Therefore, in order to overcome this situation and to involve the rural women more intensely in economic activities and matters that concern the rural community, one of the initiatives taken by this Ministry was the introduction of an exclusive programme for women viz., Development of Women and Children in Rural Areas. Since economic empowerment involves provision of additional channels of funds in the form of working capital and credit, training, employment, management skill etc., DWCRA with exclusive focus on economic empowerment of women provides all these inputs by considering women as critical to development. This intervention alms at not only raising the incomes of rural women of poor households, but also enabling organized participation of groups of women in the programmes of credit, skill training and infrastructure support for self employment, who cannot take up economic activities individually or on their own. DWCRA was introduced for ensuring that the benefits of IRDP programme reach women directly. The programme seeks to improve the access of rural women to health, education, safe drinking water, sanitation, nutrition etc., thereby bringing about an enhancement in the quality of the general wellbeing of women and children.

**Strategy**

The basic unit under DWCRA is a group of 10- 15 poor women who have come together to help each other in order to use their collective strength to break social bonds that have denied them income generating and self-fulfilling opportunities. The group size may be smaller in difficult terrain and far-flung areas. One woman amongst the members functions as the group organiser who helps in the choice of activity, procurement of raw-material, marketing of products. Before undertaking the activities women are made aware of the objectives and benefits of group formation under the scheme; understanding their potential and recognising their strength. At the operational level inputs/coaching for such an exercise by the group is given by Gram Sevika for a period of two years, who not only creates a group but also nurtures the group and orients them in availing of benefits of various other programmes/schemes.

**Implementing agency and staffing pattern**

DWCRA is being implemented by the District Rural Development Agencies. To facilitate the implementation of the scheme, one post of Assistant Project Officer (Woman) has been sanctioned to be part of the DRDA team. One additional post of Gram Sevika has also been sanctioned at the block level to look after the activities of the groups. This is in addition to the two Gram Sevikas in the normal Block pattern.

The Assistant Project Officer (APO), the additional Gram Sevika along with two Gram Sevikas and Mukhya Sevika already available with the CD Block form a team to help in the implementation of DWCRA. They conduct preliminary surveys of the area, and establish contacts with the rural women, identifying their constraints and needs. The team is responsible for monitoring and follow up. The APO is to help in establishing contacts with different agencies, in moblization of resources and training facilities, marketing of the products of the DWCRA groups and also to look after the day to day administration of the scheme within the DRDA. Implementation of DWCRA is the overall responsibility of the entire DRDA team headed by the Project Officer or Project Director.

**Community based convergent services**

The Community Based Convergent Services (CBCS), as a component of DWCRA was started in 1991 in a few districts of the country as a pilot programme. The objective was to create greater awareness among the village communities to enable them to demand social services provided by the State in a better manner and also share responsibilities in the management and implementation of these services, thus leading to sustainable development. Traditional methods like visuals, role play, folk art, puppetry dance and drama etc. are some of the means employed for sensitizing the community to the basic needs. The programme seeks to strengthen existing organizations of rural poor women, encourage women's groups to articulate their felt needs, raise the level of social consciousness, orient the community and formal community organization towards DWCRA and thereby improve the social and economic status of women. The programmes of ICDS, Rajiv Gandhi National Drinking Water Mission, National Literacy Mission are some of the programmes which are sought to be converged at the grassroots level. 298 districts have been covered so far under the scheme of Community Based Convergent Services (CBCS) with cent per cent Central assistance at Rs.5.00 lakhs per district.

**Child care activities**

Child Care Activities (CCA) has been incorporated in

DWCRA programme during 1995-96 with the following objectives :-

- To provide creche services for children of working DWCRA women.
- Setting up of literacy centres for DWCRA women with specific emphasis on girl child dropouts and illiterate members of the DWCRA groups.
- Filling up critical gaps in the areas of immunization, nutrition etc. for the children of DWCRA members with special focus and emphasis on the girl child to reduce gender disparities in the infant girl child care.
- To provide some relief to the physically handicapped children of DWCRA members.
- To provide immediate relief and pay for legal assistance in case of redressal of physical abuse of the girl child.

Children below 6 years are the target group under Child Care Activities. Each DRDA is to receive Rs. 1.50 lakhs (Rs. 1.00 lakh as Central Share and Rs.50,000 as State Share) for Child Care Activities.

**Funding pattern**

Each DWCRA group gets Rs.25,000 as Revolving Fund to meet capital expenditure requirement of economic activities. Expenditure on revolving fund was being shared equally by the Central Government, State Government and UNICEF till 1994-95. UNICEF assistance was not available from 1. 1.96. The Revolving Fund has been increased from Rs. 15,000 to Rs.25,000 from 1995-96. Presently, the expenditure for Revolving Fund is being shared by the Centre and State on 50:50 basis.

**Marketing of products**

Since the focal point of the scheme is income-generating

activities for women, it is necessary that their activities must be economically viable. Marketing of products of the women's group is, therefore, very important. The interest of women in the programme can be sustained only when a proper market outlet is available for their products. Some State Governments like Haryana, Andhra Pradesh have issued orders declaring the DWCRA groups as approved sources for the supply of bulk articles required by the Government Departments. The Gram Shree Melas organised by CAPART are also used as outlets for the sale of DWCRA products. Setting up of supportive institutions for marketing like District Supply and Marketing Societies (DSMS) are being encouraged by the States. These district level agencies must be multifaceted and also support non-credit inputs like purchase of raw materials and sale of goods where sectoral linkages cannot be established. Recently, efforts are also on at state level to create market for the products manufactured under DWCRA/ Integrated Rural Development Programme. The State of Kerala and Orissa have created State Level organizations like KERAMS and ORAMS. The State of Andhra Pradesh is encouraging organization and melas. A DWCRA Mela was organised, with the State Government support at Hyderabad which has reported very good response. The State of Haryana encourages DWCRA groups for supply of nutrition providers for ICDS programme. The momentum has to be sustained if the money invested through DWCRA groups has to receive significant returns. A wide range of DWCRA products need improvement in designing and packaging. Such improvements need to be carried out by involving professional bodies. The supply of raw material and its quality, quality control of finished products is an area of concern.

**Allocation and release of funds under DWCRA for the year 1998-99**

The BE for the programmes is Rs. 100 crores. Central allocation has been made to assist 61850 groups. Accordingly, an amount of Rs.77.97 crores has been allocated for Income Generating Activities. By the end of December, 1998, an amount of Rs.31.9053 crores has been released to 401 districts as first instalment and an amount of Rs.5.7273 crores to 60 districts as second instalment as per each DRDA fulfilling eligibility conditions such as submission of audit reports, utilization certificate and certain minimum percentage of expenditure against available funds with them. Thus a total of Rs.37.6286 crores has been released for Income Generating Activities during the year 1998-99 by the end of December, 1998.

Similarly an amount of Rs. 1.4 crores was released for CCA to those DRDAs who have submitted statements of expenditure for the funds released earlier. An amount of Rs. 1 crore has been released to CAPART to support NCO activities.

**Coverage**

Initially no specific coverage of vulnerable groups such as SC/STs was fixed. However, during the year 1997-98, it has been made compulsory that 50% of the groups have to be women belonging to SC/ST. Priority has to be given to physically handicapped persons and also girls and women rehabilitated from prostitution. The coverage achieved during each plan period is shown as below :

**Training of rural youth for self-employment**

Started as a Centrally sponsored scheme on 15th August, 1979, Training of Rural Youth for Self-Employment (TRYSEM) aims at providing basic technical and entrepreneurial skills to the rural youth from families below the poverty line to enable them to take up self employment in the broad fields of agriculture and allied sectors, industries, services and business activities. This objective was subsequently enlarged in the year 1983 to include taking up of wage employment also to the trained youth. TRYSEM plays an important role in facilitating diversification of activities taken up under IRDR Diversification away from the primary sector to secondary and tertiary sectors requires acquisition or upgradation of skills relevant to industries and business enterprises. TRYSEM seeks to impart new skills and upgrade existing skills of beneficiaries who are by and large attuned only to stagnant levels of agricultural or artisan skills.

**Salient features**

The rural youth in the age group of 18-35 years from families below poverty line are enlisted for training under the scheme. The minimum age for providing training under TRYSEM is relaxed to 46 years for inmates of orphanages in rural areas. The upper age limit of 35 years is relaxed to 45 years in case of widows, freed bonded labourers, freed convicts, persons displaced due to large development projects and cured leprosy patients. There is no age limit for rural artisans. A minimum of 50% of selected youths should belong to the Scheduled Caste and Scheduled Tribe communities, 40% should be women and 3% of the trainees should be physically handicapped persons.

The duration of training courses is normally six months. However, the State Level Co-ordination Committee (SLCC) can change the duration and prescribe duration for new trades. There are no educational qualifications prescribed for selection of trainees.

The TRYSEM trainees are paid a stipend varying from Rs. 200 to Rs. 500 per month during the training. To enable the participants to take up employment there is a provision of Rs. 800 as an allowance for purchase of toolkits by the trainees.

**Pattern of assistance**

**(a) Recurring expenses**

The share of the Centre and States is on 50:50 basis. In case of UTs the funding is 100% by the Centre. The assistance is released to the DRDAs in two instalments.

**(b) Non recurring expenses for TRYSEM training infrastructure**

The assistance to the State Government is on 50:50 basis and the Central share is limited to Rs. 20 lakhs per Exclusive TRYSEM Training Centre (ETTC) or 50% of the total cost of the centre whichever is less. The funds are released directly to the State Governments.

**Performance during the eighth five year plan**

During the Eighth Plan Period (1992-93 to 1996-97) total releases by the Centre and State Governments were Rs. 353.94 crores out of which Rs. 365.80 crores have been utilised which is 103.35%. During the same period against the target of 16.12 lakhs rural youth, 15.17 lakhs youth have been trained which is 94.10%. Details are given below :

**Performance during 1998-99**

Total allocation under the scheme of TRYSEM (Recurring Expenses) during 1998-99 is Rs. 89.76 crores out of which Rs. 45.00 crores, is the central allocation. As per the reports received from the States/UTs 0.66 lakh rural youth have been trained upto November, 98. Details are given in the Annexure-XII and XIII. No funds under TRYSEM (infrastructure) have been released during 199899 up to December 1998.

**Monitoring and supervision**

At the State level a sub-Committee of the SLCC, is constituted exclusively for TRYSEM. An official of the rank of Project Director (DRDA), designated as Director (TRYSEM) functions at the State Headquarters as part of IRDP monitoring cell. At the District level there is TRYSEM Committee under the Chairmanship of the Chairman of the DRDA. Regular monthly monitoring is done by the Ministry of Rural Areas and Employment. Area Officers nominated for various States by this Ministry also regularly inspect the implementation of the scheme in the field during their visits to the States.

**Steps for strengthening the scheme of TRYSEM**

1. The stipend rates, honorarium and other allowances etc. under the TRYSEM Recurring expenses have been enhanced appreciably from I June 1994 with a view to make the training more effective and meaningful.
2. States and Union Territories have been asked to set up a subcommittee under the SLCC exclusively for TRYSEM. A District Level Committee exclusively for TRYSEM already exists.
3. The State/Union Territories have been advised to explore the possibilities of setting up of production groups from amongst TRYSEM trainees for undertaking the ancillary activities like manufacture and assembly of modern items of production.
4. A scheme regarding setting up of Exclusive TRYSEM Training Centres in each block, where no organised training facility exists, to strengthen training infrastructure under TRYSEM for imparting training to the rural youth in different traditional trades has been introduced.

**Linkage with IRDP**

The linkage forged between TRYSEM and IRDP has so far been weak. The fourth round of IRDP Concurrent Evaluation revealed that only 3.88% of IRDP beneficiaries received training under TRYSEM. The findings of the 'Quick Evaluation of TRYSEM (June_ August 1993) also indicate that of the total number of beneficiaries who got training under TRYSEM roughly 53.57% trained youth did not apply for assistance under IRDP and of the remaining youth only about 50% were given assistance under IRDP. To ensure proper linkage of TRYSEM with IRDP, it has been made incumbent on the DRDAs, the block authorities and the training institutions to complete all the required formalities for sanction of IRDP loans to TRYSEM trainees. During the training period itself, the loan application forms will be sent to the banks so that the bankers in turn can interact with the trainees. This will significantly reduce the chances of such sponsored applications being rejected later and generate interest in the trainees to take up self-employment.

**Supply of improved toolkits to rural artisans**

The scheme was launched as a sub-scheme of IRDP in July, 1992, with the objective to enabling the rural artisans Below Poverty Line to enhance the quality of their products, increase their production and income and ensure a better quality of life with the use of improved tools. This will also help reduce their migration to urban areas.

**Salient features**

Artisans from a variety of crafts, except weaving, tailoring, needle-workers and beedi-workers are to be supplied with suitable improved hand tools or a set of tools. The average cost of a toolkit is Rs.2,000 and in case of power driven tools the average-cost is Rs.4,500. 90% of the cost of the toolkit is a subsidy from the Government of India and 10% is to be contributed by the beneficiary and there is no State share. The unit cost is to be fixed by the District Rural Development Agency (DRDA) concerned. DRDA is the implementing agency.

Prototypes of improved tools in pottery, carpentry, blacksmithy, leather work, woodcraft, metal craft and lacquerware have been developed by the National Small Industries Corporation, Regional Design and Technical Development Centres under the Development Commissioner (Handicrafts) and similar other organisations. The State Governments have been authorised to choose models/tools, which suit the needs of their artisans.

**Target group**

There is 50% reservation for SC and ST communities. Wherever SC/ST persons are not available, the DRDA Governing body can decide to allocate the percentage meant for SC/ST to other categories of artisans. There is no provision of reservation for women and physically handicapped persons. However, if eligible, preference will be given to such persons over other persons.

**Monitoring and supervision**

Regular monthly monitoring is done by the Ministry of Rural Areas and Employment. State and District Level Committees have been set up by the State Governments for implementation and monitoring of the scheme. Area officers nominated for various States by this Ministry also regularly inspect the implementation of the scheme in the field during their visits to the States.

**Performance during eighth five year plan**

During the Eighth Five Year Plan (1992-93 to 1996-97) a sum of Rs. 149.07 crores was released out of which Rs. 120.08 crores has been utilised which works out to be

80.55%. Against the target of covering 8.32 lakh beneficiaries, 6.52 lakh beneficiaries have been covered which works out to be 78.36%. Details are given below:

**Performance during 1998-99**

Allocation under the scheme during 1998-99 is Rs. 60 crores, which has been revised to Rs. 59.73 crores. An amount of Rs. 59 crores has been earmarked as subsidy for purchase of toolkits and Rs. 0.73 crore is earmarked for Research and Development of Toolkits and Evaluation of the scheme. An amount of Rs. 26.87 crores has been released as subsidy for purchase of toolkits to the States/UTs upto December 1998. Under the Research, Development and Evaluation head no funds have been released upto December. On the basis of the information available as per the reports last received, an expenditure of Rs.25.14 crores had been incurred upto November 1998. This accounts for an achievement of 52.78% in financial terms and 40% in physical terms. Details of achievement are given in the Annexure-XIV and XV.

**Areas identified for further improvement**

Based on the feedback gathered and with a view to further improving the implementation of the scheme and its efficacy, the following areas would receive attention in the Ninth Plan:

- The source of supply of toolkits would be wholly guided by the quality and cost parameters, the reputation and expertise of manufacturers, timely delivery and pre-delivery extension and post-delivery service facilities offered and suitability of the toolkits to the need of specific artisan groups.
- While it may be true that a majority of the rural artisans would be illiterate and therefore, cannot have access to documented literature, the need for such literature with plenty of graphics and

illustrations cannot be discounted altogether. Efforts should therefore be made to prepare such literature and supply a copy to the artisans covered.

- Marketing linkages need to be established for more effective use of improved toolkits so that higher productivity and enhanced production can be absorbed leading to higher earnings for artisans. State Governments have been advised to make institutional arrangements for establishing such linkages.
- The State Governments have been requested to interact with the Department of Science and Technology, NSIC and IITs for the development of appropriate technology and designs for improved toolkits for various artisan groups.
- The Scheme would henceforth place due emphasis on the choice of the artisans. The designing and manufacture of tools should at least emerge from a wider level of consultations with groups of artisans. The process of consultation should be continued even after the supply of tools have been effected to find out whether these have fulfilled the objectives of the scheme and the needs of the artisans.
- There are pockets of rural technology, which have survived the onslaught of modern technological innovations by virtue of their sturdiness and locale specific utility. These need to be identified and replicated elsewhere.
- The scheme's objective also needs to include upgradation of skills through technological innovations resulting in additional income generation. The scheme would aim at capturing markets beyond the nearest rural areas, wherever feasible.

- Research and Development must be given due emphasis. States have been advised to take the initiative in developing toolkits at least in the case of one artisan trade to start with. Similar initiatives will have to be taken by the Small Industries Services Institutes.
- State Governments have been advised to sponsor evaluation of the scheme through institutions having an expertise in the field, experience of extension work and involvement in the field of technological and marketing promotion.
- For dissemination of technology, States have been advised to organise exhibitions in several locations on important occasions.

**Ganga Kalyan Yojana**

Ganga Kalyan Yojana (GKY) was launched as a sub-scheme of Integrated Rural Development Programme (IRDP) during 1996-97 with effect from 1.2.1997 and is being continued as an independent scheme with effect from 1.4.1997.

**Objective**

The objective of the scheme is to provide irrigation through exploitation of groundwater (borewells and tubewells) to individuals and groups of beneficiaries of small and marginal farmers belonging to the below poverty line.

**Programme strategy**

The individual/groups are assisted through subsidy by Government and term credit by financial institutions including SC/ST/BC Finance and Development Corporation.

**Target group**

The beneficiaries under the scheme are small and

marginal farmers living below the poverty line, other than those who have already been assisted under any minor irrigation programme of State or Central Government.

**Safeguards for SCs and STs**

At least 50% of the funds have been earmarked for SCs and STs.

**Funding pattern**

The funding pattern is 80:20 Le 80% by Central Government and 20% by the State Government.

**Allocation of funds to the states**

The funds are allocated to the States according to the criteria fixed for IRDP allocation. The States are required to make district-wise allocations taking into consideration the potential for exploitation of groundwater resources, economic viability of exploiting such potential and other relevant considerations.

**Subsidy**

75% subsidy is allowed for SCs/STs and physically disabled groups and 50% for others. The monetary ceiling of subsidy per group (5 to 15 members) is Rs. 40,000 and for individual beneficiaries the subsidy is Rs. 5,000 per acre of land under the scheme subject to a ceiling of Rs. 12,500 per beneficiary.

5% of the project cost per annum is permissible as additional subsidy for SC/ST/Physically disabled groups as part of operation and maintenance cost for 3 years. For other groups and individual schemes, no subsidy on operation and maintenance is admissible.

**Implementing agency**

The scheme is being implemented by the DRDAs/ Zilla Parishads.

**Financial progress**

During the financial year 1997-98, a Central allocation of Rs. 20,000 lakhs was made which was scaled down to Rs. 10,000 lakhs in view of the lack of gearing up the scheme by the States and also the budgetary cuts imposed by Finance. The whole amount of Rs. 10,000 lakhs was released till 31st March, 1998. Against, this, the total utilisation of Rs. 566.65 lakhs has been incurred by the States as per the reports received.

During 1998-99, the Central allocation under the scheme is Rs. 94 lakhs which has been reduced to Rs. I lakh only at Revised Estimate stage. The reasons for such reduction is mainly on account of huge unspent balance available with the implementing agencies. The reasons for huge unspent balance is operational difficulties faced by the States in the implementation of the scheme.

**Physical progress**

The States/UTs were made responsible to fix the Suitable physical targets for the DRDAs/ZPs. During 1997-98, 1674 individual projects and 92 group projects under the scheme were implemented. During 1998-99, 2261 individual projects and 72 group projects have been taken up by the States.

**Outlay for 1999-2000**

The proposed Central Outlay of the scheme for the year 1999-2000 has not yet been finalised. Moreover, the scheme is proposed to be merged into IRDR.

**Rural housing**

Housing is one of the most serious challenges facing India's sociopolitical economy today, While food security has been largely achieved and clothing today is not a serious problem for the poor, shelter remains beyond the reach of millions in India even after 50 years of the country's independence. This is a matter not merely of deep concern but also a matter that requires immediate attention and urgent action. For a normal citizen, owning a house provides significant economic security and status in society. For shelterless persons, a house brings about a profound social change in their existence, endowing them with an identity, thus integrating them with their immediate social milieu.

**Housing shortage**

According to the 1991 Census, the rural housing shortage was 13.72 million consisting of 3.41 million households without houses and 10.31 million living in unserviceable kutcha houses. It has also been estimated that another 10.75 million houses would be needed to cover the population growth during 1991-2002, at the rate of an annual growth of 0.89 million houselessness. Thus, a total of 24.47 million houses need to be constructed or upgraded to achieve the target of providing shelter to all in the rural areas by 2002 A.D. Of the above 24.47 million houses, 5.7 million houses have been added by various agencies until 31.3.1997. It is anticipated that around 6.17 million houses will be added by different agencies by 2002. Thus the housing shortage to be tackled is 12.60 million houses, of which 10.31 million houses need up-gradation and 2.29 million new houses will need to be constructed.

**Indira Awaas Yojana**

The Government of India Is implementing Indira Awaas Yojana (IAY) since the year 1985-86 with the objective of providing dwelling units free of cost to the members of Scheduled Castes, Scheduled Tribes and freed bonded labourers living below the poverty fine in rural areas. From the year 1993-94, its scope has been extended to cover non-scheduled castes and scheduled tribes rural poor subject to the condition that the benefits of the scheme have also been extended to families of servicemen of the armed and paramilitary forces killed in action. 3% of the houses are reserved for the below poverty line disabled persons living in rural areas.

IAY operates as a 100% subsidized centrally sponsored programme with the resources being shared on 80:20 basis between Centre and the States. Funds under the scheme allocated to the States/UTs are further distributed to the districts in proportion to the SC/ST population in the district.

The allotment of house under the scheme is done in the name of the female member of the beneficiary household. Alternatively, it can be allotted in the joint name of both the husband and wife. The beneficiaries are to be involved from the very beginning in construction work and, have to make their own arrangements for construction to suit their requirements. As far as possible houses are built in dusters so as to facilitate provision of common facilities. The permissible construction assistance per house is Rs.20,000 in plain areas and Rs.22,000 in hilly or difficult areas.

District Rural Development Agencies/Zilla Parishads on the basis of allocations made and targets fixed shall decide the number of houses to be constructed Panchayatwise under IAY during a particular financial year. The same is intimated to the Gram Panchayat. Thereafter, the Gram Sabha select the beneficiaries from the list of eligible households according to IAY guidelines and as per priorities fixed, restricting this number to the target allotted. No approval of the Panchayat Samiti is required. The Panchayat Samiti is however, sent a list of selected beneficiaries for their information.

The nutritional status of women and children in rural areas is a matter of concern. Most of the rural women and children belonging to families below poverty line are found to be suffering from various ailments related to malnutrition. It is, therefore, necessary to focus attention on the need for improvement in nutritional status of our rural population by encouraging the cultivation of fruits and vegetables which can be grown easily in the backyard of rural houses. Accordingly instructions have been issued to implementing agencies for popularising the production of fruits and vegetables at household level particularly in houses constructed under IAY.

The IAY is implemented through District Rural Development Agencies specially set up in each district of the country for the implementation of Rural Development Programmes or through Zilla Parishads. At the field level the Block machinery is entrusted with the responsibility for implementing the programme. At the village level the Gram Sabha is responsible for selection of beneficiaries.

Fuel efficient chullahs have been developed and are being manufactured at several places. The Department of Non-Conventional Energy Sources is encouraging installation of such chullahs. It is ensured that every house constructed under the Yojana is provided with the fuel efficient chullah.

Construction of sanitary latrines forms an integral part of IAY house. It has, however, been observed that in a large number of cases either the sanitary latrines in these houses are not constructed or if they are constructed, these are not put to proper use which is mainly due to the old habits of the people.

While fixing technical specifications, efforts are to be made to utilise to the maximum extent, local materials and low cost technology developed by various institutions. Technology using bricks, cement and steel on large scale is not to be encouraged. As far as possible, cement is substituted by lime and lime surkhi manufactured locally. Due to increase in price of bricks, it is considered desirable to substitute burnt bricks with sun dried bricks of earth-soil-cement. Bricks manufactured by the beneficiaries themselves instead of its purchase may also be undertaken for reduction of cost and better wage employment.

**Programme performance**

The IAY has proved to be a popular programme and targets have exceeded in almost every year since its inception. A total of around 48 lakh houses have been constructed from 1985-86 till date under the scheme.

During 1998-99 allocation under IAY is Rs. 1484 crores with a target of constructing 987022 houses under the scheme. An amount of Rs. 1004 crores has been released to various States/UTs upto November, 98 and about 354683 houses have been constructed with reported expenditure of around Rs.769.54 crores till date. Financial and Physical performance under IAY during the current year (up to November, 98) is given at Annexure-XVI and XVII.

| *Year* | *Expenditure (Rs. In crore)* | *No. of houses built* |
|---|---|---|
| 1985-86 | 57.93 | 51252 |
| 1986-87 | 149.18 | 160197 |
| 1987-88 | 235.37 | 169302 |
| 1988-89 | 149.65 | 139192 |
| 1989-90 | 188.50 | 186023 |
| 1990-91 | 213.07 | 181800 |
| 1991-92 | 263.01 | 207299 |
| 1992-93 | 238.84 | 192585 |
| 1993-94 | 481.00 | 372535 |
| 1994-95 | 500.38 | 390482 |
| 1995-96 | 1166.36 | 863889 |
| 1996-97 | 1385.92 | 806290 |
| 1997-98 | 1596.44 | 767649 |
| 1998-99* | 769.54 | 354683 |
| Total | 7395.19 | 4843178 |

In addition to regular monitoring of the programme by the Ministry, the programme has been evaluated by the Programme Evaluation Organization of the Planning Commission which carried out a Quick Study of the IAY in 1992-93. According to the evaluation done by the Planning Commission, 86.4% of the houses constructed under the Yojana were occupied and lived in. Again about 84% of the households expressed satisfaction/ partial satisfaction with the houses given to them.

**Organisation of training course/study tours**

The Ministry of Rural Areas and Employment along with the Human Settlement Management Institute (HSMI) of Housing and Urban Development Corporation Ltd. (HUDCO) has organised two Training Programmes on "Rural Housing Project Formulation" of one week duration each in Hyderabad and Guwahati. The course is meant for middle level executive and professionals working in DRDAs, Zilla Parishads, Housing Boards, Financial Institutions, Planning and Development authorities, engineers, architects, NGOs etc. involved in implementation of rural housing and rural infirastructural development projects.

Besides, the Ministry of Rural Areas and Employment in coordination with Nirmithi National Institute of Habitat Management, Thiruvananthapuram organised a Study Tour to Kerala State Nirmithi Kendra (KESNIK) from 7th - 9th October, 1998 in order to sensitize the State Secretaries of Housing Heads of Housing Departments etc. about alternative cost, effective environment friendly technologies, materials and designs.

**New initiatives**

Government has recognized shelter as a basic human requirement which needs to be met on a priority basis. It has announced a National Housing and Habitat policy which aims at providing 'Housing for All' and to facilitate construction of 13 lakh additional housing units in rural areas annually with an emphasis on extending benefits to the poor and the deprived. An Action Plan for Rural Housing has accordingly been prepared. The Action Plan comprising of a series of recommendations for policy, Institutional and Schematic interventions has attempted to address the various issues related to Rural Housing in a holistic fashion and yet emerge with workable and practical interventions. Among the highlights of the Action Plan for the construction of 13 lakh additional houses in rural areas are:

**Conversion of unserviceable Kutcha houses into semi-pucca/ Pucca houses**

There are 103.1 lakh unserviceable kutcha houses requiring upgradation in the rural areas. It is therefore, proposed to convert unserviceable kutcha houses to semi-pucca/pucca houses under this scheme with an assistance of Rs. 10,000 per unit utilising the 20% of available funds for IAY. Conversion will necessarily include a provision of sanitary latrine and smokeless chullah.

**Credit-cum-subsidy component of IAY**

There are a large number of households in the rural areas who have not been covered under IAY, since they do not fall within the Below Poverty Line category. They also do not have high repayment capacity to take benefit of loan based programmes as offered by housing finance institutions. The needs of this large majority located just above the poverty line can be met through a sub-scheme of IAY, which is part credit and part subsidy based. The Finance Minister in his Budget Speech had also announced the credit-cum-subsidy scheme. Furthermore, the introduction of a part Credit and part Subsidy based sub-scheme would be an important step in the direction of redefining the role of Government from that of a 'provider' to a 'facilitator' as envisaged in the new National Housing and Habitat Policy, 1998. It is, therefore, proposed to initiate a Credit-cum-Subsidy component of IAY, which will be targeted to the group just above the poverty line having income limit of Rs. 32,000 annually. It is proposed that the upper ceiling limit of assistance will be restricted to assistance limit under Indira Awaas Yojana (presently Rs. 20,000 for plain areas and Rs. 22,000 for hilly/ difficult areas). The subsidy will be restricted to a maximum of 50% of IAY assistance limit.

**Innovative stream for Rural housing and habitat development**

Presently under IAY, it is left to the beneficiary to select building/ housing design technology and materials. In fact houses being built under IAY suffer from inadequacies such as the use of expensive materials, technology and design, lack of thermal comfort and the inability to withstand natural calamities. An important and collinear area of concern which needs to be tackled along with housing is the deteriorating habitat and non availability of quality infrastructure support services. In view of this, an Innovative Stream for Rural Housing and Habitat Development is proposed to be initiated.

Under this scheme it is proposed to provide financial assistance for efforts initiated on a project basis by organizations such as HUDCO/Building Material Technology Promotion Council (BMTPC)/Central Building Research Institute (CBRI)/NGOs etc.

**Institutional mechanisms for improved shelter delivery**

At present there are virtually no institutional structures available in the country to support rural housing initiatives, whether we consider housing finance or the areas of housing construction technology, designs or habitat. A series of initiatives are therefore being proposed to address these glaring inadequacies.

**Setting up of Rural building centres.**

The primary objectives of setting up of a building centre are:

i) Technology transfer and information dissemination
ii) Skill up-gradation through training and
iii) Production of cost effective and environment friendly material components

In other words, a building centre will be involved in transfer of technology from 'lab to land', production of cost effective building materials for sale and providing training to carpenters, masons, etc.

The Rural Building Centre Programme is proposed to be implemented through one or more agencies contributing to the rural housing/rural development programmes such as HUDCO, BMTPC or well known State organisations involved in setting up of such centres. These rural building Centres are intended to be located within the close reach of rural populations. It is proposed to provide one time grant for setting up of a building centre at the State of Rs. 5 lakhs.

**National mission for rural housing**

The National Housing and Habitat Policy, 1998 states: "At present the rural housing and to a large extent informal housing do not benefit from the outcome of research and development. Efforts will be made to disseminate information about new technologies and provide training to construction workers in the use of new technologies. In this regard a mission approach may be adopted." Adoption of a 'mission' approach will significantly alter the Rural Housing scenario, by enabling the induction of Science and Technology inputs on a continuous basis into the sector and providing convergence to technology, habitat and energy related issues. Moreover, this will sought to be achieved within a specified timeframe and through community intermediation. It is, therefore, proposed to set up a National Mission for Rural Housing.

Construction designs, materials and technologies are culturally rooted and region specific, these need to be documented/located with reference to past practice and accumulated knowledge systems and thereafter disseminated through a people centered, region specific information, education and communication strategy. Hence housing and habitat related problems would be dealt with through the coordinated effort of various agencies and local communities, within specified time frames and low cost, replicable solutions evolved. A threefold strategy of strengthening of supply lines for technologies, materials, awareness creation among the rural populace and improvement in skills of rural sector professionals will be its centrepiece. This will enable a qualitative improvement in both quality of construction techniques, habitats and in maintenance practices.

**Setting up of rural housing and habitat development corporation**

Presently the outreach of housing finance institutions in the rural areas is negligible. There is virtually no institutional finance going in for the creation of infrastructure support services in the rural areas. For instance, the definition adopted by the National Housing Bank for rural areas, enables it to extend loaning under the Golden jubilee Rural Housing Finance Scheme to residents of townships having population up to 50,000. It would be pertinent to mention that about 83% urban local bodies fall in this category. To facilitate and coordinate the rural housing programme, through a multi-pronged approach of evolving strategies for extending the outreach of housing finance in the rural areas, sourcing of capital from both internal and external sources and the development of a menu approach for housing and habitat development, it is proposed to set up a Rural Housing and Habitat Development Corporation under the administrative control of the Ministry of Rural Areas and Employment. The setting up of a separate Rural Housing and Habitat Development Corporation dedicated to the cause of enabling the creation of quality and cost effective rural human settlements will go a long way in achieving the set goals of 'Housing for All'.

## Special area development programmes

### Drought phone areas programme

Drought Prone Areas Programme (DPAP) is one of the area development programmes launched by the Government in 1973-74 to tackle the special problems faced by those fragile areas which are constantly affected by severe drought conditions. These areas are characterized by large human and cattle populations which are continuously putting heavy pressure on the already fragile natural resource base for food, fodder and fuel. This continuous biotic pressure is leading to fast and continuous depletion of vegetative cover, less and less rainfall, increasing soil erosion and fast receding ground water levels due to continuous exploitation without any effort to recharge the under ground acquifers.

Though the Programme created some positive impact in terms of creating durable 'public assets in the programme areas, the overall impact of the programme in effectively containing the adverse effects of drought was found to be not very encouraging. In addition, many of the programme States had also been demanding inclusion of additional areas under the programme.

Keeping this in view a High Level Technical Committee under the Chairmanship of Prof. C.H. Hanumantha Rao, Ex-Member, Planning Commission critically reviewed the contents, methodology and implementation processes of all area development programmes and suggested suitable measures for improvement. Based on the recommendations of the Hanumantha Rao Committee, comprehensive Guidelines for Watershed Development commonly applicable to the DPAP, DDP IWDP, EAS (50% allocation in DPAP and DDP areas) were issued in October, 1994 which came into effect from 1995-96.

**Objectives**

The basic objective of the programme is to minimise the adverse effects of drought on production of crops and livestock and productivity of land, water and human resources ultimately leading to the drought proofing of the affected areas. The programme also aims to promote overall economic development and improving the socioeconomic conditions of the resource poor and disadvantaged sections inhabiting the programme areas.

**Strategy**

The common Guidelines for Watershed Development provide for a uniform strategy in the implementation of all area development programmes viz. DPAP, DDP, IWDP and EAS. The main features of this strategy are:

- Area development programmes to be implemented exclusively on watershed basis.
- Programme activities to be confined to the identified watershed of about 500 hectares and are to be executed on a project basis spanning over a period of four years.
- Watershed project to cover a village, as far as possible.

- Elaborate institutional mechanisms at various levels clearly defined for effective participation of the local people and the Panchayati Raj institutions in all stages of project management.
- DRDA/ZP to be the nodal Government agency at the district level to act as a facilitator and provider of finances and technical assistance to the people's organizations executing the watershed projects.

**Coverage**

At present, DPAP is in operation in 947 blocks of 155 districts in 13 States. The corresponding physical area for treatment under the programme works out to approximately 7.45 lakh square kilometers. The States where DPAP is under implementation along with number of districts and blocks may be seen in the Table.

| S.No. | Name of State | Districts | Blocks |
|---|---|---|---|
| 1. | Andhra Pradesh | 11 | 94 |
| 2. | Bihar | 16 | 121 |
| 3. | Gujarat | 10 | 52 |
| 4. | Himachal Pradesh | 3 | 9 |
| 5. | Jammu & Kashmir | 2 | 22 |
| 6. | Karnataka | 11 | 81 |
| 7. | Madhya Pradesh | 25 | 134 |
| 8. | Maharashtra | 22 | 148 |
| 9. | Orissa | 8 | 47 |
| | 10. Rajasthan | 10 | 32 |
| 11. | Tamil Nadu | 15 | 80 |
| 12. | Uttar Pradesh | 18 | 91 |
| 13. | West Bengal | 4 | 36 |
| | Total | 155 | 947 |

**Funding pattern**

The programme allocation is shared on 50:50 basis between the Centre and the State Governments. The cost norms adopted under DPAP for various ecosystems depending on the severity of the problem are as below :

| *S. No.* | *Ecosystem type* | *Per Ha. cost Average (Rs.)* | *Watershed project cost (Rs. In lakhs)* |
|---|---|---|---|
| 1. | Semi-Arid Region | 4,000 | 20.00 |
| 2. | Dry-Sub-Humid Region | 3,000 | 15.00 |
| 3. | Dry Sub-Humid (Hill) Region | 4,000 | 20.00 |

**Physical and financial performance**

Under DPAP, 6454 Watershed Projects have been sanctioned in four different batches - two batches in 1995-96 and one batch in 1996-97 and 1997-98. Against this, 5956 Watershed Projects have so far been taken-up by the programme States and were under various stages of implementation during 1998-99. Table - 4.2 shows the number of Watershed Projects sanctioned and taken up during the last four years since the introduction of the new Guidelines.

In addition, financial assistance of Rs.10 crores was provided to CAPART during 1997-98 for execution of 400 watershed projects through the voluntary sector. Against this provision, CAPART had so far sanctioned 41 watershed projects at a total cost of Rs. 183.50 lakhs and released Rs. 69.59 lakhs to the implementing agencies.

There are two districts, Doda and Udhampur, in Jammu and Kashmir where DPAP is being implemented. But the State does not figure in the above table as the Government of Jammu and Kashmir continues to follow the old Guidelines in the implementation of DPAP during 1998-99 also due to the disturbed conditions prevailing in these districts. The State is expected to operationalise the new watershed guidelines from the next financial year.

The Statement at Annexure-XVIII provides State-wise physical and financial performance under DPAP during 1998-99.

**Desert development programme**

*Introduction*

Over the years, the increase in human and livestock population in desert areas has placed the natural resources of the region under great stress. The major problems are continuous depletion of vegetative cover, increase in soil erosion and fall in ground water table. All these factors account for diminishing productivity of land and loss of natural resources. The problems would have been worse but for the introduction of some specific highly focused area development programmes in these areas. On the recommendations of the National Commission on Agriculture in it's Interim Report (1974) and Final Report (1976), the Desert Development Programme (DDP) was started in the year 1977-78. The programme was started both in the hot desert areas of Rajasthan, Gujarat and Haryana, and the cold desert areas of Jammu & Kashmir and Himachal Pradesh. The objective of the programme has been to mitigate adverse effects of desertification and adverse climatic conditions on crops, human and livestock population, combating desertification and restoring ecological balance of the area.

In hot sandy desert areas, sand dune stabilization and shelter belt plantations were given greater weightage. On the other hand, in cold desert areas, since rainfall is negligible, crop cultivation and afforestation could be taken up only through assured irrigation. In these areas, the main activity was water resources development by construction of channels for diversion of water flow from the glacier and springs to the fields and lift irrigation works in the valleys.

Though the Programme created good impact in the areas treated, overall impact in the identified areas in the country was not very encouraging. Some State Governments had also been requesting this Ministry for inclusion of additional areas under the programme. With a view to identifying the infirmities in the programme and also to consider the cases for inclusion of additional areas, a Technical Committee on the DPAP and the DDP was constituted in 1993-94 under the Chairmanship of Prof. C.H. Hanumantha Rao, Ex-Member, Planning Commission. The Committee submitted its Report in April, 1994.

The main reasons identified by the Committee for the far from satisfactory results under the programme was that area development was not taken up on watershed basis and the involvement of the local people both in planning and execution of the programme was virtually nonexistent. Besides inadequacy of funds, non-availability of trained personnel and taking up of too many activities, which were neither properly integrated nor necessarily related to the objectives of the programme, were also identified as contributory factors towards reducing the impact of the programme.

Based on the recommendations of the Committee, new districts/blocks were included under DDP and a fresh set of Guidelines for Watershed Development applicable to DPAP, DDP, IWDP and EAS (50%) were issued in October, 1994. These Guidelines were made applicable from the year 1995-96.

**Objectives**

In a broad sense, the objectives of the programme are to promote the economic development of village community, restore ecological balance and improve the economic conditions of resource poor and disadvantaged section of society through creation, widening and equitable distribution of resources and increased employment opportunities. DDP has been envisaged as an essentially land-based activity and conceived as a long-term measure for restoration of ecological balance by conserving, developing and harnessing land, water, livestock and human resources. Objectives of the programme have been recast as under :-

- Combating drought and desertification.
- Encouraging restoration of ecological balance.
- Mitigating the adverse effects of drought and adverse edapho-climatic conditions on crops and livestock, and productivity of land, water and human resources.
- Promoting economic development of village community.
- Improving socioeconomic conditions of the resource poor and disadvantaged sections of village community viz. assetless and women.

**Strategy**

Although the DDP has been under implementation in several areas, its impact had been felt only in the areas actually treated by core activities. Growing population and poverty compounded the problem by increasing pressure on fragile ecosystems. On the basis of lessons learnt, the major elements of new strategy are :-

- Area development under the programme will be on watershed basis only and a watershed project of about 500 hectares would be the field unit for implementation and it will be developed in four years.
- The strategy adopted to achieve these objectives involved development of the programme area on watershed basis. However, in some sandy areas where it is not physically feasible to demarcate a

watershed, programme is to be implemented by adopting either a cluster of village or an Index Catchment as the unit of planning.

- There would be direct participation of the local people in planning and development of watersheds and maintenance of assets after the project is completed through Watershed Association (WA) comprising of all adults residing within watershed project area and its executive body named as Watershed Committee (WC).
- The Zilla Parishads, Panchayat Samitis and Gram Panchayats have the right to monitor and review the programme at district, blocks and village levels. The Panchayati Raj Institutions can also function as Project Implementation Agencies (PIA) if they so desire.
- Similarly, in the new system of programme implementation a voluntary agency can be selected as a Project Implementation Agency by the DRDA/ Zilla Parishad. The voluntary agencies have an effective role particularly in motivating people, community organizations and training.
- Keeping in view the problem of sand dune stabilization in 10 districts of Rajasthan, 50% of funds under DDP for implementation of watershed projects allocated to each concerned district, has been permitted for three activities namely; sand dune stabilization, shelter belt creation and afforestation.

**Coverage**

Under DDP 227 blocks of 36 districts having an area of 457,432 sq.kms. in 7 States are covered. The States where DDP is under implementation are Andhra Pradesh, Gujarat, Haryana, Himachal Pradesh, Jammu and Kashmir, Karnataka and Rajasthan.

**Number of districts and blocks covered under DDP**

| S.N. | Name of the State | District | Blocks |
|---|---|---|---|
| 1. | Andhra Pradesh | 1 | 16 |
| 2. | Gujarat | 6 | 47 |
| 3. | Haryana | 6 | 44 |
| 4. | Himachal Pradesh | 2 | 3 |
| 5. | Jammu & Kashmir | 2 | 10, |
| 6. | Karnataka | 3 | 22 |
| 7. | Rajasthan | 16 | 85 |
| | Total | 36 | 227 |

**Guidelines for watershed development**

Main features of new Guidelines for Watershed Development are :-

- At the district level the District Rural Development Agency/Zilla Parishad will be in overall charge of implementation of the programme. The DRDA/ZP will be advised in regard to selection of Project Implementation Agencies (PIAs), approval of Watershed Plans, training, publicity etc., by a district level Watershed Development Advisory Committee under the chairmanship of Project Director, DRDA/CEO, ZP.
- The DRDA/ZP will select the PIAs which could be besides DRDA/ZP itself, other line departments, autonomous organizations, public sector undertakings, voluntary organizations, cooperatives, banks, etc. The PIA will remain in-charge of implementation of the Watershed Projects (WPs). A multi-disciplinary team designated as Watershed Development Team (WDT) shall assist each PIA in the implementation of these WPs.
- Planning and implementation of the Watershed Project will be done with the technical support of multi-disciplinary Watershed Development Team by

the WA comprising all adult members of the village(s) in the watershed area. 75% of the project fund will be spent directly by the Watershed Association on the development works of each project.

- The Watershed Committee comprising of 10- 2 nominated members by the Watershed Association from amongst the user groups, self-help groups, with representation from Gram Panchayat, Watershed Development Team, women, Scheduled Castes, and Scheduled Tribes will be the executive body of the Watershed Association.
- As per Guidelines for Watershed Development issued by this Ministry, 10% of the total project cost is earmarked for administrative expenditure, 5% for community organization works, another 5% for training to people associated with the implementation of Watershed Projects and 80% for works.
- As regards the Panchayati Raj Institutions (PRIs), the Zilla Parishad at the district level may remain overall in-charge of implementation. The Panchayat Samiti and Gram Panchayat will have the right to monitor and review the implementation of programme and can take the responsibility of implementing the projects as PIAs.

The Guidelines also provide for an elaborate institutional arrangement at the, Centre for monitoring, review and policy making, at the State level for monitoring and review of programmes and at the district level for selecting Watershed Projects and Project Implementation Agencies, monitoring and review of the implementation of the programme. Problem of inadequacy of funds has been tackled by allowing utilization of 50% of the Employment Assurance Scheme

(EAS) funds for the development of watersheds. Training has been made a continuous process and 5% of the funds of each project has been earmarked for training of the WDT members, field functionaries and the local people. There is an inbuilt provision in the guidelines for maintenance of assets created under the watershed development projects.

**People's participation**

The guidelines for Watershed Development issued by this Ministry is an instrument, which provides an opportunity to local people to not only involve themselves in the implementation of the programme but is a tool for capacity building and empowerment of participating village community. The critical key factor in the implementation is people's participation in all aspects of the programme. It has been envisaged under the Guidelines that the local people through User Groups and Self-help Groups formed by the Watershed Association shall execute the whole work of Watershed Development Projects.

Under the new Guidelines, area development on watershed basis has been made mandatory. To ensure people's participation, an elaborate institutional mechanism at various levels has been prescribed which include the formation of Watershed Association and a Watershed Committee for each watershed project. Watershed Association comprises of all adults residing within a watershed project area. Watershed Committee is the executive body of the Watershed Association constituted by it by nominating 10- 12 members from amongst the Self-help Groups (3-4), User Groups (45), Gram Panchayat (2-3) and a member of the Watershed Development Team (WDT). This Committee has been made responsible for planning and development of Watershed Projects with the technical assistance from the

Project Implementation Agency. PIA provides technical input through a Watershed Development Team having four experts in the disciplines of Animal Sciences, Plant Sciences, Civil/ Agricultural Engineering and Social Sciences.

**Role of Panchayati Raj institutions**

Panchayati Raj Institution have been assigned very active role at the district, block and village levels in the programme. The State Governments have been authorized to empower the Zilla Parishads to discharge all functions of the District Rural Development Agencies (DRDAs) for planning and development of the watershed projects. In that capacity, the Zilla Parishad will select the Watershed Projects and the Project Implementation Agencies, approve Watershed Plans, release funds to the PIAs and the Watershed Committees and monitor and review the implementation of the programme. The Panchayat Samitis have been given the right to monitor the implementation of the programme at the block level and give guidance for integration of other area development programmes. At the village level, the Gram Panchayat is to be fully involved in mobilizing the community, training, dovetailing of other programmes and maintenance of common property resources such as pasture lands, fisheries tanks, plantation etc. The Gram Panchayat has been entrusted with the task of monitoring the implementation of the programme.

In addition to the above mentioned functions, the Panchayati Raj Institutions are also entitled to take on the responsibility of planning and development of a cluster of watershed projects. In the capacity of a Project Implementation Agency, the Zilla Parishad/ Panchayat Samiti/Gram Panchayat concerned shall be subjected to the complete discipline and control of DRDA as any other PIA. They will have to constitute Watershed

Development Team on the same lines as any other PIA and shall accordingly be entitled to demand and receive the prescribed administrative cost for each project.

**Finding pattern**

The DDP is a Centrally Sponsored Programme and funds are released to DRDAs/ZPs for implementation of the programme. The Central share under each type of project area based on the ecosystem type is as under :-

| *S.No.* | *Type of ecosystem* | *Central share* |
|---|---|---|
| 1. | Hot arid (non-aandy) areas | 75% |
| 2. | Hot arid (sandy) areas | 100% |
| 3. | Cold arid areas | 100% |

The State-wise number of Watershed Projects to be taken up has been arrived at on the basis of the following criteria fixed at block level.

| *Area of block (Sq.kms.)* | *No. of WPs to be taken up* | *Block allocation (Rs. in lakhs)* |
|---|---|---|
| Upto 400 | 3 | 16.86 |
| 401-800 | 5 | 28.10 |
| Above 800 | 6 | 22.72 |

In different ecosystems, project cost has been fixed according to the severity of the problems. At present the following rates are applicable in different areas:-

| *S. No.* | *Ecosystem Type* | *Per ha. cost (Rs.) Average* | *Watershed project cost (Rs. in lakhs)* |
|---|---|---|---|
| 1. | Hot sandy aricl region | 5,000 | 25.00 |
| 2. | Hot arid region | 4,500 | 22.50 |
| 3. | Cold arid region | 5,000 | 25.00 |

**Achievements**

Under DDP, a number of projects have been targeted and sanctioned for implementation in identified areas. All these projects are envisaged to be completed in a 4-year period and are at different stages of implementation.

The year 1995-96 was the first year of implementation under the new Guidelines for Watershed Development. A considerable amount of time was therefore, spent on preparatory works, making institutional arrangement viz. selection of watersheds and PIAs, imparting training, community organizations and planning before commencement of actual works. This led to slow down in expenditure. The details of budgetary provision and expenditure incurred during in the last three years are given below :-

*(Rs. in lakhs)*

| *Year* | *Budget* | *Release* |
|---|---|---|
| 1994-95 | 8,400.00 | 8,459.55 |
| 1995-96 | 10,000.00 | 10,100.00 |
| 1996-97 | 65,00.00 | 6,536.38 |
| 1997-98 | 7,000.00 | 7,000.00 |

Since inception till 1994-95 as core sector activities, 1.85 lakh ha. under land resource development, 0.83 lakh ha. under water resource development and 2.85 lakh ha. under afforestation and pasture development have been developed. Since inception till 3 1 st March' 1998, a total sum of Rs.845 crores has been spent on the programme. In 1997-98, a sum of Rs.70 crores was released to different DRDAs/ZPs. During 1998-99, a provision of Rs. 90 crores has been made. In the Ninth Five Year Plan (1997-2002), a sum of Rs. 1,430 crores has been proposed.

# 2

# India's Population: Issues and Options

According to Planning Commission estimates, population figures are expected to go up from 856 million in 1991-92 to 938 million in 1996-97, showing an annual average growth rate of 18 per cent. If the growth rate remains around two per cent, this figure will go up to 955 million, According to current indications, the actual figure will be in between these two figures since the death rate has fallen below even the 2000-2001 and in any case will be below the rate of around two per cent as estimated by the current UN projections, of around 1,042 million in that year. If India is able to achieve a population growth rate of around 1.6 percent in the decade 2000-2001 to2010-2011, its population will reach 1,171 million, if the Planning Commission projections are used as a base. Even if this target is exceeded, the figure will be less than 1,224 million as estimated by the UN. These projections have not incorporated the detail of the 1991 census. The Registrar—General's Working Group on Population Projections set up conventionally by the Planning Commission, will have to firm up these alternative conjectural projections, in terms of underlying fertility, mortality and expected life span-behaviour, by age—group and rural-urban categories.

The other major category needing examination on this kind of perspective is the land or resource base of the economy. The Planning Commission has correctly projected that the net area sown or arable land of the country will remain constant at 141 million hectares. Growth in net area sown at around one per cent annually in the early period of planing fell to around 0.6 per cent and then to 0.3 per cent in subsequent decades and is now not growing at all. It is reasonable to assume that the exploitation of the geographical area of the country or the extensive land frontier has reached its limits. This is an important issue, the implications of which are not being realized with the urgency they deserve, since at a basic level resource constraints of a more severe kind faced by certain East Asian economies are now being approached in India. Organizations, communities, households and individuals will have to grasp this fact and live with it.

The intensive frontier for land use, however remains. It has been known for example that cropping intensity depends on irrigatin. Thus gross cropped area or harvested area has been shown in the past to be strongly determined statistically, in an econometric sense, by net irrigated area and irrigation intensity. This fundamental relationship can be used to project the intensive resource base of the economy.

Recognizing these problems the Finance Minister has been persuaded to introduce an Accelerated Irrigation Benefit Programme in the Annual Plan for this year. An outlay of Rs. 800 crore has ben provided for large irrigation project where substantial achievement can be expected—say in completing a section of the canal systems in the next two or three years and Rs. 100 crore for delivering water to the field in the next two agricultural years. These programmes will be strictly monitored. More important, a blue ribbon com-mission has been set up with the following terms of reference:

— To prepare an Integrated Water Plan for development of water resources for drinking, irrigation, industrial, flood control and other uses;

— To suggest modalities for transfer of surplus water to water-deficit basins by interlinking of rivers for achieving the above objectives;

— To identify important ongoing projects as well as new projects which should be completed on a priority basis together with phasing;

— Identify a technological and interdisciplinary research plan for the water sector with a view to maximizing the benefits;

— To suggest physical and financial resource generation strategies for the water sector; and

— Any other related issue.

The projections assume a vastly improved performance on the land and water management frontiers. It needs to be remembered that the balance ground water reserves towards the later half of the nineties will be nore and more limited. A very dramatic effort will be needed to harvest and carefully use the available water. Otherwise, the projected increase in cropping intensity will simply not take place. Cropping intensity increased from around 1.3 in the early nineties. In the nixt two decades, this effort needs to be considerably strengthened, so that cropping intensity can increase from 1.3 to 1.5. Harvesting of rainwater, recycling water from agricultural drainage systems, more judicious use of water for cropping, will all be required, Non-agricultural use of water will have to be far more econmical.

Another way of looking at the severe land constraint

is to see that a net area sown per person will go down from around 0.17 ha to around 0.10 ha. The gross area sown per person currently around 0.2 ha will, even if cropping intensity increases very rapidly, go down to around 0.15-0.18 ha.

It has been shown elsewhere that limited co-operation in waer use has been successful in many watershed projects in resolving the land constraint. The same is true of lower level surface irrigation systems. Community involvement is also important for judicous management of aquifer systems and ground water use. In many cases, land management questions are equally important and are inextricably linked with water management, eg land shaping in hill slopes and on farm investment in irrigation commands.

The technology interface is important, both for land and water management and for cropping and non-crop farm systems that are optimal, in this class of issues. While a lot of research has been done and is available, the real issues are policy rules for fast replicability of existing knowledge and success stories. Community institutions have to be at the heart of this process. ICAR, its centres and sponsored institutions, have not easily participated in this process.

Work force: This kind of development is simply not possible if the functional literacy skills of the farm population arenot improved and if the peasant who works on the land, does not have rights to make improvements on it. There are a number of significant examples where based on local initiative, educational and training institutions led to knowledge-based growth in rural areas. These include the Charotar Vidya Mandal at Vallabh Vidyanagar (later Sardar Patel University), Dharamasthala Educational Trust (efforts of Veerendra Heggade) and many co-operative sponsored institutions in Maharashtra (for example the Pravara Ecucational Trust at Loni). Recognizing the importance of such efforts, the government of India has set up a National Council for Rural Institutes. The ICAR and its affiliates must be one of the major thrust institutions in this effort and its educational and extension wings must sponsor, acredit and support the effort.

The government's Basic Minimum Services (BMSDs) Programme also has the same objective. It consists of the following programmes which need integration with our agricultural strategy:

— 100 per cent coverage of provision of safe drinking water in rural and urban areas.

— 100 per cent coverage of primary health service facilities in rural and urban areas.

— Universalization of primary education.

— Provision of public housing assistance to all shelterless poor families.

— Extension of mid day meal programme in primary school to all rural blocks and urban slums and desadvantaged sections.

— Provision of connectivity to all unconnected villages and habitations.

—s Streamlining the public distribution system with the focus on the poor.

India's population, as on 1 March 1991 stood at 846.30 million (439.23 million males and 407.07 million females). This includes the projected population of 7.72 million of Jammu and Kashmir. The second largest populous country, India is the home of 16 per cent of world's population. The country, however, accounts for 2.42 per cent of the total world area.

The population of India as recorded at each decenial census from 1901 has grown steadily except for a decrease during 1911-21. In absolute terms the country's population has increased by 162.97 million during the decade 1981-91. An encouraging feature revealed by the provisional results is the decline in growth rate of the population in the last decade compared to 1971-81. It marginally decreased from 24.66 per cent recorded in 1971-81 to 23.85 per cent during 1981-91.

In most states the growth rate declined during the decade. However, Andhra Pradesh, Arunachal Pradesh, Madhya Pradesh, Maharashtra, Nagaland, Tripura, West Bengal, Daman and Diu, Lakshadweep and Pondicherry which account for one third of the country's population, recorded increase in growth rate. Nagaland registered the highest growth rate of 56.08 per cent while Keral the lowest 14.32 per cent.

The NSS estimates of per capita consumption of different sections of the urban population in 1967-68 suffer from similar underestimation. In column 2 of the Table we have reproduced the NSS estimates of per capita consumption of the urban population in 1960-61 only slightly revised to bring them in accord with the official estimate of per capita national consumption. In column 2 are given the NSS estimates of per capita consumption in 1967-68 at 1960-61 prices. It will be seen that the NSS estimate of per capita urban consumption in 1967-68 (Rs. 325.7) is 8.6 per cent below the NSS estimate of urban consumption in 1960-61. Therefore, the estimate in 1967-68 is clearly an underestimate. The nature of underestimation becomes evident from column 4 where the NSS estimates for 1967-68 are expressed as percentages of corresponding estimates for 1960-61. These percentages increase progressively from 77.2 per cent for the poorest 5 per cent to 99.6 for the population lying between 60-70. Thereafter the percentages decline rapidly, implying that the upper middle and the richer sections of the urban population did not do comparatively as well as the middle sections. This is incredible and the conclusion is inevitable that the underestimation of urban consumption has been more serious in the case of the upper middle and the richer sections than in the case of other sections.

Hence, the NSS estimates of urban consumption in 1967-68 need to be revised. As in the case of the NSS estimates for rural consumption, we shall do the necessary revision conservatively in two steps. In the first stage (columns 5 and 6), we suppose that the percentages in column (4) should not decline as they do after reaching the value 99.6 for the class 60-70; hence we hold them at 99.6 for all classes above 60-70. The results are given in colum (5). It will be seen that this revision causes the NSS estimate for 1967-68 to rise from Rs. 325.7 to Rs. 346.7. It is nevertheless still below the estimate of per capita consumption in 1967-68 namely Rs. 364.9. In fact, it needs to be raised by 5.25 per cent to bring it to that level. We do this by raising uniformly the revised estimates of consumption of all sections (column 6) by 5.25 per cent.

The results are eye-opening. The lower middle and poorer sections constituting the bottom 40 per cent of the ruban population have not benefited at all by the economic development of the past decade. Indeed, the evidence is that their per capita consumption has declined and greatly so among the poorest 10 per cent. This is not impossible. It is this class which sufferes from rise in prices as was witnessed in the past decade. There are other important reasons for such serious deterioration in the living standards at the bottom of the urban population. We shall refer to them a little later.

Other sections of the urban population have

benefited variously. The per capita consumption of the middle sections lying between 40-60 increased by between 1.0 and 3.0 per cent; of the upper middle and the richer sections constituting the top 40 per cent of the urban population, the per capita consumption increased by 4.8 per cent. All visible and audible evidence points to the possibility that the consumption of the richer sections, the top 10 per cent or the top 5 per cent certainly, has increased much more. But in the absence of positive evidence, we prefer to be conservative. We should be thankful that statistcis could catch even as much of the reality as we have been able to discover.

The statistical evidence on growth of inequality is thus clear. A superficial examination and comparison of the NSS estimates of consumer expenditure in 1960-61 and 1967-68, as is commonly done, gives an impression that the inequalities in the distribution of consumer expenditure have narrowed down during the past decade. Unfortunately this is not true. The NSS estimates of consumption in 1967-68 are gross underestimates and the underestimation is particularly serious in the case of consumption of the upper middle and richer classes. The statistical evidence on both these counts is conclusive. Hence the NSS estimates of per capita consumer expenditure in 1967-68 must be corrected for underestimation.

As we have seen, even a conservative revision makes clear that all sections of the population have not benefited equally from the economic development of the past decade. The gains of development have remained largely confined to the upper middle and the richer sections constituting the top 40 per cent of the population. While the overall per capita consumption increased by about 3.9 per cent in seven years, the consumption of the upper 40 per cent of the rural population increased by at least 4.4 per cent and that of the upper 40 per cent of the urban population increased by at least 4.8 per cent. These increases are not extraordinary and they certainly are not undesirable. Unfortunately they have remained largely confined to the upper middle and richer sections of the population. The middle, lower middle and poorer sections of the rural population showed much smaller increases in their per capita consumption and the per capita consumption of the poorest 5 per cent actually declined a little. The situation in urban areas appears even more serious. The per capita consumption of the lower middle and poorer sections constituting the bottom 40 per cent of the urban population declined and the consumption of the poorest 10 per cent declined by as much as 15 to 20 per cent. Such unequal distribution of the gains of development inevitably leads to growing inequality and a widening gulf between the rich and the poor.

**Urban situation**

We have earlier noted that, during the period from 1960-61 to 1967-68, the rural-urban disparity has narrowed down a little. Thus, while in 1960-61 the per capita urban consumer expenditure was 37.7 per cent higher than the per capita rural consumer expenditure, in 1967-68 the urban per capita expenditure was only 35.9 per cent higher than the rural per capita expenditure. We shall now examine how this slight reduction in the rural-urban differential came about. In particular, we shall ask whether the reduction in the rural-urban differential came about because of a reduction in the differential between the rural-urban rich or the rural-urban poor. We have put together the relevant data. In columns (4) and (7) of the Table we have expressed the per capita urban consumer expenditure as per cent of the per capita rural consumer expenditure for each of the 12 sections into which we have divided the population.

To begin with, we should not that even in 1960-61, the rural-urban differential was much greater between the rural-urban rich than between the rural-urban poor. For instance, the per capita consumer expenditure of the 30 per cent urban poor was then about 27 per cent higher than the per capita consumer expenditure of their rural counterparts. On the other hand, the per capita consumer expenditure of the 20 per cent urban rich was then about 47 per cent higher than the per capita consumer expenditure of their rural counterparts.

The corresponding data for 1967-68 are given in column (7) of the Table. It will be noticed that the differential between the rural and urban upper middle and richer classes was practically the same in 1967-68 as it was in 1960-61 It increased only slightly. The urban upper middle and richer classes seem to have done compartively a little better than their counterparts in rural areas. But the situation is quite the contrary in respect of the middle, the lower middle and the poorer sections. These classes in urban areas have done distinctly worse comparatively to their counterparts in rural areas so that the differential between them has narrowed down. This is more true of the lower middle than the middle classes and even more true of the poorer classes than the lower middle classes. The narrowing down of the rural-urban differential is on account of the lower middle and poorer classes in urban areas having thus moved closer to their rural counterparts.

What has happened to the 10 per cent poorest in rural and urban areas is the most striking. As we have noted, the 10 per cent rural poor have stayed practically where they were at the beginning of the decade. On the other hand, the 10 per cent urban poor have difinitely suffered. As a result, they have moved close to the rural poor. In 1960-61, the consumption of the urban 5 per cent poorest was 27.2 per cent higher than the consumption of their rural counterparts; in 1967-68, it was only 4.5 per cent higher. The same is true of the 5 per cent poor next above them. In 1960-61, their consumption was 29.2 per cent higher then their counterparts in the rural areas; in 1967-68, it was only 10.2 per cent higher. These small margins are certainly not adequate to compensate the higher cost of urban living at this level. It means that in 1967-68 the living standard of the 10 per cent urban poor was worse than that of their rural counterparts.

It is necessary to understand the meaning of this deterioration in the living standards of the urban poor. It does not necessarily mean that the same people were worse off in 1967-68 in comparison with their condition in 1960-61. This is not imposible. But more generaliy it means that new migrants have moved from the rural area into the growing urban centres and have been compelled to accept life at a level much below what used to be the case a decade ago and hardly distinguishable from the life they left behind and to escape which they moved into the cities. It is thus that the rural-urban disparities have somewhat narrowed down.

We should conclude. During the past decade, the per capita private consumer expenditure increased by less than half a per cent per annum. Moreover, the small gains have not been equitably distributed among all sections of the population. The condition of the bottom 20 per cent rural poor has remained more or less stagnant. The condition of the bottom 20 per cent urban poor has definitely deteriorated; and for another 20 per cent of the urban population, it has remained more or less stagnant. Thus, while the character of rural poverty has remained the same as before, the character of urban poverty has deepened further. This is the consequence of the continuous migration of the rural poor into the urban areas in search of a livelihood, their failure to find adequate means to support themselves there and the resulting growth of pavement and slum life in the cities. All the latent dissatisfaction about the slow progress of the economy and the silent frustration about its failure to give the poor a fair deal, let alone special attention, appear to be gathering in this form. Its shape today is probably no more than hideous; allowed to grow unheeded and unrelieved, it will inevitably turn ugly.

The Urban land (Ceiling and Regulation) Act, 1976 came into force on 17 February 1976. It applies to all the state governments and union territories except Jammu and Kashmir, Kerala, Nagaland and Sikkim hich have not adopted the Act so far. It also excludes Tamil Nadu which had enacted its own law in 1978. The Act was enacted in order to prevent concentration of urban land in the hands of a few persons and also to curb speculation and profiteering therein with a view to bring about an equitable distribution of urban land to sub-serve the common good. The Act is mainly implemented by the state governments through the competent authorities appointed by them for performing various functions under the provisions of the Act.

As per the information furnished by various state governments/union territories, 2,19,506 hectare of land has been estimated as excess vacant land. Out of this, 40,480 hectare of excess vacant land has been vested in the state governments/union territories. The state governments/union territories have acquired physically 14,816 hectare of excess vacant land. On the front of the social housing, 2,980 schemes were approved involving 5,320 hectare of vacant land for the purpose of construction of 4,02,449 dwelling units for the weaker sections of society. In order to make the Act more workable and to simplify the procedure various amendments to the Act have been fomulated and are under consideration of the Government.

Urban Water Supply and Sanitation is a State subject. Schemes are formulated, implemented, operated and maintained by the state governments/union territory administrations. Funds are provided for the purpose under the state plans. As per the information available, the coverage of urban water supply and sanitation till December 1991 was 85 per cent and 46 per cent respectively. The working group for the formulation of the Eighth Plan recommended to provide drinking water facilities to cent per cent population and with sewerage and sanitation facilities to 75 per cent of the urban population by the end of the Eighth Plan (1992-97). In order to achieve the objective, the Working Group envisaged amount of Rs. 23,634.56 crore for the Eighth Plan. However, only an outlay of * Rs. 1,114.54 crore has been provided for the Annual Plan 1993-94 under the state sector. During 1994-95, an amount of Rs. 16.99 crore was distributed amongst those staes which were considered earlier for the first instalment. Various training programmes have been initiated for human resource development in planning, design, operation and maintenance and management of urban water supply and sanitation schemes. The Government has introduced use of micro-computer for planning and designing of water supply distribution and sewerage systems besides imparting training to pubblic health engineers. Financial assistance was provided to several state agencies dealing in urban water supply and sanitation sector for procuring micro-computers. The agencies have procured the computers and accessories and installed them in their organisations.

The Ministry sponsors research and development projects to various institutions in the country in order to develop appropriate technologies in the field of water supply and sanitation which can be applied not only in implementation of the project but also in their operation and maintenance and to acheive an overall improvement in the sector. The Urban Development Ministry has developed a Managment Information System (Mis) which has been disseminated to state public health engineering departments and water supply and sewerage boards for implementation. The Ministry provides technical advice and accords technical approval for urban water supply and sanitation schemes in order to get loan assistance from LIC, World Bank and other bilateral agencies.

The Scheme of Urban basic Services for the Poor (UBSP) was launched in 1990-91. The scheme is based on the covergent provision of social and physical inputs in low income, urban neighbourhoods through the programmes of various specialist departments with the active participation of community groups. The cardinal objective of scheme is to improve the overall quality of life of slum dewllers. The Cabinet has approved the scheme for the Eighth Plan period. From the inception of the Eighth Five Year Plan, the programme is being implemented on a 60:40 sharing basis between the Central and state governments. Further, the per capita expenditure will be Rs. 75 in the first year and Rs. 50/- from the second year onwards after the basic infrastructure hs been established. A total outlay of Rs. 100 crore has been provided for the scheme for the Eighth Plan period. The scheme is to be implemented in collaboration with the state sector scheme of Environmental Improvement of Urban Slums and the Centrally-sponsored scheme of Nehru Rozgar Yojana. By the end of the Eighth Plan period, it is expected that the benefit of the scheme will extend to urban areas having a total slum population of about 70 lakh and, on a national basis, targets 500 cities and towns. The National Plan of Action (NPA) on Children which is a follow-up of the promises made by the global fraternity at the World Summit for Children in 1990, reiterates and re-affirms

India's commitment to the cause of women and child development. NPA goals became opertional from early 1992. One of the major objectives of the UBSP scheme is to achieve the goals of the NPA on Children in the urban poor localities by planning and organising various programmes being implemented by different ministries/ departments.

Upto March 1995, over 3,622 neighbourhood development committees comprising primarily of urban poor women have been set up in around 283 towns taken up for provision of basic services all over the country. This represnets community based structures covering around 48.26 akh low income women and children. It is expected that approximately 70 lakh beneficiaries will be covered under UBSP programme by; the end of Eighth Five Year Plan. On a national basis, the Eighth Five Year Plan targets 500cities and towns. Around 2,997 mini plans have already been prepared and 460 community organisers are in the field working as catalysts for enriching community participation. In order to monitor the scheme a National Level Monitoring Committee has been set up under the Chairmanship of Secretary, Ministry of Urban Affairs and Employment.

The Scheme of Urban Micro-Enterprises (SUME) is being implemented from June 1990 under the Nehru Rozgar Yojana (NRY). The scheme covers unemployed urban poor whose family income is less than Rs. 11,850 per annum in metropolitan areas, cities and towns, not covered by Integrated Rural Development Programme (IRDP).

Under the scheme, subsidy at the rate of 25 per cent of the project cost is given to each beneficiary subject to the ceiling of Rs. 5,000 for SCs/STc and women beneficiaries and Rs. 4,000 for others. Repayment is made in three to five years with the suitable monthly/quarterly instalments depending upon the surplus cash generation. The applications are sponsored by the Urban Local Bodies (ULBs) viz., Nagar Panchayats and Municipalities which act as nodal agency. Applicants should * have lived in the locality at least for three years. The security for the loan will be the asset created out of the loan and no security or third party guarantee is necessary. While 30 per cent of the funds would be utilised for women beneficiaries, SCs/STs are to be given weightage in proportion to their population share in total urban poor of the ULB concerned. During 1993-94, an amount of Rs. 12,647.69 lakh was sanctioned against 1,78,956 applications.

Prime Minister's Rozgar Yojana (PMRY) for educated unemployed youth was launched on 2 October 1993. the objective of the scheme is to provide sustained employment to about 10 lakh educated unemployed urban youth in micro-enterprises during the Eight Five Year Plan. These enterprises cover manufacturing, service and business ventures. The scheme was implemented in urban areas during 1993-94 and from 1 April 1994, throughout the country. Self-Employment Scheme for Educated Unemployed Youth (SEPUY) has been subsumed with PMRY from 1 April 1994. The salient features of the scheme are: (i) Youth between the age of 18 and 35 belonging to families having incomes of less than RS. 24,000 per annum would be eligijble for assistance under the scheme; (ii) These educated unemployed entrepreneurs would be given a subsidy of 15 per cent subject to a ceiling of Rs. 7,500 each for starting the micro-enterprises; (iii) They would be required to bring in five per cent of the project cost as margin money; (vi) Each entrepreneur will be eligible for a loan upto a ceiling of Rs. one lakh and this loan would not require a collateral gurantee; (v) The entrepreneurs selected under the scheme would be provided training before the loan is granted; (vi) Not more than 30 per cent of the micro-enterprises would be from the business sector; (vii) Besides matric passed or failed students and ITI passed youth, all the persons who have undergone Government sponsored technical courses for a minimum duration of six months will be eligible for assistance under the scheme; (viii) Reputed NGOs would also be associated in the implementation of the scheme especially in the selection training of entrepreneurs and preparation of the project under the scheme; (ix) A reservation of 22.5 per cent for SCs/STs and 27 per cent for other backward castes (OBCs) has been provided; (x) Women shuld be given preference and the beneficiary should have been a permanent resident of the urban area for three years. Upto December 1994, 60,513 applicants have been sanctioned loans amounting to Rs. 32,226.65 lakh (by all Indian scheduled commercial banks).

With approximately 27 per cent of its population living in urban areas, India is one of the least urban countries, but with an urban population of 217 million (1991) it is also a country with one of the largest urban populations. India's towns and cities could, by themselves, make up the third largest nation of the world.

Urban India consists of close to 3500 towns varying in size from the smallest district towns with a population of 5,000 to the large urban agglomerations exceeding 10 million people. Nearly two-thirds of the urban population is concentrated in 317 'Class I' towns, or cities with a population of over 100,000 of which half lives in 23 metropolitan areas with populations exceeding 1 million. The four largest cities—Bombay, Calcutta, Delhi and Madras—between them account for one sixth of the urban total. the Class I towns are the fastest growing urban areas in India. Greater Bombay, with apopulation of 12.57 million, and Calcutta with 10.86 million, are among the largest metropolitan areas in the world.

While over the past four decades the popultion of India has more than doubled, during the same period the urban population has more than quadrupled. The growth has come as much from net migration as from natural increase (about 40 per cent each), with the balance due to reclassification and inclusion of new towns.

The National Commission on Urbanization (1988) states that "these urban centres have also generated tha most brutal and inhuman living conditions, with large sections of the citizens living in squatter settlements. The overcrowding in the slums and the desperate lack of water and sanitation leads not only to severe health problems but to abject degradation of human life." It further remarks that "in the decades to come, who knows how much political tension and physical viloence will be triggered off by the flrgrant display of wealth which coexists with the rising expectations of the poor and with the appalling conditions of congestion and pollution which form their environment?"

The estimate of proportion of urban people living in slums varies from about 20 per cent to 30 per cent. Looked at by class of town, the highest percentage of people living in slum areas is in the cities with a million plus population and the least in towns with less than 100,000 population. The growth rate of the slum population, largely through continuing in migration, is significantly faster than that of other segments of the urban population. While this phenomenon is in no way unique to India, it is the sheer size of the problem in India that is staggering.

About 27 per cent of the urban population lives below the poverty line, 30-40 per cent of the population of the larger metropolitan areas live in slums, 27 per cent does not have access to water-borne sanitation. Indian cities also have very high levels of air and water pollution. As a result, the environment that the rural migrant has to live in, is as harsh a choice between environment and development as one can pose.

And yet the choice is made. It is made by over 13,500 people each day who move from rural to urban environments and the several million who continue to live in the highly degraded areas of urban India. The urban slum is their 'gateway'. It is the 'solution' rather than the 'problem' of urban living. It is both a low cost housing solution and a low cost transportation solution, as the slum is usually close to the place of work. But it makes nevertheless for squalid surroundings. It is a price that is paid, and paid consciously—because the option, where it even exists, is worse. Urban poverty is preferred to rural poverty.

Air pollution is a problem in some urban areas. Heavy vehicles cause 47 per cent of the pollution while accounting for 8 per cent of the total number of vehicles on Indian roads. The production of automobiles in India has increase from 1,891 in 1955 to 116,564 in 1988. Two and three wheelers constituting 63 per cent of the number of vehicles cause 13 per cent of the total pollution. While this pollution does cause localized problems, the number of vehicles is so small that it has negligible impact at the global level. Efficient public transport options, which will cut down on both fossil fuel consumption and pollution need to be explored.

The noise levels in many of the Indian cities is much above the safe limit. This is due to diverse factors which include industrial manufacturing activities, excessive use of vehicle horns, and unregulated use of loudspeakers at social, political and religious events. Awareness must be created in this regard.

The question that is difficult to understand is not so much why the poor decide to stay in slums, but rather how much remains to be done about improving conditions in these areas. The Report of the National Commission on Urbanization feels that "For whatever reason, resource allocation in the urban field seems to follow a problem rather than anticipate it." Furthermore, "the inefficiency of our cities and towns is being perpetuated by obsolete, rigid and irrational laws, regulatory provisions and norms. The urban centres, with their concentration of diverse activities, should be generators of wealth; instead, they have degenerated into parasites looking elsewhere for support."

The family Welfare Programme has helped in containing the growth rate of population. Total Fertility Rate has declined from 4.5 in 1981 to 3.5 in 1993 as per the estimates of Sample Registration System (SRS). The Crude Birth Rate has decreased from 33.9 per provisional estimates of the SRS. The Crude Death Rate has also declined from 12.5 to 9 per thousand population over the same period. The Infant MOrtality Rate dropped from 110 per thousand live births in 1981 to 74 in 1995. The annual average exponential population growth rate has come down marginally from 2.22 per cent during 1971-81 to 2.14 per cent during 1981-91. The population, however, continues to grow as the decline in birth rate has not been as rapid as the decline in the death rate.

There are, however, inter-State differences in the achievements of the Family Welfare Programme. At one end of the spectrum are the States like Kerala, Tamil Nadu and Goa which have already achieved replacement level of fertility. At the other end, are the large States like Uttar Pradesh, Madhya Pradesh, Rajasthan and Bihar where fertility levels and bjirth rates continue to be higher than the national average. Therefore, decline in the rate of growth of population for the country as a whole depends upon how the large northern States perform in the family welfare programmes in the future. Unless effective steps are taken to bring about significant improvements in the programme, the performance in containing the growth of population at the All India level may not change significantly.

Recognising the close relationship between high birth rates and high rnfant mortality, high priority has been accorded to the Maternal and Child Health (MCH) programme since 1985. In order to achieves the main objective of MCH, (i.e. to improve the health status of women and children and to reduce maternal, infant and child morbidity and mortality rates), the Universal Immunisation Programme (UIP) was launched in 1985. From the year 1992-93 the UIP has been strengthened and expanded into the Child Survival and Safe Motherhood (CSSM) programme. Under this programme, apart from strengthening the existing MCH, initiative has been taken to expand the pilot projects on Acute Respiratory Infection Control and Traditional Birth Attendants training. For this, a provision of Rs.350 crore has been made in the 1996-97 budget as against Rs.220 crore in 1995-96 (BE).

From 1.4.1996, the Family Welfare Programme is being implemented on the basis of the "Target Free Approach" (TFA). This approach envisages replacement of the system of setting contraceptive targets from the top by a system of decentralised participatory planning at the Primary Health Centre level.

Pursuant to the World Health Organisation (WHO) goal to eradicate poliomyelitis (polio, a major crippling childhood disease) by the year 2000 A.D., the Pulse Polio Immunization (PPI) was launched in 1995-96. About 87 million children aged 0-3 years were administered as supplemented dose of oral polio vaccine on 9.12.1995 and

93 million on 20.1.1996, irrespective of their routine immunisation status. Since PPI received an overwhelming response from the public, the exercise was repeated on 7.12.1996 and 18,1.1997 covering about 120 million children in the age group of 0-5 years.

A Special School Health Check-up Scheme for Primary School Children was carried out in 27 States/ UTs in July 1996, and in the remaining 5 States between August and October 1996. The objectives of this Scheme were to detect common health related problems among primary school children; to conduct screening of children for appropriate referral and check up; to generate health awareness in the community; and to ensure arrangements for follow up and treatment at higher level medical facilities. Reports from 441 districts show 75.9 per cent coverage of schools and 84.9 per cent coverage of enrolled children.

In order to foster community involvement in the Family Welfare Programme, two new schemes have been started on a pilot basis. Under one of these, one revenue village in every district, among villages with a population of 500 or more, will be given an award of Rs. 2 lakh for achieving a reduction in the Crude Birth rate, Infant Mortality Rate and Child Mortality Rate. The second schemes aims to integrate family welfare and health care into the ongoing National Wastershed Development Project for Rainfed Areas (NWDPRA) of the Ministry of Agriculture. Under this scheme, the watershed level community based management structures, known as the 'Mitra Krishak Mandal' (MKM) will conduct surveys and prepare watershed level family welfare and health care plans. An amount of Rs. 5000 will be given to each village in the watershed areas, for specified activities like emergency obstetric care and purchase of essential medicines.

The Prenatal Diagnostic Techniques (Regulation and Preventation of Misuse) Act, 1994, has been brought into force from 1st January, 1996. This Act makes it illegal to use prenatal diagnostic techniques like amniocentesis for determining the sex of the foetus, a practice that often leads to abortion of female foetuses. Statutory machinery for implementation of the Act has been established.

Uttar Pradesh continued to be the largest state, population wise with 16.44 per cent people of the country living there (13,91,12,287) followed by Bihar with 10.21 per cent (8,63,74,465) and Maharashtra with 9.33 per cent (7,89,37,187). West Bengal occupied fourth place accounting for 8.04 per cent (6,80,77,965) of the country's population followed by Andhra Pradesh with 7.86 per cent (6,65,08,008). Ranking of the states and union territories according to population size is in table 2.

Bombay metropolis continued to be the most populated city of the country with urban population of 12.60 million, Calcutta taking the second place having 11.02 million. Delhi ranks third with a population (urban) of 8.42 million followed by Madras 5.42 million.

**Population factors**

One of the important indices of population concentration is the density of population. It is defined as the number of persons per square kilometre. The population density has gone up from 216 in 1981 to 267 persons in 1991 (excluding Assam and J&K). In 1901 it was 77 persons per sq km followed by Chandigarh (5,632). Lakshadweep which has the smallest population size is the fourth most densely populated area with a density of 1,616 persons per sq km. Arunachal Pradesh is the most sparsely populated area of the country with 10 persons per sq km.

The 10 heavily populated districts of the country are Calcutta, Madras, Greater Bombay, Hyderabad, Delhi,

Chandigarh, Mahe, Howrah, Kanpur City and Bangalore. All of them have density of above 2,000 persons per square kilometre and 5.01 per cent of the country's population lives in these districts. The average density of these districts is 6,888.

In any study of the population, analysis of the sex composition plays a vital role. The sex composition of the population is affected by the differentials in the mortality conditions of males and females, sex selective migration and the sex ration at birth.

Sex ratio is defined as the number of females per 1000 males. In India, it has generally been adverse to women. The ratio has also declined over the years except in 1981 when it slightly improved to 934 from 927. In 1991, there has been a fall by seven points to 927 per thousand males. But Kerala represented a different spectrum. The state has a higher number of females than males, 1,036 females for thousand males.

In the Indian context, a sex ratio of 950 and above can be considered as favourable to females. The states and union terrtories coming under this category besides Kerala are Himachal Pradesh (976), Andhra Pradesh (972), Goa (967), Karnataka (960), Manipur (958), Orissa, (971), Tamil Nadu (974),

Dadra and Nagar Haveli (952), Daman and Diu (969) and Pondicherry (979). Chandigarh accounted for the lowest number of females per thousand males with 790.

**Socio-economic dynamics**

Overall economic growth in terms of Gross Domestic Product (GDP) at constant factor cost improved from 0.8% in 1991-92 to 6.3% in 1994-95 and 7% in 1995-96 aided by a growth rate of 2.4% by agriculture and allied sectors, 11.7% by industry and construction sector and 7% by services. Overall economic growth during the first four year of the 8th Plan (1992-97) averaged 5.9% per annum compared with the planned target of 5.6%.

The domestic savings rate measured in terms of gross domestic savings as a proportion of GDP at current market prices increased from an average rate of 21.3% in 1992-93 and 1993-94 to 24.4% in 1994-95. The rate of domestic investment measured in terms of gross domestic capital formation as a proportion of GDP at current market prices increased from 21.6% in 1993-94 to 25.2% in 1994-95.

Industrial production which was virtually stagnant in 1991-92 increased by 9.4% and 12.1% in 1995-96 supported by a growth rate of 6.9% in mining, 13.6% in manufacturing and 8.1% in electricity generation. As per the latest information available, industrial growth deceleration to 8.5% in April-June 1996 due to deceleration of growth rates in all the sub-sectors (3.6% in mining, 10.4% manufacturing and 2.2% in electricity generation). As per growth rates by use-based classification, capital goods sector recorded a growth rate of 14.2%, intermediate goods 11.9%, consumer durables 11.1% and consumer non-durables 8.6% in April-June 1996. However, the growth rate of basic goods sub-sector having a weight of 39.4% in the overall industrial production was only 4% in April-June 1996.

Seven infrastructural sectors, namely, electricity, coal, steel, cement, crude oil and petroleum product & fertilizer with a combined weight of 31% in the Index of Industrial Production (IIP) recorded a growth rate of 7.8% in 1995-96. But their growth rate decelerated to 3.2% in April-August 1996 due to poor performance of electricity generation (growth rate of only 2.4%) and crude oil production (decline of production by 10.4%).

The outlook of agricultural production in 1996-97 is excellent with foodgrains output likely to reach 197 million tonnes compared with 185 million tonnes in 1995-96. This is primarily due to this year's rainfall distribution being the best in the past five years. The late withdrawal of monsoon has further ensured bright prospects for rabi production this year.

The estimate of foodgrains production in 1995-96 has been scaled down to 185 million tonnes representing a sharp decline of nearly 6 million tonnes over the prec * eeding year. The shortfall was substantial (about 3 million tonnes) in wheat output, besides short-fall of production of rice and coarse cereals. Consequently wheat procurement dropped steeply to 8.2 million tonnes compared to 12.3 million tonnes in the preceding year. Public stock (Central Pool) of foodgrains was about 22.1 million tonnes as on September 1, 1996.

There are 23 districts in Assam of which Cachar, Karimganj and Hailakandi are the three plain districts and Karbi Anglong and North Cachar Hills are the two hill districts in its southern part. Karbi Anglong is known as the biggest district in southern Assam covering an area of 10,434 sq. kms in contrast to Hailakandi being the smallest district with the area of 378 sq. kms. The two hill districts cover 68% of the total area in South Assam. Out of 33 lakh population, 75% of it live in the three plain districts and the district Cachar alone gives shelter to 36.7% of its total population.

Over the years there has been consistent rise of both population and density in South Assam. The density of populaltion has increased from 75 per sq. km. in 1960–61 to 98 per sq. km. in 1970–71 and further to 149 per sq. km. in 1990–91 as against the corresponding figures of 286 persons in all Assam and 267 persons at the all India level. In contrast Karimganj has been observed to be the most thickly populated district in South Assam with the highest density of 457 persons per sq. km.

Out of 33 lakh population in South Assam, 15.89 lakh are living in the Cachar district alone as against 0.69 lakh in N.C. Hlls. The percentage of female population to total population is varying from district to district from the lowest of 46.16% to the highest of 48.61%. It is estimated that 76% of the total female population are living in the plain districts and percentage of female has been higher in rural areas than that of the urban areas in all the five districts in South Assam.

Urbanization is one of the important indcators of development in an economy. South Assam's economy being a part of the Indian economy is no exception to this. It is found that about 3.2 lakh population in South Assam are living in the urban areas. Among these urbanites 37.4% are living in the Cachar district and 22.1% in Karbi Anglong. It is estimated that 67% of the total urbanites are lliving in the plain districts only. The extent of urbanization is found to be too less in Kailakandi and N.C. Hills in comparison to other three districts in South Assam.

According to 1960-61 census reports, there were only one lakh of urban population in South Assam. However, there has been slow but a continuous rise in their number over different census periods. The number has increased from 1.51 lakh in 1970–71 to 3.19 lakh in 1990–91. In other words, the percentage of urban population to total population has increased from 6.04% to only 9.64% in 1990–91. The figure of 9.64% is comparatively too low to the al India average of 25.7% and all Assam average of 11.1%. The highest growth rate of urban population of 22.87% is observed in the N.C. Hills district. Growth of urban population has been observed to be relatively higher in the hill districts than that of the plain districts.

Literacy being another important indicator of socio–economic development reflects the relative position of the region in the country. It is estimated that 14.5 lakh of people in South Assam are literate of which 40.4% are living in the Cacher district alone. Only a measure 4.8% of the total literates live in N.C. Hills. It also reveals that 79% of the total literate in South Assam live in the three plain districts. There has been slow but a steady rise in the growth of literacy in the region. During 1960–61 the lliteracy rate was at the level of 26.7%. This was increased to 28.5% in 1970–71 and further to 43.9% in 1990–91. Comparing this literacy rate of 43.9% in South Assam with the corresponding rate of 42.5% in Assam and that of 52.2% in India it can be said that not only South Assam but also the whole of the Assam state is lagging behind in this respect. Moreover, within South Assam the lowest literacy rate of 35.9% is observed in the Karbi Anglong district as against 48.3% in Cachar.

Surprisingly female literacy is much better in this part of the state in Assam. It is estimated that 5.6 lakh females are literates. The percentage of female literacy is relatively at a higher level of 38.4% as against the corresponding rates of 35.2% in Assam and that of 24.8% at the all India level. However, it is in much worse a positon compared to Nagaland and Mizoram where the rates are 45.5% and 64.1% respectively. As far as different districts are concerned, there is no significant variation in the female literacy rates in South Assam.

The Central Statistical Organisation (CSO) conducted the first economic census in 1977 to bridge the data gaps in the unorganised sectors of non-agricultural economy. The economic census was aimed at providing basic information on distribution of non-agricultural enterprises and to provide a frame for follow-up surveys for collection of detailed information about the structure of enterprises, investments, input, output, emploument, etc. The first economic census was followed by two sample surveys-one in 1978-79 relating to unorganised manufacturing and the second in 979-80 devoted to trade, transport, hotels and restaurants, storage and warehousing and services.

The second Economic Census was conducted in 1980 during the houselisting operations of 1981 Population Census with increased scope and coverage. It covered all enterprises (establishments and own-account enterprises) in the non-agricultural sector excluding crop production and plantation. Based on the information thrown up by this Census, three follow-up surveys were carried out, one in 1983-84 on hotels and restaurants, transport, storage and warehousing and services; second in 1984-85 on unorganised manufacturing and third in 1985-86 on wholesale and retail trade. The frame of 1980 Census was updated during 1987-88 in 64 towns. On the basis of Economic Census 1980 and updated frame, four sample surveys were conducted.

The third Economic Census 1990 was conducted along with the houselisting operations of 1991 Population Census in all states/union territories except Jammu and Kashmir. The data processing of Economic Census 1990 was undertaken in a decentralised manner by state/ union territories. Some of the states/union territories utilised the services of Regional Computer Centres at Calcutta and Chandigarh. The all India results of Economic Census 1990 brought out shortly by the CSO for which processing and tabulation has been done by the Computer Centre, Department of SAtatistics. On the basis of the frame thrown up by Economic Census 1990, a follow-up survey covering sectors of mining and quarrying and storage and warehousing was conducted during 1992-93 and another survey on hotels and restaurants and transport was conducted during January to September, 1994.

According to 1980 Economic Census, there were 18.4 million enterprises in the country (excluding Assam) employing 53.6 million persons. Among these, these were 16.9 million enterprises (58.4 per cent in rural areas) engaged in non-agricultural activitties employing 50.7 million persons (43.3 per cent in rural areas). As per of the results of Economic Census 1990, there were 25 million enterprises out of which 22.7 million were in the non-agricultural sector. The total number of persons usually working were of the order of 72.1 million out of which 40.2 million were hired workers. A total of 17.7 million enterprises operated without any hired labour on a regular basis and were mainly run by the households themselves.

Ministry of Finance is responsible for administration of finances of the Government. It is concerned with all economic and financial matters affecting the country as a whole including mobilisation of resources for development and other purposes. It regulates expenditure of Government including transfer of resources to the states. This Ministry comprises three departments, namely, (i) Economic Affairs, (ii) Expenditure and (iii) Revenue.

The Department of Economic Affairs consists of seven main divisions namely, (i) Economic, (ii) Banking, (iii) Insurance, (iv) Budget, (v) Investment, (vi) External Finance and (vii) Currency and Coinage. This Department inter alia monitors current economic trends and advises Government on all matters of internal and external economic management including working of commercial banks, term-lending institutions, investments regulations, external assistance, etc. Preparation of the Budget of the Union of India as well as the state governments and union territory administrations with legislature when under President's rule and their presentation to Parliament is also the responsibility of this Department.

The Department of Expenditure comprises eight main divisions, namely, (i) Plan finance Division, (ii) Establishment Division, (iii) Cost Accounts Branch, (iv) Controller General of Accounts, (v) Finance Commission Division, (vi) Implementation Cell, (vii) Integrated Finance Division and (viii) Staff Inspection Unit.

Department of Revenue exercises control in respect of revenue matters relating to direct and indirect Union taxes through two statutory boards namely, Central Board of Direct Taxes and the Central Board of Excise and Customs. This Department is also entrusted with the administration and enforcement of controls and regulatory measures provided in the enactments concerning Central sales tax, stamp duties, gold control, foreign exchange and other relevant fiscal statutes. Control over production and disposal of opium and its products is also vested with this Department.

Industrial production grew by 9.7 per cent in the first seven months of 1996—97, 1.9 percentage points slower than the 11.7 per cent growth in the first seven months of the previous year, which was the highest in 25 years. The growth of 9.5 to 10.5 per cent would still be the second highest growth rate in 25 years. It says, "the good performance of industrial production in 1996—97 is due entirely to the manufacturing sector, which has maintained its high growth." During the first seven months of the year the rate of growth of the manufacturing sector was 12.1 per cent, virtually the same as 12.3 per cent in 1995—96.

The Survey attributes the slowing of industrial production to the dramatic fall in the rate of growth of electricity production and a slowing down of growth in the mining sector, mainly because of the 10 per cent decline in crude oil production. During the first seven months of the year, electricity production has grown only by 3.4 per cent compared to 10.1 per cent in the corresponding period of 1995—96. If despite slowdown of electricity generation, manufacturing has recorded good growth, one possible reason could be captive generation, which is increasingly being used as a backup to public supply, the Survey adds. This hypothesis is supported by the growth of about 22 per cent in the volume of diesel imports.

Another noteworthy aspect of industrial production in 1996—97 has been acceleration in the rate of growth of capital goods production to 16.5 per cent from 15 per cent in the first seven months of the previous year. In contrast capital goods inports have declined by six per cent in the first seven months of the year. This according to the Survey, shows the increased competitiveness of the domestic capital goods industry.

The Survey also refers to the deceleration in the growth rate in the production of consumer durables, such as cars, to 9.8 per cent in the first seven months of 1996—97, compared to 30.2 per cent in the first seven months of the previous year. The delisensing of investment in consumer durable and decontrol of imports of parts of these goods, contributed to boom in investment and production in the sector. The decline in growth during 1996—97 suggests that the pent—up demand in the domestic economy has been met. Further growth will depend on increased cost competitiveness, which requires fuller exploitation of the comparative advantage that India has in the production of labour—intensive parts. Some analysts, however, seen in the sudden saturation of the demand a falacy in the general belief of the size of the middle class with good purchasing power, estimated at 200 million.

The Survey rates as poor the overall performance of the core and infrastructure sectors during the first 8 months of 1996—97 (April—November). Six industries, namely electricity generation, coal, steel, crude oil, petroleum products and cement, with a combined weight of 28.8 per cent in the Index of Industrial Production (IIP), averaged a growth of 4.1 poer cent in April—November, 1995. It says the previous Surveys had emphasised the need to accelerate, widen and deepen reforms of th non—tradable infrastructure and energy sectors, to avert an impending mismatch between economic growth and provision of these services. The new government, it says has repeatedly stressed its firm determination to reform the infrastructure and energy sectors and has take a number of policy decisions and new initiatives.

The Survey says continuing restraint on money supply growth is among the factors that have kept the prices in check. Despite the recent rising trend inthe growth of WPI, the average inflation for 1996—97 is expected to be at least one percentage point less than the average inflation in the previous year. There was complete change in the sectoral pattern of price changes du;ring 1996—97. The annual rate of inflation accelerated sharply in the "fuel, power, light and lubricants" and primary articles, while decelerating in the "manufactures" group. The annual rate of price increase in the fuel—power group went up to 17.4 per cent in January 1997 from 1.1 per cent a year ago because of administered price increase, while that of primary articles to 11.7 per cent from 2.6 per cent. The rate of growth in prices of manufactured goods declined to 3.6 poer cent from 6.9 per cent in the previous year. The rise in prices of primary goods has largely been due to rise in prices of cereals and fruits and vegetables.

Money supply growth has been higher in 1996—97 than in 1995—96, the Survey says, adding "Upto the fornight ended January 17, 1997, broad money (M3) grew by 10.6 per cent as against 8.2 per cent growth in the corresponding period of 1995—96. The average call money rate declined from a high of 13.75 per cent at the beginning of the currently financial year to a range of 5 to 11 per cent in September 1996 and ruled between 10 and 11 per cent in December 1996, before falling to low single digits in January 1997. The reversal of the 1997—96 excess demand for funds for investment in 1996–97 has led to a general softening of interest rates during the year. The cut—off yields on 91—day treasury bills has come down from 12.4 per cent in the first week of July to around 7.5 per cent at the end of January 1997.

Control over fiscal deficit was identified by the Update to the Economic Survey, presented by the United Front Government last year as one of the three challenges for economicpolicy. The Budget for 1996—97 envisaged a reduction of the fiscal dificit by 0.8 per cent of GDP to 5 per cent from 5.8 per cent in 1995—96 (RE). The primary deficit is also budgeted to fall from 1.1 poer cent of GDP to 0.2 per cent, while the revenue deficit to 2.5 per cent of GDP from 3 per cent in 1995—96.

The reduction in fiscal deficit has been attempted through an increase in revenues coupled with a reduction in expenditure. Revenue receipts (net) are budgeted to increase by 18.3 per cent during 1996—97 (BE). Despite a larger outgo on account of interest payments, subsidies and provision for revision of salaries and pension, total revenue expenditure is budgeted to grow at a lower rate of 12.7 per cent compared to 17.5 per cent in the previously year (RE). This deceleration in the growth of revenue expenditure has led to a decline in revenue expenditure to GDP ratio from 13.1 per cent in 1995—96 to 12.9 per cent in 1996—97 (BE). This favourable outcome, the Survey claims, is largely on account of containment of non—interest, non—plan expenditure growth at 9.3 per cent during 1996—97, about half the growth of 18.6 per cent in 1995—96 (RE). Consequently, non–interest revenue expenditure as a proportion of GDP is budgeted to fall to 8.1 per cent from 8.3 per cent in 1996—97 (RE). The revenue deficit is budgeted to fall by 0.5 per cent point of GDP. One may, however, note that the comparison of Budget estimates (BE) with Revenue Estimates (RE) is not very realistic.

Attainment of industrialisation over the last 48 years has been striking feature of Indian economic development process which was launched as a conscious and deliberate policy in the early fifties. In pursuance of this policy, large investment has been made in building up capacity over a wide spectrum of industries. Industrial production has made rapid strides in terms of variety, quality and quantity. There has been a substantial diversification of industrial base during this period with the consequent ability to produce a very broad range of industrial goods. Self-reliance has been achieved in basic and capital good. Indigenous capabilities have now been established to the point of virtual self-sufficiency so that further expansion in various sectors such as mining, irrigation, power chemicals, transport and communication can be based primarily on indigenous equipment. Process of industrialisation has also fostered entrepreneurship and development of a wide variety of technical, managerial and operative skills. Today, the country is in a position to provide consultancy services as well as managers, technicians and skilled workers for setting up industrial projects aborad.

The Industrial Policy Resolution of 1948 marked the beginning of the evolution of Indian Industrial Policy. The resolution not only defined the broad contours of the policy, it delineated the role of the State in the industrial development both as an entrepreneur and as an authority.

Successive policy resolutions also reiterated this basic tilt in favour of the public sector. The Industrial Policy Resolution of 1956 gave the public sector a strategic role in the economy. It categorised industries which would be the exclusive responsibility of state or would progressively come under state control and others. Earmarking the pre-eminent position to the public sector, it envisaged private sector co-existing with the State and thus attempted to give the policy framework flexibility.

The Industrial Policy initiatives undertaken by Government since July 1991 have been designed to build on the past industrial achievements and to accelerate the process of making Indian industry internatinally competitive. It recognises the strength and maturity of the industry and attempts to provide the competitive stimulus for higher growth. The thrust of these initiatives has been to increase domestic and external competition through extensive application of market mechanism and facilitating forging of dynamic relationships with foreign investors and suppliers of technology. The process of reform has been continuous.

As on 31 March 1993 there were 245 central public sector undertakings, comprising of eight in the construction sector, 72 in services and remaining 165 in the manufacturing. The number of CPSUs as indicated above exclude nine companies, six insurance companies and three financial institutions with Central Government investment but without direct responsibility of management.

The total capital employed in the 245 CPSUs increased from Rs. 1,179.91 billion in 1991-92 to Rs.

1,399.33 billion in 1992-93. The overall rate of return on capital employed in the PSUs also increased from 2.0 per cent in 1991-92 to 2.43 per cent in 1992-93.

The number of small scale units as at the end of 31 March 1994 were 2.38 million comprising of 1.77 million registered units and 0.61 un-registered. The overall production in the small scale sector during 1993-94 has been estimated to have reached Rs. 2,416.5 billion. The total value of exports of these units has been Rs. 177.85 billion in 1992-93.

**Agriculture**

The rate of agricultural growth of the order of around 3.2 per cent per annum during the fifties was derived from acreage increases to the extent of 70 per cent. In the sixties, the rate of growth which was only 2.1 per cent in this sector and did not neutralize even the rate of increase of population in that decade, could be derived from acreage increase to the extent of 30 per cent only. The scope for any further increase in acreage for increasing agricultural peoduction has exhausted in the seventies and the entire increase in farm production had to come from improvement in per acre productivity. This has required high level of capital–intensive effort in the development of the agricultural sector.

According to a competent study, the capital output ratio in Indian agriculture has already touched the figure of four and is close to the same scale as is required in industry. For the same reason, the fact has to be reckoned with that absorption of labour in agriculture through a significant rise in yields on land has tended to be a comparatively limited and expensive process and this process alone cannot be relied upon to solve the growing unemployment problem. The running controversy on priorities as between agriculture and industry, in particular heavy industry, is thus futile and misleading in the context of the realities of Indian economic situation and its growth prospects. The idea that India enjoys a comparative advantage in agricultural output inIndia is now crucially dependent on growth of inputs from industry. The need is thus not to fforeclose available resources in the economy for the so called development needs of the agricultural sector but to mop up a substained part of the surpluses and incremental incomes generating in the agricultural sector to meet the investment requirements of infrastructural development, including heavy and intermediate goods industries,to inputs for agriculture at a rapid and accelerating pace.

If much credit is taken for achieving self—sufficiency in food grains relative to effective domestic demand, there is now much brave talk of making India one of the few "grain powers" in the world even while large number of Indian people still do not have access to adequate food. Agriculture in India will have to go a long way yet before it can feed the Indian people. It is too early to talk of India becoming a "grain power." But the official policy has already veered to the postion that the government would not come in the way of the farmers exporting their produce and these exports would not be banned "merely" for bringing supplies and prices down for the domestic consumers. The upshot has been that while good grains have been exported, two million tonnes of wheat are being imported in the current year, 1996—97 to meet even the effective demand in the domestic market. The danger inherent in this position is not imaginary.

The widening disparities in incomes and levels of living combined with growing concentration of land and the swelling ranks of landless rural labourers are manifest. It is not amiss either to consider the pricing of agricultural produce, more especially food grains—the primary wage goods—and examine its influence on the general price trend and structure of relative prices in the Indian economy. The Agricultural Prices Commission, to start with, recommended a particular set of prices based on its studies of the cost of production, fair return to the farmer and fair prices for the consumer. It has been a practice, by and large, to improve upon the prices recommended by the APC in order to provide additional incentives to the surplus farmers to increase production for the market. After the launching of the so—called economic reforms in 1991, however, the baalance between the claims of the surplus farmer and the consumer has been tilting sharply in favour of the former and the inflationary impact of "incentive prices" for good grains and other agricultural produce has been ignored. Subsidised farming by way of what are called "incentive prices" for farm produce and subsidised inputs for agriculture like chemical fertilizers, private irrigation facilities like tubewells and pumpsets, power andcomparative soft—term credit, was conceived in the wake of the disastrous drought years of 1964-65 as the means of stimulating agricultural production for the market and securing control over a substantial part of the marketable surpluses so produced.

There were probably compelling reasons under the given ownership pattern in cultivable land for adopting this strategy when shortages of agricultural commodities, especially of food grains, ad emerged as an endemic problem of the economy—its stability and further growth. But the concomitant of this development has been the growing commercialization of agriculture and emergence within it to prominence of that segment of farmers with their commercial interests which produce and control agricultural surpluses. In the course of time, however, as shortage in cereals or other crops are overcome relative, of course, to effective market demand at the present low-level of purchasing power in the economy, the system of subsidised production and marketing in agriculture has become in essence a mechanism to ensure to the surplus producer a monopoly to all the gains arising from incrreases in production and productivity.

Among the vast numbers of Indian farmers, only a small fraction, and more than 10 per cent of the total, commanding the best cultivable land produces for the market on any scale. They also monopolise the subsidised supply of inputs and credit and benefits of infrastructural facilities such as irrigation and power created by public investment.

Agricultural crop production in 1996—97 is expected to show good recovery from the slower growth in 1995—96. Growth is projected at 3 per cent after a fall of 0.4 per cent in 1995—96. The sharp decline in foodgrains production by 3.4 per cent, which was responsible for the slow growth in 1995—96, is expected to be reversed by an increased of 3.3 per cent in 1996—97. Foodgrains production is expected to recovery is primarily due to coarse cereals, as well as an anticipated rise in wheat production which suffered a sharp setback in 1995—96.

As the agricultureal year runs from July to June, the estimates for 1995—96 were only firmed up after the end of the financial year. A large downward revision (of 3 million tonnes) was made in the estimate of wheat production for 1995—96. The revision was unexpected and unexplained, because average rainfall in 1995—96 was quite normal. The revision, late in calendar year 1996, also created severe problems for the management of the food economy.

Commercial crop production has done extremely

well in 1996—97 with oilseeds and cotton expected to reach record levels of 24.1 million tonnes and 14.3 million tonnes, respectively. Jute and mesta have also shown a growth of 3.4 per cent this year. Sugarcane output is, however, unlikely to maintain the record level of 283 million tonnes attained in 1995—96.

Industrial production (as measured by the index of industrial production–IIP), grew by 9.8 per cent in the first seven months of 1996—97, 1.9 percentage points slower than the 11.7 per cent growth in the in the corresponding period of 1995—96. The good performance of industrial production in 1996—97 is due entirely to the manufacturing sector, which has maintained its high growth.

The slowing of industrial production is clearly attributable to the dramatic fall in the rate of growth of electricity production and a slowing of growth in the mining sector mainly because of the 10 per cent decline in crude oil production. During the first seven months of 1996—97, electricity production (as measured by the index) has grown by only 3.4 per cent compared to the 10.1 per cent growth in the corresponding period of 1995—96. It is somewhat surprising that manufacturing sector growth has been barely affected by the slow growth in electricity production. One possibility is that captive electricity generation, which is increasingly used as a back—up to public supply, has substituted for the lack of generation by electricity boards. The high growth of diesel imports, about 22 per cent by volume in the first seven months of 1996—97 (with total refinery throughput growing in the normal range of around 4 per cent), is consistent with this hypothesis. At present, electricity statistics incorporate little or no data on captive power generation.

Another noteworthy aspect of industrial growth this

year is the acceleration in the rate of growth of capital goods production to 16.6 per cent in the first seven months of this year from 15 per cent in the first seven months of last year. This has off—set the decline in the rate of growth of consumer goods and basic goos. In contrast, capital goods imports have declined by 6 per cent in the first seven months of 1996—97. This shows the increased competitiveness of the domestic capital goods industry.

The overall performance of the core and infrastructure sectors during the first 8 months of 1996—97 (April—November) has been poor. Six industries namely, electricity generation, coal, steel, crude oil, petroleum products and cement, with a combined weight of 28.8 per cent in the Index of Industrial Production (IIP), averaged a growth of 4.1 per cent in April—November, 1996, less than half the 8.9 per cent, in April—November, 1995. The deceleration in the growth rate of these infrastructure industries is mainly due to a decline in crude oil production and power generation. Hydro power generation declined by 7.7 per cent, and thermal power generation grew by only 6.4 per cent in the April—November, 1996 as compared to 14.6 per cent in the April—March, 1995—96. Coal, cement and refineries' throughput have grown faster in April—November, 1996—97 compared to the corresponding period of 1995—96. Growth of sectors such as railways, ports and telecommunications, which do not appear in the IIP, also slowed. The rate of growth of railways' revenue earning goods traffic decelerated marginally from 7 per cent during 1995—96 to 6.3 per cent for April-November 1996. Growth of cargo handled at major ports and new telephone connections provided decelerated more sharply to 4.7 per cent in April—November, 1996 (from 9.1 per cent in 1995—96) and 8.3 per cent in April—November, 1996 (from 23.3 per cent in 1995–96), respectively. The slower growth in cargo handled by ports in probably the result of a deceleration in the growth of external trade. The telecomunications slowdown, however, suggests that the pace of implementation of telecommunications reform needs to be accelerated and its scope widened to include Department of Telecommunications as a service provider. Given the parlous financial state of many public utilities, particularly the State Electricity Boards, the possibility of crises worsens with each passing year. The new government has repeatedly stressed its firm determination to reform the infrastructure and energy sectors. In line with this commitment, a number of policy decisions have been taken and new initiatives launched.

High Yielding Variety Programme was started in 1966-67 as a major plan of agriculture strategy for increasing production of foodgrains in the country. Cropwise details are shown in table 3. The programme is supported through a number of Centrally-sponsored schemes and thrust has been shifted from single crop to cropping system approach since 1994-95. Identifying potential areas, the country has been grouped in three major cereal based cropping systems viz., (i) Integrated Cereal Development Programme in Rice Based Cropping System Areas (ICDP-Rice); (ii) Integrated Cereal Development Programme in Wheat Based Cropping System Areas (ICDP-Wheat); and (iii) Integrated Cereal Development Programme in Coarse Cereal Based Cropping System Areas (ICDP-Coarse Cereal).

These thrust programmes are designed to increase the productivity and production of foodgrains through adoption of latest scientific production technology. Minikit demonstration programme aims at popularising newly released varietity and getting the newly released evolved varieties tested under field conditions. For this a large number of seed minikits containing 0.25 kg to 10 kg seed are distributed at a nominal cost to farmers. State level training programmes are being organised at agricultural universities and ICAR research institutes in collaboration with concerned state agriculture departments to disseminate the latest crop production technology to the district/block level extension officers.

About 990 lakh hecare area in the country is rainfed accounting for 70 per cent of the net sown area of 1,410.6 lakh hectare. Crops grown and cropping practices followed in these areas entirely depend on the rainfall which is often erratic and unpredictable. Bulk of the crops like rice, jawar, bajara, other millets, pulses, oilseeds and cotton are grown in this area under rainfed conditions. Farmers in these areas, particularly, small and marginal, are still practising subsistence farming and are in the vertex of vicious circle. Wide fluctuations in production occur in these areas year after year. Increasing and stabilising agricultural production in these areas is, therefore, of crucial importance.

Government has given high priority for the development of dryland areas and, therefore, several programmes and projects have been launched for utilisation of potential of these areas for: (i) realising the projected requirement of about 240 mt of annual food production by 2000 AD and to smoothen out fluctuation in annual production; (ii) reducing regional disparities between irrigated and vast rainfed areas; (iii) restoring ecological balance by greening rainfed areas through appropriate mixture of trees, shrubs and grasses; and (iv) generating employment for rural masses and reducing large-scale migration from rural areas to already congested cities and towns. Holistic approach for integrated farming system development on watershed basis in rainfed areas would be main pursuit of the development activities under the National Watershed Development Project for Rainfed Areas (NWDPRA) in the Eighth Plan.

**Allied sectors**

The gross value of output from livestock sector (at current prices) is estimated to account for 26 per cent of the total value of output from Agriculture sector. This excludes the contribution of animal draught power. Animal husbandary is an important source of self employment and subsidiary occupation in rural and semi-urban areas and more so for people living in the drought prone, hilly, tribal and other poorly developed areas, where crop production on its own may not sustain them fully. As revealed by NSS, 1987-88 was 4.15 per cent as against 1.1 per cent for the agriculture sectore as a whole. The recent Land and Livestock Holding Survey (NSS, forth-eitghth round) further reveals that during eighties there was a substantial growth of dairy farming in the country.

The ratio of in-milk bovine stock to 100 households rose from 37 in 1981-82 to 46 in 1991-92. It also highlighted that the rise in ratio during eighties was most pronounced in the states with relvatively high average in milk stock, like Punjab, Haryana and Fajasthan. On the other hand, there was little improvement in the ratio in Kerala, Orissa and Tamil Nadu. The marginal and small holdings constitute the core of the milk production sector accounting for about 66 per cent of the in-milk bovine stock (1991-92 estimate).

In 1995-96, the country produced 66 million tonnes of milk. This represents an average annual growth of 4.5 per cent since 1990-91.

Poultry Farming has become an important activity providing additional income to the weaker sections of the population in rural and semi-urban areas. Poultry farming has made good progess due to research and developmental efforts of the Government and the organised private sector. Egg production is expected to have increased to about 27 billion during 1995-96. Land and Livestock Holding Survey (NSS, forty eighth round, October, 1996) point out that there has been a rapid growth in poultry farming during 1970s and 1980s. The poultry stock per hundred households rose steadily from 107 in 1971-72 to 195 in 1991-92. In 1991-92, the marginal category of farm households (constituting 48 per cent of the households) alone accounted for 55 per cent of poultry stock.

Under the cattle insurance policy, cover is provided for the sum insured or the market value of the animal at the time of death, whichever is less. Animals are normally insured upto 100 per cent of their market value. General Insurance Corporation (GIC) implements various cattle insurance programmes through its four companies under their "Market Agreement on Cattle Insurance". Buffaloes, calves/heifers, stud bulls, bullocks etc. of specified age groups are insured against death due to accidents inclusive of natural causes like fire, lighting, floods, storm, earthquakes, famine diseases, surgical operation, riot, strike and civil commotion and risk of breeding an calving. Insurance policy can also be extended to cover permanent total disability on payment of extra premium. Cattle purchase under poverty allevation programmes are insured under Master Policy. The animals are insured at concessional rate and part of the premium is subsidised by the Government. Under the Cattle Insurance Scheme, at present, about 10 per cent of the total cattle population is covered. The projected target for insuring cattle during 1996-97 was 88 lakhs out of which 48 lakhs was for 'scheme' animals and 40 likhs for 'non-scheme' animals. The position regarding number of cattel covered, premium collected and claims paid during the past 5 years. After taking into account management expenses and incentives, the scheme is presently operating on no-profit-no-loss basis. The scheme is thus operated by the Insurance Companies on their own risk.

India is the seventh largest producer of fish in the world and, perhaps, second in Inland fish production. Fishery sector plays a vital role in sustaining a fairly large proportion of population along the long 8129 kms. coast line. The contribution of fisheries to the net domestic product has increased from Rs. 1479 crore in 1984-85 to Rs. 9826 crore in 1994-95 at current in 1994-95 at current prices showing about six and a half times increase in ten years. The trend of fish production and exports. The target for fish production in 1996-97 is 51.40 lakh tonnes comprising 28.57 lakh tonnes from marine and 22.83 lakh tonnes from Inland waters. An area of 3.86 lakh hactares has been brought under scientific fish culture and 5.04 lakh farmers have been trained in improved practices upto 1995-96 through active support provided under Fish Farmers Development Agencies. Development of brackish water aquaculture through Brakish Water Fish Farmers Development Agencies have been established in the coastal states for providing a package of technical, financial and extension support for shrimp farming. A shrimp and fish culture project is under implementation with the World Bank assistance in 5 states.

**Agriculture census: research and education**

The Department of Agriculture and Cooperation has been conducting agricultural census in each of the Plan period since 1970-71 in collaboration with states and union territories on the recommendation of Food and Agriculture Organisation (FAO) of the United Nations. The censuses in 1970-71 and 1980-81 were organised as part of the World Agricultural Census Programme sponsored by the FAO. They were conducted on complete enumeration basis in states where the land records are maintained. In other states information was collected from 20 per cent villages on enquiry method. The other two censuses with agricultural years 1976-77 and 1985-86 as reference periods were conducted on a census-cum-sample basis to reduce the burden in collection and processing of primary data and also to keep costs low. The Fifth Agricultural Census with reference period 1990-91 has also been taken up on a census-cum-sample basis and the field work is completed in most of the *states/UTs. The data on number and area the states/UTs except Assam and Bihar. All the tables generated from the data relating to Agricultural Census 1990-91 have also been received from 22 states/UTs and the tabulation work in the remaining states/UTs is in progress.

Agricultural census seeks to collect information on distribution of holdings and area operated along with the related characteristics such as tenancy and terms of leasing, and use and cropping pattern, irrigation and source of irrigation, etc., by different size classes. The data is utilised for formulation of poverty alleviation programmes in generral and relief to small and marginal farmers in particular. As part of the agricultural census scheme, an input survey was also conducted for the first time in 1976-77 with a two per cent sample of villages as the first stage of selection. The second and third input surveys with reference periods 1981-82 and 1986-87 were also conducted as part of agricultural censuses 1980-81 and 1985-86 respectively in seven per cent of the total villages in the country. An All India bulletin on input survey, 1986-87 containing detailed results has also been prepared. The fourth input survey with reference period 1991-92 is in progress in seven per cent sample of villages in the country. The field work of Input Survey 1991-92 has been completed in all the states/UTs except Assam and Bihar and tabulation work is also in progress in those states/UTs where the field work has been completed.

The results relating to number and area of operational holdings of agricultural Census 1990-91, have been finalised for All India (in the case of Assam and Bihar, the data of Agricultural Census 1985-86 have been taken). According to the results of the Agricultural Census 1990-91 the total number of operational holdings in the country has increased from 972 lakh in 1985-86 to 1,053 lakh in 1990-91. Operated area on the other hand had risen only marginally, i.e., by about 0.6 per cent. Rise in number of holdings without corresponding increase in area clearly showed pressure of population on land with average size of holding declining from 1.69 hectare in 1985-86 to 1.57 hectare in 1990-91.

Holdings operated by the scheduled casted and scheduled tribes households increased both in number as well as area operated during 1990-91 as compared to 1985-86. In the case of scheduled castes there has been an increase of 9.2 per cent in the number of holdings while the increase in the area operated by them was 3.6 per cent from 1985-86 to 1990-91. On the other hand the scheduled tribes holdings increased by 11.6 per cent while the area operated by them increased by 3.8 per cent during 1990-91 as compared to 1985-86. According to the Agricultural Census 1990-91, the area operated by scheduled caste holdings accounted for 7.9 per cent while the area operated by scheduled tribes clearly accounted for 10.8 per cent of the total operated area. This clearly shows that there has been an improvement in the status of these social groups in the operation of land which may be attributed to various land reforms and other measures taken by the Government.

The Department of Agricultural Research and Education set up in 1973 in the Ministry of Agriculture is responsible for coordinating research and educational activities in agriculture, animal husbandary and fisheries. Besides, it helps to bring about inter-departmental and inter-institutional collaboration with national and international agencies engaged in the same and allied fields. The Department provides government support, service and linkage to the Indian Council of Agricultural Research (ICAR).

Indian Council of Agricultural Research (ICAR), the main organisation of the Department of Agricultural Research and Education (DARE) of the Ministry of Agriculture has played pivotal role in developing agricultural technologies, input materials and critical scientific mass leading to self sufficiency in food. The ICAR is an autonomous apex body at national level which promotes science and technology programmes in the areas of agricultural research, education and extension education. The Council is directly involved in undertaking fundamental as well as applied reasearches in the traditional and frontier areas to offer solution to problems relating to the conservation and management of resources and productivity of crops, animals, fisheries etc. The activities of the ICAR organised into eight subject matter divisions, namely, Division of Crop Sciences, Horticulture, Soil Agronomy and Agro-forestry, Agricultural Engineering, Animal Sciences, Fisheries, Agricultural Extension and Agricultural Education.

The research is carried out through a chain of 45 institutes, four bureaux, nine project directorates (PD), 30 national research centres (NRCs) and 79 All India Coordinated Research Projects (AICRPs) located throughout the country, mostly at 27 state agricultural universities (SAUs) at their 200 zonal research stations. As part of promotional activity, the Council is also helping the SAUs in improving their infrastructural facilities as well as regional research capabilities.

The whole country has been divided into 120 distinct agro-climatic zones and in each of them, a multi-disciplinary regional research station has been established under on-going national agricultural research project. These stations carry out research on multi-dimensional problems of local importance and on factors acting as constraints to the enhancement of agricultural production in a given zone.

For transfer of new improved agricultural technologies developed, the ICAR has created integrated programme of Krishi Vigyan Kendras (KVKs), (183 on-going and 78 newly sanctioned). To train the trainers, there are eight trainers training centres (TTCs). Four of the ICAR institutes have Deemed-to-be University (DUs) status offering graduate and post-graduate education. SAUs allied field making the country self-sufficient in agricultural human resource. ICAR channelises Central assistance to SAUs for strengthening, promoting agriculture education, research and extension.

The educational programmes at the national level are by and large being conducted through 28 agricultural universities located in various states. This includes the North Eastern Hill University (NEHU), Manipur. Four of ICAR's institutes, viz. Indian Agricultural Research Institute, New Delhi, Indian Veterinary Research Institute, Izatnagar. National Dairy Research Institute, Karnal and Central Institute of Fishery Education, Bombay, also perform educational functions and offer post-graduate and basic programmes in the capacity of well-recognised deemed university and award degrees.

Under the SAUs, there are 61 agricultural colleges, 30 veterinary colleges, 16 agricultural engineering colleges, 18 home science colleges, nine fisheries colleges, eight dairy technology colleges, 13 colleges of forestry, eight colleges of horticulture and one college each in the field of sericulture, food science and technology. At present, the admission capacity at the under-graduate and post-graduate levels are 9.715 and 4,500 respectively excluding the capacity of admission in the colleges of central university.

**Urban fringe**

Urban fringe has been existing since the emergence of urban civilisation. However, its importance in the planning process has been realised only in recent times, particularly in the wake of the Industrial Revolution. No doubt, the concept of fringe is prevalent more in metropolitan and big cities than in small cities and towns.

It is now established that industrialisation and urbanisation are inter-related and irreversible processes. These are two sides of the same coin. A small town grows into a big town, a big town intoa city, and then it acquires the status of a metropolis and a mega city. Rapid urbanisation in the country has been accompanied by the emergence of urban fringe and slums in the cities. The existing areas of these cities are put under much pressure, causing excessive clustering and haphazard urban growth. The study on Management of Urban Fringe Land Development in selected Metropolitan cities undertaken by TCPO indicates that too much pressure on urban land during the last two decades has resulted into a decline in the per capita availability of urban land. As of now, a significant percentage 30% to 50% of population in metropolitan cities live in the slum areas in most deplorable and sub-standard conditions.

The emergence of urban fringe depends on various factors like growth of industrial, commercial and institutional activities in the fringe area, the availability of transportation facilities, proximity to the city, the existing spatial capacity of the city to absorb growing population, increasing economic activities and the basic infrastructural facilities being provided in the fringe areas, as well as in the city, etc. Therefore, it is difficult to assign a spatial boundary to define urban fringe.

According to Lewis Keeble the urban fringe is defined "as the land surrounding the town which is not considered as a part of it but whose use is influenced directly by the town". Richard Mayers considers the urban fringe "as the zone between the country and the city while to Andrews the rural urban fringe outward from the economic city in which there is an interminingling of charteristically agriculture and urban land uses." George Wherewein defines the fringe "as the area of transition between well recognised urban land uses and the area devoted to agriculture".

As such there is no exact definition for urban fringe land. It seems it is not possible also. This is because no one can exactly say as to what distance ithe fringe land should extend from the city boundary. One may say that fringe land should include those areas which fall on the fringe of the city, that is the areas falling just out side the boundary of the city. But the question is upto what distance one should go? Some people define fringe areas as those areas which are not contiguous to the existing built up areas of the city, but those which are likely to become contiguous if provided with the right injection of investment towards the right injection of investmnet towards the development of physical and social infrastructure. The structure plan for the Madras Metropolitan Areas has defined urban fringe as those areas that are experiencing considerable pressure form the process of urbanisation.

During initial staes, the urban fringe land would be mostly under agricultural use. However, once migration of population form nearby areas into the fringe land starts, the available land in taken over for housing, commercial, institutional and industial uses.

During recent years, the trend towards rural-to-urban migration as well as urban-to-urban migraton is on the increase and the mobility characteristics are particularly strong towards metropolitan cities. Statistics show populaltion increase annually at national level—2%, at Urban level—3% and in metropolitan cities level—9%. As such, the existing areas of these cities are put under much pressure, causing excessive clustering and haphazard urban growth. According to 1991 census (provisional figures), about 65% of the total urban population live in Class-I cities and 50.6 per cent of urban population live in 23 metropolitan cities alone. Even though the rate of growth to over 40% in 12 metropolitan cities during 1971-81 has been less than the growth of urban population of 46%, the absolute addition of about 12 million people representing 24% of the total addition to urban population is distinctly very high. By the year 2000, India's urban population is excepted to be 325 million, twice the 1981 level, and more than half of India's population growth will occur in urban areas only.

It could be seen from this data that the pressure on land in urban areas had increased manifold during the last two decades resulting in further decline in the availability of per capita urban land. Further, nearly 30 to 50 per cent of the urban population in these cities has been living in slum areas with poor and sub-standard living conditions, with civic amenities far from satisfactory. The density of population in slums is also very high. Hence, the imbalance between the rapid growth or urban population in the metropolitan cities and relatively slow process of development of additional land for housing, commercial and other purposes has given rise to the following major problems in the metropolitan cities:

— Acute shortage of serviced land for residential, commercial and industrial purposes, resulting in urban sprawl and invasion on urban fringe.

— Continuous increase in density and loss of open spaces, more demand for land for housing and transportation have resulted in large conversion of land in the fringe.

— High land values due to ever-increasing gap between demand and supply of land for various uses.

— Increasing pressure on physical and social infrastructure due to massive spill-over, population pressure/economic activities etc.

— Acute shortage of housing, resulting in unauthorised construction, squatter settlements, up-coming of slums and even invasion of villages by the spill over population/economic activities etc.

— Inadequate finances/investment in urban infrastructure led to the concomitant problems of unplanned urban development on the green-belt leading to serious environmental/ecological problems.

— Fast urbanisation, coupled with sky rocketing land prices has deprived the poor/low income families to have access to shelter or even serviced land. Hence, not only the weaker section of the society but lower, middle income group of society but lower, middle income group of society have also started on public/private land, generally on the urban fringe. The Land Acquisition of land have further acted as a major constraint in smooth and expeditious a acquisition of land and making it available for urban development.

The TCPO's study on Management of Urban Fringe Land Development in selected Metropolitan Cities of India namely Madras, Hyderabad, Pune, Indore, Lucknow, and Jaipur was taken up to analyse the efficacy of existing policies and programmes in making serviced land available at affordable prices to the poor for utilisation of land, availability of vacant land, unutilised land for meeting future demand etc. The study has gone into the spatial problems of inner city, density pattern, migration, of various infrastructural facilities like water supply, transport, sewerage, drainage, electricity, roads and other physical amenities in the cities. An attempt has been made in the study to analyse the effects on the management of green-belt, environment and land use transformation, provision of water and transportation for land development. The findings of study are briefly given below:

— The fringe areas of Madras and Jaipur are inhabitated by mostly middle and higher income groups, whereas fringe areas of Hyderabad, Pune, Lucknow and Indore are dominated by poor or low-income people.

— The people living in urban fringe of these six cities are employed in private sector/informal sector. A significant proportion of the total population of these areas are also found to be self employed.

— In case of Madres and Hyderabad, a significant proportion of persons (50-70%) are employed locally. Hosever, in respect of other smaller cities, the majority of the earning members commute to the main city for work or for other purposes.

— Public transport service seems to be the most important mode of transport for work journeys performed by the households of the urban fringe areas. Public transport facilities appear to be good in the fringe areas of Hyderabad, Madras and Pune, wherwas private transport is playing important role in Jaipur, Lucknow and Indore.

— A good proportion of the households who settled in the fringe areas of Madras, Hyderabad and Jaipur have come from the main cities, whereas the households settled in the fringe areas of Pune, Lucknow and Indore have migrated from nearby rural areas.

— Growth of these urban fringe areas has taken place only around mid-1980s.

— Majority of the households in urban fringe areas of these metropolitan cities have their own houses. It shows that the priority of these households has been to have houses of their own .

— Construction in all these urban fringe areas is unauthorised. This may be due to the impression among the people that these construction or pucca houses would be regularised on the intervention of some social or political pressures later on.

— The majority of the households lack municipal or protected water supply and depend on open wells located within their premises. These households are also deprived of sewerage and drainage facilities. Majority of them have water-borne latrines connected to septic tanks.

— Fringe areas of these metropolitan cities lack adequate basic facilities like education/medicines etc. They have to depend for them on the main cities.

— The reasons for living in the fringe areas are the

high cost of urban land within city, the city life being unaffordable for the poor.

— Majority of the households of the fringe areas wanted to have domestic water connections and drainage facilities in their localities.

— Land price in the fringe areas started rising around mid-1980s. The price level between 1980-85 was steady. A sharp rise in the price of land, however, occured after 1985. The Urban Land Ceiling and Regulation Act, 1976, instead of being helpful in preventing speculative transactions relating to scarce and precious land, has added to the misery of land-speculation. Thousands of hectares of surplus land that the government proposed to aquire nder the Act was caught in the never ending rigmarole of court litigations. In two decades of its existence, the government has been able to acquire barely 15,321 hectares of the total 2.21 lakh hectares declared surplus across the country.

In we give the percentage distribution of agricultural labour households according to their annual per capita consumer expenditure in 1956-57. The distributions are given separately for the six population zones of the country.

We have earlier accepted minimum desirable consumption in rural area to be Rs. 15 per capita per month or Rs. 180 per capita per annum at 1960-61 prices. At 1956-57 prices, this is approximately equal to Rs. 150 per capita annum. Hence it will be seen that about 57 per cent of the agricultural labour households lived below the minimum. The incidence of poverty among the agricultural labour households is again somewhat different in different regions. In Central India, 68.7 per cent of the agricultural labour households and in North

India and South India, about 60.0 per cent of the agricultural labour households lived below the minimum.

It is obvious therefore that the incidence of poverty is much more common among all rural households. To judge what part of rural poverty is due to agricultural labour households, we should find the proportion of agricultural labour households among rural households living at different levels of per capita annual consumer expenditure. In we give the relevant data.

It will be seen that among rural households living at less than Rs. 100 per capita per annum, which, as we saw, corresponds to the rock-bottom of physical existence, agricultural labour households constituted more than 40 per cent. In South India, half of the rural households living at this level were agricultural labour households. Among rural households with annual per capita consumer expenditure between 101-150, agricultural labour households constituted nearly one-third. In South India, they constituted over 40 per cent of the rural households living at this level.

Among the rural households with annual per capita expenditure between Rs. 151-200, the proportion of agricultural labour households is no larger than in the general rural population. Among rural households with annual per capita consumer expenditure of more than Rs. 200, the proportion of agricultural labour households is naturally small.

Thus the rural poverty at the lowest level is largely accounted for by the agricultural labour households. Nevertheless, even at this level, they do not account for more than half the poor. The remaining rural poor are presumably small cultivators.

In we give the percentage distribution of small landowners (possessing cultivated land) according to their per capita monthly expenditure in 1955-56. It will be seen that the distribution, by consumer expenditure, of households with less than 0.5 acre of cultivated land is quite similar to that of the agricultural labour households. Indeed, these households would be classified as agricultural labour households because their main source of income would be from hired labour on other farms.

With landholdings of between 0.5 and 1.5 acres, the situation is only slightly better. Nearly 75 per cent of the households with these size holdings lived below Rs. 13 per capita per month which, in 1955-56, would be approximately the equivalent of Rs. 15 per capita per month in 1960-61.

With larger landholdings the situation naturally improves. However, even with cultivated landholdings between 3.50-4.99 acres, nearly 60 per cent of the households still lived below the minimum of Rs. 13 per capita per month.

In spite of these rather old and fragmentary data, it is clear that the rural poor consist predomnantly of agricultural labour households and small landholders with cultivated holdings of less than 5.0 acres and particularly less than 2.5 acres. The two groups would also include village artisans progressively thrown out of their traditional employment. The urban poor are only an overflow of the rural poor into the urban area. Fundamentally, they belong to the same class as the rural poor. However, as they live long enough in urban poverty, they acquire characteristics of their own. Little is known of their life and labour in the growing cities.

The National Sample Survey (NSS) offers more direct and independent estimates of private consumer expenditure. These are based on direct inquiries made from a random sample of households. The NSS estimate of per capita private consumer expenditure in 1960-61 is Rs. 278.8. The difference between this estimate and the one obtained above (Rs. 276.3) is small. Indeed, considering the entirely independent sources of data from which the two estimates are built up, the agreement between the two is remarkably close. We may therefore neglect the difference between the two.

An advantage of the NSS estimates of private consumer expenditure is that they are available for the rural and urban populations separately. In 1960-61, out of the total of 434 million population, 356 million lived in rural areas and 78 million lived in urban areas. According to the NSS estimates, the per capita private consumer expenditure of the rural population was Rs. 261.2 while that of the urban population was Rs. 359.2. Thus, the per capita consumer expenditure of the urban population was about 37.7 per cent higher than that of the rural population. This does not however mean that the urban population on an average was so much better off than the rural population. The prices of consumer goods and services are usually higher in the urban area than in the rural area. This must be allowed for before judging the relative levels of living in the urban and the rural areas.

Another advantage of the NSS estimates of private consumer expenditure is that they enable us to obtain a distribution of the rural and urban populations according to per capita consumer expenditure. In we give the distribution of the rural and urban populations according to the monthly per capita consumer expenditure in 1960-61. For each monthly expenditure class, the average annual per capita expenditure is also shown for convenience of reference.

Thus, according to the National Sample Survey, the per capita rural consumption in 1960-61 was Rs. 261.2 per annum; and nearly two-thirds (more than 63.26 per cent) of the rural population lived below this average. Similarly, the per capita urban consumption in 1960-61 was Rs. 359.2 per annum; and nearly two-thirds (more than 64.51 per cent) of the urban population lived below this average. Of course, this is in the nature of the distribution and it only means that the country is poor. But sizable sections of the population are much poorer. Thus, in 1960-61, 6.38 per cent of the rural population had per capita consumer expenditure of less than Rs. 8 per month which is 27 paise per day. Another 11.95 per cent had per capita consumer expenditure less than Rs. 11 per month which is 37 paise per day. Another 9.88 per cent had per capita consumer expenditure less than Rs. 13 per month which is 43 paise per day. Yet another 9.82 per cent of the population had per capita consumer expediture less than Rs. 15 per month which is 50 paise per day. The four classes mentioned above constituted a little under 40 per cent (38.03) of the rural population. In 1960-61, they lived with less than 50 paise per day per capita.

The situation in the urban areas was in fact a little worse. Apparently, only 21.69 per cent of the urban population had per capita consumer expenditure of less than Rs. 15 per month or 50 paise per day. However, as we shall presently see, the cost of urban living at this level is at least 50 per cent more so that the equivalent consumer expenditure in urban area would be Rs. 22.5 per month or 75 paise per day. It will be seen that in 1960-61, about 50 per cent of the urban population lived below this level.

People not familiar with these sections of the population, say the 40 per cent poorest rural population and the 50 per cent poorest urban population, have wondered how men at all subsist at these levels. Therefore, when somebody occasionally brings these facts to public notice, some of them are shocked and are righteously indignant; others simply do not believe. Nevertheless, such are the facts of poverty in this country.

It will therefore be worthwhile examining, even if briefly, the standard and quality of living at this level. A simple index to judge the standard of living is the distribution of the total consumer expenditure between major items such as food, fuel, clothing, etc. The poor must devote a large part of their expenditure to food so that little is left for anything else. In we give the distribution of the rural consumer expenditure between major items of expenditure at different levels of total expenditure are given in.

It will be noticed that, in 1960-61, the poorest households having per capita monthly expenditure less than Rs. 8 constituted 6.38 per cent of the rural population and 2.15 per cent of the urban population. Their annual per capita expenditure was less than Rs. 80 (Rs. 79.3 in rural area and Rs. 77.6 in urban area). More than 90 per cent of this small expenditure is devoted to food and fuel for cooking. In rural area, 64.42 per cent of the total expenditure at this level is spent on foodgrains and substitutes such as tapioca; another 18.25 per cent is spent on other items of food and 8.74 per cent is spent on fuel and light. The distribution of urban consumer expenditure at this level is quite similar. Evidently, this is the rock bottom of physical existence and there is little room for variation.

If we leave out this rock bottom, the pattern of consumer expenditure begings to show marked differences between rural and urban living. As we move up from the poorest to the somewhat better, the proportion of expenditure on food and especially on foodgrains declines in both rural and urban areas; but it declines much more rapidly in the urban than in the rural case. For rural households with per capita monthly expenditure of Rs. 18-21 or annual per capita expenditure of Rs. 237.3, which is a little below the average (Rs. 261.2), about half (50.31 per cent) of the total expenditure is spent on foodgrains and substitutes, and about a quarter (24.10 per cent) on the other items of food. At this level, about 75.0 per cent of the expenditure is spent on food and if we add to it the expendirture on fuel and light (6.67 per cent), more than 80.0 per cent is spent on sheer physical existence.

In urban area, the proportion spent on foodgrains and substitutes declines rather rapidly and is partly made up by increased proportion of expenditure on other items of food. For households with monthly per capita expenditure of Rs. 24-28, or annual per capita expenditure of Rs. 315.4, which is a little below the average (Rs. 359.2), about a third (32.72 per cent) of the total expenditure is spent on foodgrains and substitutes and another one-third (34.56 per cent) on other items of food. Their expenditure on fuel and light accounts for nearly 7.0 per cent. Hence, even in urban areas, the households living a little below the average seem to spend almost 75.0 per cent of their total expenditure on bare physical existence.

A distinguished study group set up by the Government of India in July 1962 has deliberated on the question of what should be regarded the nationally desirable minimum level of consumer expenditure. The study group recommended that a per capita monthly consumer expenditure of Rs. 20 (at 1960-61 prices) should be deemed the national minimum. The basis of this determination is not known. Apparently, the study group also did not make a distinction between rural and urban living costs. In our computation above, we have regarded that level of consumer expenditure desirable which secures a diet adequate at least in respect of calories. In 1960-61, this was Rs. 170 per capita per annum for rural households and Rs. 271 per capita per annum for urban households. It will be noticed that the rural minimum determined by us is considerably below that proposed by the study group while the urban minimum determined by us is a little above that proposed by the study group. In deference, we propose to revise the rural minimum slightly upwards to Rs. 180 per annum or Rs. 15 per month. We may also round off the urban minimum to Rs. 270 per annum or Rs. 22.5 per month. With these minima, it seems that, in 1960-61, about 40 per cent of the rural population and about 50 per cent of the urban population lived below the desirable minimum.

The cost of minimum living varies not only between rural and urban areas but also between rural or urban areas of different States. As we shall presently see, the level of per capita consumer expenditure at which a diet with 2,250 calories is attained differs considerably from State to state. This is partly due to differences in prices and partly due to differnces in consumer preferences in the sense that consumers in some States seem to attach a higher priority to food than do consumers in some other States.

The results of the National Sample Survey for 1960-61 are not published in sufficient detail to bring out these differences between States. However, the results for 1961-62 are available in sufficient detail. They give State-wise data on quantities of various items of food consumed at various per capita consumer expenditure levels. It is therefore possible to find for each State the level of consumer expenditure at which a diet with 2,250 calories is reached and the proportion of the population having consumer expenditure below this level. The results for the rural population are shown in.

In this shown, for each State, the monthly per capita expenditure class in which a diet with 2,250 calories is reached (column 2). In subsequent columns of the are shown the per capita total annual consumer expenditure (column 3), the calorie equivalent of daily diet (column 4), and the proportion of the population lying below this level (column 5). For computing this proportion, we have taken into account half the population lying in the monthly per capita expenditure class mentioned in column 2 together with the population falling in the lower classes. It will be seen that, in different States, the food consumption reaches the desired *level also varies greatly from State to State. Some of the differences are worth noting.

In Jammu-Kashmir, Punjab, Gujarat, Mysore, Bihar and Orissa, the desired calorie-level is achieved at about the same level of total consumer expenditure (Rs. 13-15 per capita per month). Nevertheless, the proportion of population lying below this level varies from 43.88 per cent in Orissa and 37.88 per cent in Bihar to 19.09 per cent in Gujarat and less than 14.0 per cent in Punjab and Jammu-Kashmir. In West Bengal, the desired calorie-level is reached at a slightly higher expenditure level (Rs. 15-18 per capita per month) and the proportion lying below this level is 44.09 per cent which is close to the situation in Orissa. In Assam, the desired calorie-level is reached at an even higher expenditure level (Rs. 18-21 per month per capita) and the proportion of population lying below the desired level is also somewhat higher, namely 47.57 per cent. In Madras, Maharashtra and Andhra Pradesh, the desired calorie-level is reached at about the same expenditure level (Rs. 18-21 per month per capita), but the proportion of population lying below this level is much greater in these States–55.19 per cent in Tamil Nadu, 61.04 per cent in Maharashtra and 62.14 per cent in Andhra Pradesh.

At the other end are Uttar Pradesh, Madhya Pradesh and Rajasthan. In these States, the desired calorie-level is achieved at much lower expenditure levels (Rs. 11-13 per capita per month in Uttar Pradesh and Madhya Pradesh, and Rs. 8-11 in Rajasthan) and the proportion of population lying below this level is also much smaller (25.79 per cent in Madhya Pradesh, 18.13 per cent in Uttar Pradesh and 13.29 in Rajasthan).

The case of Kerala is extreme and peculiar. Here the desired calorie-level is reached not until the total expenditure is as high as Rs. 34-43 per capita per month. Consequently, 90.75 per cent of the rural population of the State appear to have diets below the desired level. This may be true. It happens because, in Kerala, tapioca is widely used as a subsitute for foodgrains and, weight for weight, tapioca has a calorie value only one-third that of foodgrains. It is possible therefore that in Kerala 90 per cent of the rural population in fact lives on diet inadequate even in respect of calories. Alternatively, it is possible that the National Sample Survey has underestimated certain items of food such as banana, coconut, and fish entering into the diets of these people and that consequently the extent of malnutrition in Kerala has been somewhat exaggerated in the above figures.

If we apply the State-wise estimates of the proportion of the rural population living on inadequate diets to the State-wise rural population in 1960-61, it seems that, in that year, 135 million rural people, which is about 38 per cent of the total rural population, lived on diets inadequate even in respect of calories.

As in the case of the rural population so in the case of the urban population, the level of consumer expenditure at which the diet reaches adequacy in respect of calories varies greatly from State to State. The relevant data derived from the National Sample Survey for 1961-62 are given in. It is clear that the level of consumer expenditure at which the diet reaches adequacy in calories and the proportion of the urban population living below this level vary greatly from State to State. But everywhere the incidence of poverty is much greater in the urban areas than in the rural areas.

If we apply the State-wise estimates of the proportion of the urban population living on inadequate diets to the State-wise urban population in 1960-61, it seems that, in year, 135 million rural people, which is about 38 per cent of the total rural population, lived on diets inadequate even in respect of calories.

As in the case of the rural population so in the case of the urban population, the level of consumer expenditure at which the diet reaches adequacy in respect of calories varies greatly from State to State. The relevant data derived from the National Sample Survey for 1961-62 are given in. It is clear that the level of consumer expenditure at which the diet reaches adequacy in calories and the proportion of the urban population living below this level vary greatly from State of State. But everywhere the incidence of poverty is much greater in the urban areas than in the rural areas.

If was apply the State-wise estimates of the proportion of the urban population living on inadequate diets to the State-wise urban population in 1960-61, it seems that, in that year, 42 million urban people, which is about 54 per cent of the total urban population, lived on diets inadequate even in respect of calories. Adding this number to the estimate of rual population living on inadequate diets, namely 135 million, it seems that in 1960-61, between 175 million to 180 million people in the country lived on diets inadequate even in respect of calories. This briefly is the measure of the extent of poverty prevailing in the country at the beginning of the last decade.

An area of priority in the Ninth Plan is to improve project implementation and delivery mechanisms and to ensure that the intended benefits actually reach the people. Further, several social sector programmes are formulated without addressing the isssue of sustainability of benefits and most programmes run with ever-increasing government budgets and thus pre—empt resources which could find better alternative uses. The Ninth Plan must introduce necessary correctives to reverse many of the unsustainable trends in the implementation of poverty alleviation programmes. Just allotting higher outlay for rural development will mean nothing unless a major streamlining takes palce in the implementation and delivery systems.

The existion schemes whose delivery costs are disproportionately high or which fail to make the desired impact should be considered for reorientation and discontinuation. It is necessary to shelve such schemes whose delivery cost exceeds, say 15 to 20 oer cent of the total cost of operating the programme. Monitoring and evaluation of programmes have to be made equally effective and purposeful. Therefore, the Centre, States and the grass roots level organizations/institutions would need to be involved to ensure the effectiveness of the system. It is encouraging that the Planning Commission would bring out compendium of evaluation studies and give wider publicity of the findings of research studies conducted and sponsored by it. This would be helpful for a meaningful public debate on issues involved.

An overall increase in the level of real wages of the unorgainzed workers will also help empowering them to be able to secure maximum advantage from the other developmental programmes of the government. The very concepts of democratic decentralozation and empowerment of the people imply a steady reducation in the paternalistic role of the State and increased emphasis on empowerment of the people themselves. It is hoped that during the Ninth Plan there will be much more attention on bringing about awareness among the unorganized workers as also on providing effective redressal mechanisms to enforce their rights. The approach document of the Plan rightly observes that one of the most important weaknesses of the Indian social sector programmes has been is inabiligy to inform the target benefiviaries about the schemes that are available and to which they have a rightful clain. The Ninth Plan will, hopefully, stress the creation and deployment of an effective information dissemination system,and the necessary redressal mechanism for making the demands effective.

Finally, of course, there is no unique way to describe an ideal gorwth process. It can be hoped that the Ninth Plan will lay down foundations for a more progressive process of planning than has been the case so far. Growth involves a dynamic interaction of linked changes. The economic endocrine gland has to be clear as to how much other matters mingt have advanced. As such, it can also be argued that little attention is required to any particular rate of economic growth so long as it is positive.

Wouldn't it then make little sense to worry whether a baby will end up five or six feet tall when the real anxiety should be whether the baby can be safely brought through the problems of infancy, childhood and adolescence? The slower rate of growth, once under way, can pick-up speed and, of course, can slow down too. But the higher gorwth rate has the prospect of slowing down only. It is desirable to have a steady growth as it has more possibility of ending up with the fastest rate of growth of the economy just as the movement on a highway gives to the motorest the highest speed. The crux of planning is to find the turnpike and reach it. Also gorwth is no longer the guarantor of trickle down effects. To what extent these plan promises are taken care of in the Ninth Plan, can be anybody's guess.

Against the per capita net availability of 501.9 gms of cereals the estimated consumption of cereals was of the order of 394 gms i.e. 78.6 per cent of the net availability. similarly in the case of pulses, per capita consumption was 28.05 gms. i.e. 75.8 per cent of net availability. Inequality in the consumption of foods among different income groups gets masked in the overall consumption estimates. Among the poor, nearly 80 per cent of consumption expenditure goes for food items. Recent surveys indicate:

— Percapita cereal consumption has declined over the years resulting in the aggregate energy intake of 1859 k.cal per capita as against 2200 k.cal recommended.

— 47.7 per cent of households have calorie inadequacy and 19.8 per cent of households have protein inadequacy. 19.5 per cent of households have both calorie and protein inadequacy.

— The exetent of moderate and severe growth retardation in preschool children varied from 34 per cent in Kerala to 72 per cent in Gujarat.

— 47 per cent of adults have body mass index value below 18.5 indicating large scale prevalance of chronic energy deficiency in the community.

— Haemoglobin levels among pregnant mothers reveal

that as many as 87.5 per cent of mothers were anaemic.

— About 30 per cent of infants born had low birth weight.

— 167 million people are considered to be at risk for iodine deficiency disorders and 54 million have goitre.

— Preventable blindness due to Vitamin A deficiency still large.

Looking back the distance travelled and counting on various milestones towards food security, the country can be proud of some of the achievements so far. Yet the final milestone looks to be a long march. Shrinking arable land resources, soil degradation and depletion of nutrients from the soil, poor water management and unsustainable use of ground water, loss of momentum in the growth of food output, inefficient biological utilisation of the nutrients consumed due to poor environment and growing population are some of the problems the country faces in the march towards the final milestone of a hunger-free nation. The over-exploitation of the aquifer is also leading to the leaching of high levels of arsenic from natural underground sources into thousands of village wells in West Bengal. As estimated 200,000 people already have arsenic-induced skin lesions.

It is estimated that there are about 20 million species of poants, out of which 50,000 are edible. However, we are not using more than 200 plants as food, 80 per cent of our food supply however comes only from about eight species. We are today laying much emphgasis on developing new varieties of these few plants. We should enlarge the food basket by including the excluded. Many nutritious grains fall under the classification "coarse grains". It is time we start referring to them as "nutritious grains". They are rich in micronutrients like Fe and Ca.

Seeing that between 75.0 and 80.0 per cent of the total expenditure at levels a little below the average is spent on food and its preparation, we might briefly examine the nutritional adequacy or otherwise of food at this level. In we show the per capita daily consumption of foodgrains and substitutes at different levels of expenditure. As is to be expected, the consumption of foodgrains increases as we move from the poorest to the somewhat better. This occurs much more rapidly in rural area than in the urban area. In rural area, the per capita daily cosumption of foodgrains and substitutes reaches 616 grams for households with per capita monthly expenditure of Rs. 13-15 or per capita annual expenditure of Rs. 170.8. Calculating at the rate of 3.3 calories per gram of foodgrains (including substitutes), 616 grams of foodgrains give 2,033 calories per capita per day. As we have seen, this takes up nearly 60.0 per cent of the total consumer expenditure of these households. They spend another about 20.0 per cent on other items of food such as edible oil, ghee and butter, sugar and gur, and a little milk, meat and fish. The quantities of these items are rather small and they yield about 200 calories per capita per day. Thus the entire food at this level seems to give about 2,250 calories per capita per day. Nutritional experts regard this as adequate under Indian conditions of climate, etc. It means that, in 1960-61, an annual per capita consumer expenditure of Rs. 170 was essential to give a diet adequate at least in respect of calories. At consumer expenditure below this level, the diet was inadequate even in respect of calories. With reference to the population lying in monthly per capita expenditure classes Rs. 0-8, 8-11, 11-13 and half the population lying in the class Rs. 13-15 had per capita expenditure below this level. These classes add up to 33.123 per cent of the total rural population. Thus, in 1960-61, about one-third of the rural population lived on diets inadequate even in respect of calories.

In 1993-94, the Planning Commission stated that only 18.96 per cent of the Indian people were below the poverty line. Now we are told that it is 40 per cent. A couple of shocking statistics, recently released by the National Council of Applied Economic Research (NCAER) provide a horrifying picture of where we are. The first figure is that 39 per cent of India's population of nearly one billion remain under the poverty line, a number that has not changed in a decade. In real terms, this means a very large number of Indians have an earning capacity of a couple of chapatis. According to another survey by the NCAER, 37 per cent lof the country's rural population are landless and therefore unable to grow their own crop to put off hunger.

The second figure, less publicised but avilable from international agencies, is that food grains production is 1991 million tonnes in 1994-95 to 185 million tonnes in 1995-96 and in the case of wheat from 65.5 million tonnes to 62.6 million tonnes in same period. Unsurprisingly the worst shortfalls are in the politically volatile States of Uttar Pradesh and Bihar and yet the naked face of hunger continues to be maskedby the hypocrisy that India is a food grain exporter.

Apart from the rising poulation, agro-economists put forward a number of reasons for fall in food grain production, among them soil exhaustion and the larger number of landless that are concentrated in the States of UP, Bihar and eastern India. What they don't spell out is the endemic political instability and coruption these States, and the interminable cycle of fodder scams and caste wars, that are pushing the poor deeper into the poverty trap.

Economic reports do not point out that the agricultural ministry for many years has been managed by ministers, who only represent the narrow interests of wealthy landed farmers like themselves, and have no truck with the poor landless peasants.

The Ninth Plan will be an heir to the same hypocrisy despite agriculture being put on the top by all then nine objectives of the Plan.

J. Gaur, a retired officer of Rajasthan government has a telling story about his visit to one of the villages of Dungarpur district. He was shocked to know from one of the poor schoolboys that he was served the family had ten members. This speaks volumes about our rural development and family planning programmes. The population clock outside the Capital's (Delhi) All-India Institute of Medical Sciences is galloping ahead but, for India's shoddy family planning programme, time has stood still. The latest census data is proof, if any were needed, that we are sitting on a population time bomb. By 2040, India will be the world's most populous nation. In a situation where over 18 million—or six Singapores—are being added to the population every year, it can be of little comfort to learn that curde birth rates have declined from 34.7 per cent in 1991 or indeed that fertility levels have shown a negligible decrease of two per cent in that period. If the population has to stabilize at even a staggering 100 crore by 2001-2005, the average birth rate has to be reduced to two children per woman. But so far, only Kerala and Tamil Nadu have achieved this with Madhya Pradesh stated to do so only after 2060, Rajasthan by 2048, Bihar by 2039 and Uttar Pradesh by 2100. The government has confined itself to making tall claims about running a family planning campaign which is so "people oriented" that all targets have been removed. The truth is that it is Central run and almost totally dependent on female sterilisation ignoring the variety of options which are available.

The desired goal of population as mentioned as one of the objectives of the Ninth Plan could be achieved only through the willing co-operation of the population and specially of the rural people. The magic words are 'literacy' and 'healthcare'.

There is no "political will" as is evident from the fact that no political party has cared to emphasize the need for some concrete steps to restrict population growth in their election manifestoes. There is no mention of family planning even in the Common Minimum Programme of the United Front government.

It should be a matter of deep concern for every thinking Indian that after 45 years of the so-called planning, the country does not have a comprehensive education policy. This is despite the constitutional objective to provite universal primary education and eradication of funding, enormous sums have been wasted on subsidies and populist schemes from which money is easily diverted into the pockets of corrupt politicians and officials. Even in education, priorities have been misplaced. While primary and vocational education, which would improve the skills of the work force, have been neglected, money has been spent on creating an army of inadequately unemployable at various levels. The crying need of the hour is not elaborate plans but the 'political will' to act and innovate.

The late S.K. Dey, a Minister of State in Nehru's Cabinet once visited Tamil Nadu. He met the late Kumarappa at Gandhi Niketan and with some pride of achievenment he claimed that the Community Development Programe was a grand success. Kumarappa was sharp to retort : "What is your scale for measuring the success of your projects? S.K. Dey answered by giving elaborate statistics of the miles of roads constructed, number of wells dug, school-buildings built, dispensaries opened, fertilizers distributed, improved seeds introduced, the manure pits constructed, and all the usual figures. Kumarappa looked doubtfully at S.K. Dey and said in a derisive voice, "this is your scale" and laughed. Pricked by Kumarappa's remarks, Dey asked, "what then is your scale of success?" Kumarappa in a very emphatic tone said: "Mr Dey, before I cover an area with the Community Development Programme, I would select some six poor persons, count their ribs and if after three years (or five years) of implementing the C.D. Programme, there is some flesh to cover these ribs, thn I will call it a success". Dey was dismayed and implicitly accepted that his approach was defective. Kumarappa continued to say thay S.K. Dey was "trying to throw a silk shirt on a hungry person". The essentials of development are brought out in this one sentence. In other words, villages have developed and not the villagers.

Kalia a poor villager at the time of India's Independence thought, he was poor. He was told he was not poor but needy. Then as to be called needy was self-defeating, he was addressed as deprived which was again changed to underprivileged. This term was also later changed to disadvantaged. Kalia said : "I have no dime or rupee yet but a rich vocabulary". He further said : "I have no idea of Five Year Plan". He was about 20 years of age at the time of India's Independence. Now he is about 70 years of age. In the last two-and -a-half decades, he was not able to eat chapatis with pulses. His earnings are so meagre that he is unable to afford prices to buy pulses for his family consisting of six members.

The life and vitality of human beings depend crucially on certain vitamins and minerals that help in the efficient functioning of the brain, immune system, reproduction and energy metabolism. The body needs only small amounts of these nutrients, but it cannot synthesize them. They must be provided through diet. Deficiencies of even the small amounts required cause learning disabilities, impair work capacity and bring illness and death. Micronutrient malnutrition (silent hunger) is most devastating for pre—school children and pregnant women but is also debilitating for all ages. And it is debilitating the national economy as well. The most important and well studied micro-nutrient deficiencies are vitamin A, Iodine and Iron. Virtually every developing country has deficiencies in the micro nutrients large enough to constitute a public health problem. Many developing countries have multiple deficiencies. Taken together micronutrient deficiencies affect a far greater number of people in the world than Protein-Energy malnutrition. 1.6 billion people live in areas where soils lack sufficient iodine, 655 million suffer from goitre, 26 million have had brain damage and 5.7 million cretinism. Two billion pre-school children suffer from iron deficinet anaemia. 254 million pre-school children are affected by subclinical, severe and moderate deficiencies of Vitamin A.

In India, 167 millions are exposed to the risk of Iodine deficiency of which 54 million have goitre. Surveys conducted by DGHS indicate that 186 districts are IDD endemic area with goitre rates over 10 per cent. As regards Iron deficiency anaemia, multicentre study conducted by ICMR reveal that 87.5 per cent were anaemic. Deficiency of Vitamin A has long been known to be the largest preventable cause of blindness.

The main intervention strategies against micronutrient malnutrition are:

- Diet supplementation of vulnerable population.
- Dietary improvements.
- Fortification of common foods.

The richest sources of micronutrients are green leafy vegetable and fruits. India is rich in vegetable crops, some of which have good carotene content. Future programmes with respect to horticultural products must be directed towards identifying and propagating high micro-nutrient concentration varieties. People know when they are hungry but they have no natural hunger for vitamin. A, Iron, Iodine and other micronutrients. They do not know they need them and they often do not know what foods provide them.

Deficiency in soil nutrients reflect in the plants grown in the soil. One—half of all soils in all developing countries are deficient or low in available micronutrients. Soil depletion of S, Fe, Mn, Zn and Cu are due to intensive and indiscriminate irrigation and heavy use of high analysis chemical fertilisers. This gets reflected in the plants grown in these soils. Hence, in the national soil health care programme, we should ensure that both the macro-and micro-nutrient needs of soils are addressed.

The term Green Revolution was coined by Dr. William Gadd of USA in 1968, when our farmers brought about a quantum jump in wheat production by taking to semi-dwarf, non-lodging varieties with great enthusiasm and when similar progress appeared feasible in rice. Punjab took the lead because of the scientific and educational backstopping given by the Punjab Agricultural University on the one hand and on the other, by the presence of the essential pre-requisites for progress such as land consolidation and leveling, rural communication, rural electrification and above all, owner cultivation.

Twenty eight years after the term "Green Revolution" was coined, we are in a position to draw a balance sheet and chalk out a strategy for the future. Apart from erasing the "begging bowl" image of India, the most important gain has been the saving of forests and land, thanks to the productivity improvement associated with high yielding varieties. This year, Indian farmers harvested over 60 million tonnes of wheat, as compared to 6 million tonnes at the time of our Independence in 1947. Punjab farmers have raised the average yield of wheat to over 40 quintals per hectare. Likewise, Tamil Nadu farmers have raised the average yield of rice to over 50 quintals per hectare. If the yield improvement associated with the Green Revolution in wheat and rice had not taken place, we will need another 70 million hectares to produce the wheat and rice we now harvest. Thus, the productivity inmprovement associated with the Green Revolution is best described as forest and land saving agriculture. The productivity improvement has taken place not only in wheat and rice but also in relation to milk and eggs. Only in the case of pulses, we are lagging behind.

The population of India is growing at a rate of 1.8 per cent per year. If this trend continues, our population will double itself in less than 40 years. Only Kerala, Tamil Nadu, Goa and Mizoram have so far achieved a demographic transition to low birth and death rates. Besides population increase, improved purchasing power among the poor will enhance the demand for food, since undernutrition and poverty go together. In contrast, per capita availability of arable land is shrinking. Water efficiency is still on the whole low and water disputes are growing. In addition to the gradual decline in per capita availability of land and water, various forms of biotic and abiotic stresses are spreading.

There is still a widespread mismatch between production and post-harvest technologies. In perishable commotities like fruits, vegetables, flowers, meat and other animal products, this mismatch is often severe, affecting the inyterests of both producers and consumers. This is why foreign experts frequently refer to the setting in of a fatigue of the Green Revolution. Lester Brown and Hal Kane in their book "Full House" released last year predict that at the current rate of population growth and environmental degradation coupled with an improvement in the consumption capacity of the poor, India will have to import annually over 40 million tonnes of food grains by the year 2030. This is four times the quantity we imported in 1966 i.e. before the onset of the Green Revolution. We should examine this issue seriously and should not allow complacency overtake the farm sector, just because we now have over 30 million tonnes of food grains available with Government.

Industrial countries are responsible for much of the global environmental problems such as potential changes in temperature, precipitation, sea level and incidence of ultraviolet-B radiation. While further agricultural intensification in industrialised countries will be ecologically disastrous, the failure to achieve agricultural intensification and diversification in developing countries where farming provides most of the jobs will be socially disastrous. This is because, agriculture including crop and animal husbandary, forestry and agro-forestry, fisheries and agro-industries provides livelihood to over 70 per cent of our population. The smaller the farm, the greater is the need for higher marketable surplus for increasing income.

Eleven million new livelihoods will have to be created every year in India and these have to come largely from the farm and rural industries sectors.

Importing food and other agricultural commodities will hence have the same impact as importing unemployment. Thus, what we need now is an environmentally sustainable and socially equitable green revolution or what may be termed as ever-green revolution.

Those who advocate going back to the old methods of farming ignore the fact that just a century ago when the population of undivided India was 281 million, famines claimed 30 million lives between 1870 and 1900. The famine eradication strategy of India comprising the following steps is perhaps the most important achievement of independent India:

- Enhanced production and productivity.
- Better distribution through the public distribution system.
- Adequate grain reserves.
- Purchasing power enhancement through various employment generation and guarantee schemes.
- Special intervention programmes for children, pregnant and nursing mothers and old and infirm persons.

While famines have been prevented, widespread under-nutrition prevails among the economically underprivileged. Since non-food factors like health care, environmental hygiene and literacy play an important role in promoting sustainable food security of the level of the individual, we should redefine security.

Steps for achieveing sustainable food security are as under:

First sustained physical access to food will involve a transition from chemical and machnery intensive to ecological farming technologies.

Second, the emphasis on economic access underlines the need for promo9ting sustainable livelihoods through multiple income-earning opportunities.

Third, environmental access involves on the one hand attention to soil health care, water harvesting management and the conservation of forest and biodiversity, and on the other to sanitation, environment hygiene, primary health care and primary education.

If the political vision to implement this mission is forthcoming, population stabilisation can be more readily achieved. The prediction of Margins de Condorcet made in 1975 that population will stabilise itself, if children are born for happiness and not just for existence, will then come true.

The emphasis on the individual is important, since the household is not often a homogenous unit. Women and girl children tend to suffer more from under-nutrition than men and boys. UNDP's 1995 Human Development Report contains distressing data on the growing feminisation of poverty. To give operational content to such a concept of food security, we should initiate a Hunger-Free Area Programme (HFAP) consisting of the following components:

- Ensuring sustainable availability of food production over population growth through the development and dissemination of ecotechnologies, supported by appropriate packages of services and public policies. Ecotechnology involves the blending of the ecological prudence and technologies of the past, with the best in frontier technologies, particularly biotechnology, information technology, space technology, renewablre energy technology and management technology. Without ecotechnological empowerment, farm men and women will not be able to produce more food and other agricultural commodities on an environmentally sustainable basis from less land, water and energy resources.

- Sustain the productivity of the natural resource base, by conserving and improving the ecological foundations essential for continuous advances in crop and animal productivity.
- Ensure adequacy of household incomes through promotional social security, such as accessing assets, employment and organisational and marketing empowerment. Agricultural programmes should concurrently aim at more food, more jobs and more income. Integrated attention to farm and non-farm employment and value-addition to primary agricultural commodities will be necessary to enhance income and rural livelihood security.
- Provide entitlement to food through protective social security measures to the vulnerable groups, such as employment guarantee and food for nutrition programmes.
- Introduce a National Food and Livelihood Security Act for the purpose of paying integrated attention to:

— Conservation of lands, water, forests, biodiversity and the protection of the atmosphere.

— Enchancing productivity through ecotechnologies.

— Improving distribution in order to eliminate endemic hunger.

— Maintenance of adequate food security reserves.

— Strengthneing the techno-infrastructure for better post-harvest technology and expanding the coverage of sanitary and phytosanitary measures, and

— Efficient research, education, extension, marketing systems both to take full advantage of emerging opportunities in international trade and to ensure that research and extension designed to promote public good receive adequate support.

The major problems that confront India are poverty and unemployment. And both are interrelated. There is a lot of controversy regarding the estimates of poverty in the country. Estimates of Tendulkar and Jain show that rural poverty has increased from 37.5 per cent in 1990-91 to 39.7 per cent in 1993-94. On the other hand, urban poverty has declined from 35 per cent in 1990-91 to 30.9 per cent in 1993. The upshot of the argument is that even in 1993-94, around 40 per cent of the rural population (around 250 million) and 31 per cent of the urban population were below the poverty line, or food insecure in terms of not having enough calories.

The continuance of poverty at such a colossal level has created great distortions in the economy. There are several reasons why poverty has persisted in rural areas. One obvious factor which has hurt the poor is the sharp increase in the prices of food grains. During the last five or six years, procurement prices of food grains have increased considerably recultural labourers. Secondly, the rural poor appear to have been left out of the gains of increased productivity in the agricultural sector. Thirdly, the rate of growth in employment in rural areas (both males and females), during the period 1987-88 to 1993-94 was significantly lower as comparesd to the urban areas as shown in.

According to the 50th Round of the NSSO, while 'Open' unemployment at a little over 6.0 per cent, remained more or less unchanged. And casualization increased with a corresponding decline in self-employment, both in rural and urban areas. Casual wage employment increased from 31.2 per cent in 1987-88 to

33.5 per cent in 1993-94, while self-employment declined from 53.6 per cent to 51.9 per cent. Regular salaried employment also declined from 15.2 per cent to 14.7 per cent.

The census figures have given an alarming new for Indian planners again. The data paint a dismal picture both with regard to increase in population and unemployment. By 2040, India is set to become the world's most populous country with a population of 126 crores. And as far as unemployment situation is concerned, one-third of the populztion—300 million were estimated to be without work in 1994.

This implies that unless some effective steps are taken to control population, the rate of employment will increase in future.

The approach paper, however, recognizes that a sustained and long-lasting solution to gthe problem of poverty depends on the creation of adequate employment opportunities through a broad based programme of development and economic growth. Therefore, in the Ninth Plan, a great deal of emphasis has been given to agriculture and rural development. And agriculture has been delinked from rural development in order to emphasize the development of irrigation, watershed development, animal husbandry schemes, social forestry and so on.

This study is concerned with the problem of poverty in India. It is a problem of low national income and its unequal distribution; of slow pace of development and inequitable distribution of the small gains of development. Before one discusses how to meet the threat this problem poses, one should know its dimensions and understand the process through which it seems to be deepening. We shall therefore begin with a brief review of the situation at the beginning of the sixties, that is, in 1960-61.

National income (Net National Product at Factor Cost) per capita, that is per person, is a useful summary measure to judge the well being of a people. The National Income of the Indian Union, excluding Portuguese and French territories, in 1960-61 was Rs. 13,308 crores. The corresponding population in that year (October 1, 1960) was 43.4 crores. Hece the National Income per capita in that year works out to be Rs. 306.7.

A more direct measure of the level of living of a people is per capita Private Consumer Expenditure. To arrive at this, we begin with Net Domestic Product which is only slightly different from the Net National Product and the distinction between the two need not detain us here. The whole of the Net Domestic Product is not expended domestically. A part of the goods and services produced at home is exported. On the other hand, a number or goods and services are imported. If we deduct from the Net Domestic Product the exports and add to it the imports, we get the Net Domestic Expenditure.

Again, the whole of the Net Domestic Expenditure is not Private consumer Expenditure. A part of it goes into net investment or what is called Net Domestic Capital Formation. This adds to the productive capacity of the economy and hence leads to higher national product in future. But in a given year, it does not form part of consumption. Another part of Net Domestic Expenditure is consumption by Government. This consists partly of expenditure on administration and partly of expenditure on social welfare such as education and public health. The latter is what is often termed socialised consumption and it adds to the welfare of the people. But presently it constitutes a small part of the total consumer expenditure. We may therefore neglect it. We therefore deduct from the Net Domestic Expenditure, firstly the Net Domestic Capital Formation and secondly the consumption Expenditure of Government. We thus arrive at the Private Consumer Expenditure. When this is divided by the population, we get the per capita private consumer expenditure. This provides a simple measure of the well being or standard of living of the people.

For the year 1960-61, the computation appears as under:

Thus, in 1960-61, the consumer expenditure in India amounted to Rs. 276.3 per capita per annum or 75.7 paise per day per person. This sums up the average level of living prevailing in 1960-61.

**Sustainable food security**

The commitment of the international community to ensure food and nutrition security to every child, woman and man on our planet has been reiterated at several international conferences held during this decade.

Despite such high level political reaffirmation of the need to achieve speedily the goal of "Food for All", over 800 million human beings now suffer from hunger and malnutrition. Hidden hunger, arising from the deficiency of the essential micronutrients is widespread. Endemic hunger is now more due to the lack of adequate income at the household level than due to the lack of food in the market. Both poverty as well as non-food factors such as environmental hygiene, sanitation and lack of safe drinking water are becoming major contributors of food insecurity at the level of communities and individuals. A majority of the food insecure live in Asia.

There is also increasing concern about the earth's capacity to produce adequate food for the growing population. The increase in human population, now mostly confined to the developing countries, coupled with enhanced purchasing power leading to greater capability to buy food and increasing urbanisation will lead to a higher growth rate in demand for food as well as more diversified food products in the coming millennium. Thus, on the one hand, there will be need for intensification and diversification of agriculture, particularly in the developing countries, on the other, the ecological foundations essential for sustainable advances in crop and animal productivity are getting eroded. This situation has led to the ringing of alarm bells by experts concerning the earth's capacity to produce adequate food to meet growing needs. Lester Brown has concluded; "Constraints imposed by the earth's natural systems, the environmental degradation of land and water resources and the diminshing backlog of yield-raising agricultural technologies are slowing the growth in world food production, raising questions about the earth's population carrying capacity. The earth's capacity to produce enough food to satisfy expanding demand is now emerging as the overriding environmental issue as the world approaches the 21st Century".

The year 1998 will mark the bicentenary of Malthus's essay on population. The onward march of science and technology, supported by appropriate public policies, has so far helped humankind to keep Malthusian forebodings on the population-food supply equation at bay. It is, however, becoming increasingly clear that without concerted national and global action to arrest environmental degradation, promote economic and gender equity and check population growth, the Malthusian spectre may still come true in the next century. The Food and Agriculture Organisation of the United Nations (FAO) therefore, organised a World Food Summit in Rome from November 13 to 17, 1996.

At this Summit, a Rome Declaration on World Food Security and a World Food Summit Plan of Action were adopted.

The Declaration makes a commitment to reduce the number of undernourished people to half their present level no later than 2015. It also states:

"We will pusue participatory and sustainable food, agriculture, fisheries, forestry and rural development policies and practices in high and low potential areas which are essential to adequate and reliable food supplies".

"We will strive to ensure that food, agricultural trade and overall trade policies are conducive to fostering food security for all through a fair and market-oriented world trade system".

The Plan of Action includes the following seven commitments:

- Create an enabling political, social and economic environment designed to create the best conditions for the eradication of poverty, and for durable peace.
- Implement policies aimed at eradicating poverty and inequality and improving physical and economic access to sufficient, nutritionally adequate and safe food and its effective utilization.
- Pursue participatory and sustainable food, agriculture, fisheries, forestry and rural development policies and practices in high and low potential areas.
- Ensure that food, agricultural trade and overall trade policies are conducive to fostering food security for all.
- Prevent and be prepared for national disasters and

man-made emergencies.

- Promote optimal allocation and use of public and private investments to foster human resources, sustianable food agriculture, fisheries and forestry systems, and rural development, in high and low potential areas.
- Implement, monitor and follow-up the Rome Plan of Action at all levels in cooperation with the international community.

The above plan of action integrates the principles of (a) conservation of the ecological foundations essential for sustainable advances in agricultural productivity and production, (b) sustainable production through ecotechnologies and (c) equity in acces to food through an appropriate blend of national and international action in the area of entitlements and employment. The Science Academies Summit held in Madras in July, 96, recommneded that all nations may provide an overall public policy support to action at these three levels through the enactment of a National Food and Livelihood Security Act designed to achieve the following objectives:

- That every individual has the physical, economic, social and enviormental access to balanced diet that includes the necessary macro-and micronutrients, safe drinking water, sanitation, environmental hygiene, primary health care and education so as to lead a healthy and productive life.
- That food originates from efficient and environmentally benign production technologies that conserve and enhance the natural resource base of crops, animal husbandry, forestry, inland and marine fisheries.

The Chief Minister of Tamil Nadu, India in his budget speech delivered on July 17, 1996 made the following announcement.

Feed the people who are hungary Educate the people to uplift the World"

To fulfil this dream of Mahakavi Bharatiyar, this Government will launch a new "Hunger Free Area Programme" with an aim to eradicate poverty induced hunger. A number of schemes are already under implementation to alleviate poverty and to cater to the nutrition requirements of different groups of the population. Gaps in this coverage will be identified which can then be specifically targeted under the Hunger Free Area programme. Preovision has been made in the Budget for preparing a detailed strategy to implement this programme in association with Dr. M.S. Swaminathan.

Studies at MSSRF have shown that by adding a horizontal dimension to numerous vertically structured programmes and by promoting a coalition of all concerned with ending hunger and deprivation, it is now possible to provide opportunities for a healthy and productive life for all.

The problem of food and nutrition security at the level of the individual has to be viewed in 3 dimensions. First,, inadequate purchasing power leads to calorie-protein under-nutrition. Second, the lack of the needed quantity and variety of micronutrients and vitamins in the diet leads to several nutritional disorders including blingness caused by Vitamin A deficiency. This kind of problem is referred to as "hidden hunger", a problem which affects today more than 2 billion people in the world. Third, lack of environmental hygiene and sanitation leads to a low biological absorption and retention of food, due to intestinal infection and diarrohea. Thus, both food and non-food factors assume importance in determining the r.utrition secu;rity of an individual. Concurrent action at all these levels is necessary in a Hunger-Free Area Programme. The various steps involved in this process are described below:

— Identify the basic underlying reasons for chronic under and malnutrition.

— Collate information on available programmes and opportunities for the sustainable end of hunger.

— Articulate the steps needed to provide the 'missing elements' in achieving the end of hunger.

— Mobilise local level community action and commiotment for achieving the end of endemic hunger by the end of the Ninth Five Year Plan and enlist mass media support for this purpose.

— Assess the extent of (i) Financial resources required (ii) Technical resources for technological empowerment necessary (iii) Managerial and Organisational resources needed.

— Foster the organization of a Grassroots level Coalition for Ending Hunger in each HFAP area comprising representatives of

  - Elected representatives of the people.
  - Government agencies.
  - Civil society-non-governmental organizations, voluntary agencies, services organizations like Rotary clubs, Lions clubs, etc.
  - Academia-Research, Training Instituitons and Universities.

- Corporate Sector.
- Financial Institutions and
- Mass Media.

The Coalition for Ending Hunger will be responsible for designing, implementing and monitoring the Hunger Free Area programme.

The challenge lies in converting HFAP from a concept into an operational programme. In such a programme, emphasis will have to be placed during the remaining years of this century on generating additional livelihood opportunities for those living below the poverty line in villages and towns. The increasing feminisation of poverty demands that priority attention be given to women and girl children. Based on these considerations, the following operational framework is suggested for a National Hunger-Free Area Programme.

This phase will relate tot he analysis of gaps and constraints. Under the Gap Analysis Programme, an inventory will be made of all the entitlements currently available to those living below the poverty line both through the Central and State Government programmes. The inventory will be suitably classified so as to differentiate social security and nutrition intervention programmes from those relating to employment generation.

Once the Entitlements Database is compiled detailed study based on random sampling techniques will be conducted in about 100 villages of a district to assess the extent to which the entitlements have actually reached the intended families. Within families, special studies will be conducted to ascertain the extent of male-female differences in access to entitlements. The gap between what the poor are entitled to and what they are actually receiving will be grouped according to gender and economic status (I.E., those having assets like land or livestock or fish pond or tress and those who do not own any productive asset).

Once the GAP Analysis is completed, a careful identification of the reasons for the gap and the contrainsts faced by the pooring getting their entitlements will be made. Such a gap and constraints analysis will be the starting how direct and imdirect opverty elimination programmes can be made to reach the unreached organisationfunctioning in the villages including under the GAP Analysis would be made together with an assessment of their effectiveness in serving as bridges between Government agencies and the poor. Discussions will be held with both voluntary organizations and men and women members of elected Panchayats and Nagarpalikas on how the gap can be ended and how the delivery systems of poverty in thier efficiency and impact.

This phase-II will be a strategic planning phase giving particular attention to the following:

(a) Steps needed to fill the gap between entitlements and actual delivery.

(b) Opportunities for mobilising human, financial resources in the concerned areas for improving the efficiency of delilvery of on-going programmes and for initiating new programmes to meet the unmet minimum needs of the population.

(c) Identification of methods of achieving synergy and convergence among all the programmes, whether governmental or non-governmental.

(d) Articulation of new livelihood opportunities based on both farm and non-farm occupations.

(e) Introduction of organisational and management methods which will ensure the oversight and effective participation of the primary stake holders in the implementation of programmes designed to strengthen the security of their livelihoods, and

(f) Identification of young women and men in the concerned villages for forming a Corps of Hunger Fighters. The young hunger fighters would undertake responsibilities such as creating awareness of entitlements, improving delivery systems and promoting environmental hygiene and garbage and sewage recycling.

The hunger fighters would be given a small honorarium for meeting their travel and other expenses and for compensating them for thier time. The members of the Corps of Hunger Fighters will be drawn from those who have a social or economic stake in living in their respective villages. There will be equal number of women and men in such a corps.

As a result of the work done during phases 1 and 2, awareness of the possibilities for ending hunger and deprivation, analaysis of methods of achieving the desired goals and an implementable action plan would have emerged. The Action Programme, to be effective, must emerge from discussions with the poor families and on the basis of their suggestions. The phase will therefore be opportune to establish a broad based local level Coalition for Ending Hunger and Deprivation. Such a Coalition for Ending Hunger could consist of representatives of local self-government institutions, government agencies responsible for fighting poverty and hunger, academic community, the civil society, corporate sector, women's and youth organisations, financial institutions and the mass media. Such a coalition will assign specific tasks to each member of the coalition in the areas of awareness generation, resource mobilisation task implementation, monitoring and evaluation. The Coalition will aim to add a horizontal dimension zto vertically structured government programmes. Coalition members will also help to develop methods of achieving gender equality and eliminating social evils like dowery and alcoholism.

During ths period, HFAP will be converted from a desirable concept to anb implementable local level action plan. Intensive efforts will be made to sensitise all sections of the community to the uncommon opportunities now available for achieving a sustainable end to hunger. The poor themselves will play an active role in both the planning and implementation phase. Many of the members of the grassroots level Corps of Hunger Fighters will come from landless labour families. The Corps of Hunger Fighters will include elected members of Panchayats and Nagarpalikas, so that they are able to serve as links between the elected bodies and the people. There should be a minimum of two members of the corps drawn form every village/town, so that they are able to play a role in improving environmental hygiene and sanitation as well as the health and nutrition secutity of the families living in their village/town.

Ours is a land of the young. Nearly 400 million women and men are below the age of 21. The nation's future depends upon the opportunity they get for a productive and healthy life. Youth can be attracted and retained in farming only if farming becomes and economically rewarding. This is where ecological agriculture, which is knowledge intensive, can prove to be a double advantage.

Our society is characterised by cultural, religious, linguistic and political pluralism. Political pluralism at the level of the central government provides an opportunity for elevating issues relating to hunger elimination and poverty alleviation to a level of overriding priority, transcending political frontiers and placing them at the top of the political agenda. The Government of Tamil Nadu has taken the first bold step in this directon by deciding to initiate a cencerted attempt to eliminate poverty-induced hunger. We should work for spreading the Hunger-Free Area programme throughout the country before we enter the next century.

Integrating environemntal considerations into development planning is not an easy task. Unless concern is backed by an ability to take ameliorative action, little can be achieved. India has been very conscious of this and has, over the past few decades, taken important steps to increase its capacity to handle environmental issues.

The initiatives have come equally from the Government, NGO's and individuals. Many collaborative and joint programmes exist today between the Government and the NGO's.

Environment and development problems are complex and there cannot be generalized and simplified solutions. Answers have to be found which are ecologically, economically and socio-culturally consistent in the particular milie. Given the size and diversity of a country like India, this task becomes extremely difficult.

Expertise is requied in framing appropriate policies and legislation, in planning, in creating mechanisms for implementation, in * education and public awareness. India also needs to be above to bring its perspective to global forums and participate in evolving international treaties, protocols and conventions. Most importantly, with the increasing emphasis on decentralized decision—making and the stress on micro-planning, this capacity-building is taking on a greater urgency. Capability is required to enable decisions to be made in a decentralized manner—decisions which are not imported solutions, but are appropriate to the particular situation.

Addressing the plenary session of the UN Conference on Human Environment in Stockholm in 1972, Prime Minister Indira Gandhi and said, "Even though our industrial development is in its infancy and at its most difficult stage, we are taking various steps to deal with the incipient environmental imbalances, more so because of our concern for the human species, whic is also imperilled." It was at her initiative that a National Council Environmental Planning and Coordination (NECPC) was set up in 1972 to identify and investigate the problems of preserving or improving the human environment in the country, and to propose solution to environmental problems.

Another Empowered Committee, the Tiwari Committee, was set up in 1980 to review and recommend legislative measures and administrative machinery for ensuring environmental protection. On the recommendation of this Committee, the Department of Environment was set up in 1980 as the focal agency in the administrative structure of the Central Government for planning, promotion and coordination of environmental programmes. This department became part of the new Ministry of Environment and Forest in 1985.

The Ministry is the apex body under the Government of India for planning, promotion and coordination of environmental and forestry programmes. Its activities include conservation and survey of flora and fauna, prevention and control of pollution, afforestation and regeneration of degraded areas, impact assessment, forest conservation and research, and education and information. The National Wastelands Development Board and the Ganga Project Directorate are major components of the Ministry.

Most of the states have also set up their own Departments of Environment, Pollution Control Boards and other associated bodies. Various other ministries and departments, including those of Urban Development, Oceanography, Non-Conventional Energy Sources etc., at the state and central levels, are also concerned with different aspects of the environment. Greater coordination among these various agencies—government and non-government-would strengthen environmental efforts. State Governments are in the process of involving themselves seriously in environmental planning.

The Directory of Environmental NGOs, brought out by the World Wide Fund for Nature - India (WWF-I) in 1989, lists about 850 NGOs working in this field, but there are porbably at least four times this number. Their involvement is clearly seen. As the Secretary General of WWF-I says, "India's impressively large body of NGOs is becoming active on the environmental front because fo the increasingly clear nexus between meaningful, equitable, sustainable economic growth and the conservation of the environment...For instance, the National Environmental Awareness Campaign promoted by the Ministry has successfully encouraged many NGOs whose primary concerns are rural development, appropriate technology, civil rights, women's development, tribal welfare etc. The interaction between NGOs and State Governments is largely confined to functional matters (clearance, information, advice etc.) whereas for financial and technical support various central departments and agencies have to be relied upon. However now there is a concerted effort by the Government to use their expertise for their own programmes."

NGOs range from clubs which encourage and assist in adventure travel, exploration, and dissemination of knowledge about an ecosystem to agencies which deal with various issues like creating gainful employment, wastelands development, afforestation, rehabilitation of tribals, and with preparation of educational materials and aids. They may be as small as groups of two or three persons, or as large as organizations with an eight-thousand-strong membership.

One of the most important signs of environmental awareness in India is the rise of people's movements which are challenging existing socio-political structures and development models, and are showing alternative paths. These have led not only to action at the grassroot level, but are also helping to shape developmental policies.

**Environmental degradation**

There are a host of human interventions including development activities which have resulted in considerable environmental degration. Major human interventions in forests are deforestation, commercial logging, setting up protected area, partial closure of forests, etc which are described below:

- There is increasing deforestation due to commercial exploitation, building of dams, mining and construction activities. Of the world's estimated 8.4 billion hectares of forests in 1990, tropical forests covered 1.76 billion ha. During 1981-90, tropical forests were lost at the rate of 0.8 per cent (15.4 million ha) a year, as per estimates of the World Resources Institute. The net annual deforestation during 1981-90 exceeded two per cent in 10 tropical countries of Asia and Africa.
- Commercial logging for industrial activities is increasing rapidly. Eighty-four per cent of such logging took place in closed tropical broadleaf forests in primary (undisturbed forests) during the

1980s. Logging activity is a causal factor for forest degradation and is reflected in rough wood production which increased by 19 per cent between 1979-81 to 1989-91. Globally, almost 50 per cent of such rough wood is used for industrial purposes, the rest for heating and cooking.

- Setting up of protected areas for conservation purposes has led to complications and conflict-situation with indigenous communities and also denial of many of their rights and privileges.
- Closure of parts of forests for setting up of industries or agro-based activities for private, semi-private lands, construction of railways, roads and new settlements has led to shrinkage of forest cover and increased hardship for local communities in their day-to-day existence.
- Interventions for adhering to international agreements have also alienated many local communities and some of their practices, eg, tribal hunting of wild animals which goes against biodiversity agreements.
- Policies of economic liberalization, privatization and globalization have both, directly and indirectly, led to reduction of forest cover and cuts in subsidies and grants affecting food subsidies and other welfare schemes involving poor and marginalized communities.

Human rights are a extensive as human life and, whether or not enshrined in national constitutions or bills of right or in international covenants to which nations are signatory, first order rights are inherent and inalienable. As Jefferson said, "the God that gave us life, gave us liberty at the same time". These rights are not gifted and cannot be taken away except by due process of law. To act otherwise is to violate Human Rights. There are, however, a whole series of rights, other than the basic or fundamental freedoms, which are statutory or derive from subscription to international or regional covenants.

Human Rights may be broadly classified as civil and political (so-called civil liberties and democratic rights), and social, economic and cultural. The latter include rights to development, the rights of women and children, a whole new family of environmental rights, rights to education and health, and to employment and to enjoy the fruits of labour. Both sets of rights are growing. Thus, freedom of speech and expression has developed to encompass the right to information. Privacy is now increasingly protected. There will be refinements and new situations will bring forth new rights such as now, in some societies, of pays, and may be for victims of AIDS.

A comparison of South Asian constitutions will probably indicate a broad similarity in the basic rights enunciated. Interpretations and implementation might vary. Derogations are permitted in emergency situations and these instances have been extensive in all parts of South Asia and have sometimes continued long after the proximate cause, perhaps well justified in some cases, has passed. The Indian Emergency (1975-77) and martial law or emergency regimes in Pakistan, Nepal, Bangladesh and Sri Lanka can also be cited. Many statutes contain preventive laws (preventive detention in India), and special laws may be invoked in given circumstances such as declaring certain areas to be disturbed and applying therein summary procedures (such as the Armed Forces Special Powers Act in India).

The South Asian nations are members of the United Nations and have variously subscribed to a number of international instruments including the international

Covenants on Civil and Political Rights/Economic and Social Rights, the Geneva Conventions, ILO conventions and so forth. However, retification has not always followed speedily or at all. For instance, India took a long time to ratify the Convention on the Rights of the Child and has yet to ratify the Convention Against Torture. The record of the other South Asian governments would probably reveal similar lags or omissions which need to be overcome. Even where ratifications has taken place it is not certain whether governments have cared to create public awareness about national adherence to these conventions and to explain their implications or to examine whether national laws need to be upgraded, expanded or created to give them an enforceable statutory basis. This is an exercise national governments should be asked to undertake and could be the subjects of a report of SAARC.

While human rights are proclaimed, newly-independent nations have sometimes been prone to stress sovereign or national rights, the rights of the state, over individual human rights. This was true worldwide until the second world war and in some ways continue to be so even in the more industrially advanced and politically older or mature societies because of the fears and compulsions of the cold war. With the end of the East-West divide, the West has given more emphasis to human rights and democratic governance and has come to attach trade and aid conditionalities for "good performance". While this may be justified at one level, the question that arises, as it does in the domestic domain, is who will police the policeman? Also, how far observing is the human rights record of smaller and weaker countries. Such conditionalities are also creeping into the field of environment, the rights of so-called indigenous people, a misnomer when applied to South Asian societies, and so on.

Development, gender, minority, regional and environmental rights, among others, are of great importance to South Asia where poverty, gender inequalities, disparities, illiteracy, bonded labour and child labour are widespread. Poverty robs the individual of dignity and, often, children of their childhood. While, therefore, development rights are vitally important, there are no hierarchy of rights. All rights, political, civil cultural, social and economic, are indivisible and mutually reinforcing. This is a normative value that South Asia must accept and proclaim so that one right is not used to supersede and thereby deny another.

South Asia has a number of human rights organisations, statutory and voluntary. In India, for scheduled castes and tribes and statutory bodies such as the Press Council, the Minorities Commission, the National Commission for Women, and the Commissioner for Linguistic Minorities. A statutory Human Rights Commission has been brought into being by ordinance and incorporates many improvements in relation to an earlier Bill. Pakistan has a very active non-governmental Human Rights Commission whose reports merit wider distribution in the region. The Human Rights Organisation of Nepal (HURON) played an important part in securing the change-over from the panchayati system to the vigorous multi-party democracy that was established in 1991. Bangladesh has a Coordinating Council for Human Rights (CCHRB) which aims to publish annual reports.

All the countries of South Asia are in transition and there is much ferment: violence, terrorism, ethnic discords, the rise of religious fundamentalisms, basic rights, but the exploitation of religion for partisan political ends, can be dangerous as India has discovered. Likewise caste. With the process of nation-building still underway, individual and state rights tend to clash. A more careful study of events and trends and a sharing of experience could promote clarity and wisdom in dealing with highly complex and volatile situations.

Human rights violations regrettably occur everywhere around the globe in greater or lesser measure. What matters, however, is that violation, aberrant action and derogations are brought to light by the media, the law enforcement agencies and human rights groups or by the community at large and the guilty are brought to book. While human rights mechanisms need to be strengthened or even created where necessary, human rights problems most often begin where due process and the criminal justice system break down. This then leads to false cases, torture, custodial death, extortion, rape, corruption, et al. The public preception of a breakdown in the local criminal justice system led to the Bhagalpur blindings in Bihar in the 1980s when there was widespread public approval of known criminals being blinded while in detention for fear that they would otherwise be bailed out or released and continue with their depredations.

The restoration of the efficacy, integrity and speed of the criminal justice system (including the working of the police and jails) is perhaps the single most important item that should be on the South Asian human rights agenda. For prevention is better than cure. Political interference with the police, the politicisation of crime and the criminalisation of politics have played havoc. Dealing with human rights violations then becomes a case of trying to shut the stable door after the horse has bolted. The understaffing of courts, mounting arrears and costs, and dilatory procedures are discrediting the rule of law.

Yet the judiciary has been innovative. In India, for example, public interest litigation has opened new doors, overriding former impediments of locus standi in relations to the cause of action and treating a single case as a class action. Judicial verdicts have also amplified Article 21, the Right to Life, to embrace "rights to livelihood, health, education, shelter, dignity, minimum wage, environment" (Upendra Baxi).

Environmental issues have come to the fore in South Asia with poverty, population and livestock pressures leading to deforestation, erosion of common property resources and environmental degradation generally. The land can no longer support burgeoning numbers and the region is spawning its share of inadvertent cities and threatens to (and does) explode with crime and violence. Water and energy shortages confront us and industrial, pollution and development blight are increasingly visible, though yet in the early stages. The warning signals are there.

South Asia's environmental problems are largely related to the economics of survival, poverty in a broad sense being the worst polluter. Population control and ensuring an early demographic transition are of the highest importance. Primary education and health and improving the status of women hold the key as Sri Lanka, and Kerala and Goa in India have well demonstrated. The pace of development must be hastened and the fruits of development more equitably shared. There have to be alternative sources of fodder and fuel, improved land-use patterns, better land and water management and greater emphasis on biofertilisers and integrated pest management so as to avoid incremental toxicity entering the food chain. Rivers are becoming sewers. The Ganga Action Plan, now being extended to the Yamuna, Damodar, Gomati and other rivers, represents the largest river clean-up operation ever undertaken anywhere. Conservation, substainability and maintenance of bio-diversity have become key ideas.

South Asia is setting new pollution standards and seeking to upgrade technology and maintenance systems, but there is a long way to go. Environmental groups are active and environmental awareness is spreading. Indian courts have ordered the closure of polluting industries for failure to ensure minimal emission of effluent standards despite being allowed resonable time, access to credit, and technical assistance to upgrade their technology. Environmental tribunals are contemplated.

Two problems will have to be confronted. One is internal pressure from local groups and communities to adopt alternative strategies of development: decentralised, low-energy, appropriate technology, small-is-beautiful, back-to-nature systems. While the opposition to ostentatious consumption, crass consumerism and waste is widel'y shared, there will be reservations about nostalgia, romanticising the past, overlooking the tremendous growth of population which is likely to double or triple again before it stabilises in South Asia, and ignoring the demand for minimal life styles and national infra-structure in a globalised setting. There has to be a practical via media. At the other end of the scale, the North would like to globalise tropical forests and bio-diversity and points to population growth as a looming ecological threat, leading to green house warming, a possible sea-rise, and destablising climate changes. This ignores the unsustainable life styles of the North and its massive contribution to global warming since the industrial revolution, but more particularly, in the past few decades. Global conferencing and the Rio meet have brought about some convergence, but maybe not nearly enough.

South Asia, as a clearly demacrated monsoonal geopolitical entity, should concert action on both the regional and global planes. The Himalayan-Karakoram barrier constitutes a critical watershed the greening of which should be worth something as a global carbon sink and oxygen bank. Debt-for-nature swaps and debt forgiveness by the North, linked to environmental improvement and technological upgradation in South Asia, should be jointly explored. The natural disaster study undertaken by SAARC (1989-91) marks a beginning towards collective action on environmental issues and optimal harnessing of shared natural resources such as rivers and bio-diversity.

There could be joint studies and research programmes in South Asia to meet the challenge of global warming and sea-rise effects, to fight locusts and study seismicity.

On the human rights plane, it is perhaps not widely known that a South Asian Forum for Human Rights was formally set up in Kathmandu in February, 1993, a spinoff from a suggestion mooted at the World Human Rights Congress in Delhi in 1990. This is a non-governmental body that plans to promote networking and interaction among human rights groups in the region. All the SAARC nations other than the Maldives are represented. It is still at an embryonic stage but could grow. The setting up of SAARC observer groups to monitor elections in the region represents another initiative. Perhaps the time has come to moot the establishment of a human rights cell within SAARC or more informally to gather information, liaise and sensitise governments on issues and opportunities that call for concerted action.

Human rights and environmental issues are very much on the national, regional and international agenda today. These concerns have wide linkages and need to be properly understood and fully internalised in national and regional policies and instruments.

**Disease control and health improvement**

Given the existing conditions of poor environmental sanitation and the weakness of the public health system it may not be possible to completely prevent out breaks of communicable diseases in the near future. Nevertheless, early detection and prompt response could result in rapid containment and control of the outbreak, reduction in morbidity and mortality. The building up of the disease surveillance and response mechanisms have received considerable attention during the Eighth Plan period. It is felt disease surveillance and response must be based at district level ensure prompt response. This system needs to be given the necessary back up laboratory support and epidemiological expertise so that containment measures are based on suond data and are logical. This back up system should be evolved through strengthening and optimal utilisation of the facilities and expertise available in the National Institutions/medical colleges.

Increasing incidence of hospital acquired infections and accidental infection in health care providers and waste disposers renders it imperative that efforts are made to improve infection control and waste management through utilisaton of appropriate affordable technology at all levels of health care. Planning Commission and the Ministry of Health and Family Welfare Programme have initiated steps to take up specific pilot projects.

Increasing longevity, demographic transition resulting in rapidly rising numbers of aged population, urbanisation, increasing pollution, a change over from traditional diets, sedentary life style and increase in the stress of day to day living have led to the increase in life style related disorders and noncommunicable diseases. Noncommunicable diseases such as cardio-and cerebrovascular diseases resulting in heart attacks and strokes, diabetes and common malignancies are emerging as major public health problems in the country. Pilot projects for district based integrated noncummunicable disease control programmes carried out through the existing primary and secondary level facilities, using diabetes as a model, have been initiated in the Eighth Plan. The experience gained will be used to expand such programmes.

Rapidly growing population, urbanisation, changing agricultural, industrial and water resource management, increasing use of pesticides and fossil fuels have all resulted in perceptible deterioration in the quality of environment and attendant adverse health consequences. Pilot projects exploring the dimensions of the problem and aimed at seeking realistic solutions were initiated during the Eighth Plan period. Efforts are also under way to document extent of the problem of environmental pollution and its impact on health status of the population. Prevention and management of health consequences of environmental deterioration will receive increasing attention.

Over the last two decades occupational health has received considerable attention. Continuous monitoring of safety of work environment and workers' health status, both in the organised and unorganised sector with emphasis on gender specific and child labour related issues, documenting the magnitude and types of the occupational health problems, initiating appropriate preventive and remedial measures will be developed into a structured health programme are being taken up wherever possible.

Several major development activities in any field such as Agriculture, Industries, Urban and Rural Development have resulted in environment changes;

some of these could have health implications. In order to minimise these it has been suggested that all large development projects should have Health Impact assesment and then necessary provision for health care of people involved in development activities and prevention and management of health consequences of developmental activities on the population living in the vicinity of the project should be incorporated and costed as part of the project. These suggestions are being considered by appropriate implementing agencies.

The past fifty years have witnessed the development of a vast health care infrastructure and manpower aimed at providing health care to the population. National Programmes have been evolved and implemented to control major public health problems. The investment in Public health has shown considerable increase over the plan periods. However there has not been any increase in the proportion of the Plan outlay allocated to health sector. There is an increase in the disease burden due to communicable and non-communicable disease caused by the growing population, newer diseases and changing life styles. There are evolving technologies for health care and increasing expectations of the population for health care. All these have resulted in the ever widening gap between what is possible and what is affordable. It is imperative that in the coming decades this gap is bridged and at the same time equity and excellence are ensured in health care services.

The family Welfare Programme has helped in containing the growth rate of population. Total Fertility Rate has declined from 4.5 in 1981 to 3.5 in 1993 as per the estimates of Sample Registration System (SRS). The Crude Birth Rate has decreased from 33.9 per provisional estimates of the SRS. The Crude Death Rate has also declined from 12.5 to 9 per thousand population over the same period. The Infant MOrtality Rate dropped from 110 per thousand live births in 1981 to 74 in 1995. The annual average exponential population growth rate has come down marginally from 2.22 per cent during 1971-81 to 2.14 per cent during 1981-91. The population, however, continues to grow as the decline in birth rate has not been as rapid as the decline in the death rate.

There are, however, inter-State differences in the achievements of the Family Welfare Programme. At one end of the spectrum are the States like Kerala, Tamil Nadu and Goa which have already achieved replacement level of fertility. At the other end, are the large States like Uttar Pradesh, Madhya Pradesh, Rajasthan and Bihar where fertility levels and bjirth rates continue to be higher than the national average. Therefore, decline in the rate of growth of population for the country as a whole depends upon how the large northern States perform in the family welfare programmes in the future. Unless effective steps are taken to bring about significant improvements in the programme, the performance in containing the growth of population at the All India level may not change significantly.

Recognising the close relationship between high birth rates and high rnfant mortality, high priority has been accorded to the Maternal and Child Health (MCH) programme since 1985. In order to achieves the main objective of MCH, (i.e. to improve the health status of women and children and to reduce maternal, infant and child morbidity and mortality rates), the Universal Immunisation Programme (UIP) was launched in 1985. From the year 1992-93 the UIP has been strengthened and expanded into the Child Survival and Safe Motherhood (CSSM) programme. Under this programme, apart from strengthening the existing MCH, initiative has been taken to expand the pilot projects on Acute Respiratory

Infection Control and Traditional Birth Attendants training. For this, a provision of Rs.350 crore has been made in the 1996-97 budget as against Rs.220 crore in 1995-96 (BE).

From 1.4.1996, the Family Welfare Programme is being implemented on the basis of the "Target Free Approach" (TFA). This approach envisages replacement of the system of setting contraceptive targets from the top by a system of decentralised participatory planning at the Primary Health Centre level.

Pursuant to the World Health Organisation (WHO) goal to eradicate poliomyelitis by the year 2000 A.D., the Pulse Polio Immunization (PPI) was launched in 1995-96. About 87 million children aged 0-3 years were administered as supplemented dose of oral polio vaccine on 9.12.1995 and 93 million on 20.1.1996, irrespective of their routine immunisation status. Since PPI received an overwhelming response from the public, the exercise was repeated on 7.12.1996 and 18,1.1997 covering about 120 million children in the age group of 0-5 years.

A Special School Health Check-up Scheme for Primary School Children was carried out in 27 States/ UTs in July 1996, and in the remaining 5 States between August and October 1996. The objectives of this Scheme were to detect common health related problems among primary school children; to conduct screening of children for appropriate referral and check up; to generate health awareness in the community; and to ensure arrangements for follow up and treatment at higher level medical facilities. Reports from 441 districts show 75.9 per cent coverage of schools and 84.9 per cent coverage of enrolled children.

In order to foster community involvement in the Family Welfare Programme, two new schemes have been started on a pilot basis. Under one of these, one revenue village in every district, among villages with a population of 500 or more, will be given an award of Rs. 2 lakh for achieving a reduction in the Crude Birth rate, Infant Mortality Rate and Child Mortality Rate. The second schemes aims to integrate family welfare and health care into the ongoing National Wastershed Development Project for Rainfed Areas (NWDPRA) of the Ministry of Agriculture. Under this scheme, the watershed level community based management structures, known as the 'Mitra Krishak Mandal' (MKM) will conduct surveys and prepare watershed level family welfare and health care plans. An amount of Rs. 5000 will be given to each village in the watershed areas, for specified activities like emergency obstetric care and purchase of essential medicines.

The Prenatal Diagnostic Techniques Act, 1994, has been brought into force from 1st January, 1996. This Act makes it illegal to use prenatal diagnostic techniques like amniocentesis for determining the sex of the foetus, a practice that often leads to abortion of female foetuses. Statutory machinery for implementation of the Act has been established.

# 3

# Rural Development

### Panchayati Raj

Panchayats have been the backbone of the Indian villages since the beginning of recorded history. Gandhiji, the father of the nation, in 1946 had aptly remarked that Indian Independence must begin at the bottom and every village ought to be a Republic or Panchayat having powers. Gandhiji's dream has been translated into reality with the introduction of the three-tier Panchayati Raj system to enlist people's participation in rural reconstruction.

### 73rd amendment act 1992

The passage of the Constitution (73rd Amendment) Act, 1992 marks a new era in the federal democratic set up of the country and provides constitutional status to the Panchayati Raj Institutions (PRls). Consequent upon the enactment of the Act, almost all the States/UTs, except J&K, NCT Delhi and Arunachal Pradesh have enacted their legislation. Except Assam, Arunachal Pradesh, Bihar, NCT Delhi, Pondicherry and Goa (Zilla Parishad), all other States/UTs have held elections. As a result, about 2,27,698 Panchayats at village level; 5,906 Panchayats at intermediate level and 474 Panchayats at the district level have been constituted in the country. These Panchayats are being manned by about 34 lakh elected representatives of Panchayats at all levels. Thus, this is the broadest representative base that exists in any country of the world - developed or underdeveloped. The main features of the Act are - (1) a 3-tier system of Panchayatil Raj for all States having population of over 20 lakh; 00 Panchayat elections regularly every 5 years; (iii) reservation of seats for Scheduled Castes, Scheduled Tribes and women (33%); (iv) to appoint State Finance Commission to make recommendations as regards the financial powers of the Panchayats and (v) to constitute District Planning Committee to prepare draft development plan for the district as a whole. As per the Constitution, the Panchayati Raj Institutions have been endowed with such powers and authority as may be necessary to function as institutions of self-government and contains provisions of devolution of powers and responsibilities upon Panchayats at the appropriate level with reference to (a) the preparation of plans for economic development and social justice; and (b) the implementation of such schemes for economic development and social justice as may be entrusted to them.

**Financial powers of Panchayati Raj**

Institutions Article 243-G of the Constitution of India-introduced by the 73rd Amendment - deals with the question of powers, authority and responsibilities of Panchayats. It reads thus:

"Subject to the provisions of the Constitution, the legislature of a State may, by law, endow the Panchayats with such powers and authority as may be necessary to enable them to function as institutions of self-government and such law may contain provisions for the devolution of powers and responsibilities upon Panchayats at the appropriate level, subject to such conditions as may be specified therein, with respect to - (a) the preparation of plans for economic development and social justice; and (b) the implementation of such schemes for economic development and social justice as may be entrusted to them including those in relation to the matters listed in the Eleventh Schedule".

While Article 243-G of the Constitution visualises Panchayats as institutions for self-government, it subjects the extent of devolution of powers and functions to the will of the State Legislatures.

- As per Article 243-H of the Constitution, State Legislatures have been empowered to enact laws;
- to authorise a Panchayat to levy, collect and appropriate some taxes, duties, tolls and fees;
- to assign to the Panchayat, some taxes, duties, tolls levied and collected by the State Government;
- to provide for making grants-in-aid to the Panchayats from the Consolidated Fund of the State; and
- to provide for constitution of such funds for Panchayats for crediting all money received by or on behalf of Panchayats and also the withdrawal of such money therefrom.

Article 243-1 of the Constitution provides for constitution of a State Finance Commission (SFC) to review the financial position of Panchayats and to make recommendations to the Governor regarding the principles governing the major issues mentioned in Article 243-H. State Finance Commissions of Andhra Pradesh, Assam, Gujarat, Haryana, Himachal Pradesh, Karnataka, Kerala, Madhya Pradesh, Maharashtra, Punjab, Rajasthan, Tamil Nadu, Tripura, Uttar Pradesh and West Bengal have submitted their reports to the respective State Governments. The States of Assam, Karnataka, Kerala, Madhya Pradesh, Punjab, Rajasthan,

Tamil Nadu, Tripura and West Bengal have accepted most of the recommendations of the SFCs. Andaman and Nicobar Islands, Dadra and Nagar Haveli and Daman and Diu have received Interim Reports of the SFC on which states/UTs have yet to take action. SFCs of Orissa, Goa and Sikkim have yet to submit their reports.

The Constitution requires the Central Finance Commission to recommend measures needed to augment the Consolidated Fund of a State to supplement the resources of the Panchayats, in the State on the basis of the recommendations made by the Finance Commissions of the State. The Tenth Finance Commission, for want of SFC reports, made an adhoc provision of Rs. 4381 crores to the PRIs for the period 1996-2000. All the States were released grants amounting to Rs. 1095 crores during 1996-97 to be given to the three tiers of Panchayats. However, releases during 1997-98 required the State Governments to furnish utilisation reports. Kerala, Maharashtra, Himachal Pradesh, Tamilnadu and Tripura were the only States which obtained all the four instalments during 1997-98. Andhra Pradesh and Uttar Pradesh have managed to obtain 3 out of 4 instalments. The remaining States have obtained either one or two instalments only. The State of Bihar was not released any grants during 1997-98 for want of elected PRI bodies.

The Eleventh Finance Commission which would recommend on the devolution of resources for five years commencing from Ist April, 2000, will be dealing with the mandatory subject of making recommendations for the Panchayats. It is essential that expeditious action is taken by the States in terms of acceptance of the SFC recommendations as the Eleventh Finance Commission is expected to take into account the recommendations of the SFCs and recommend suitable financial arrangements in respect of the PRIs. A comprehensive paper on the requirement of finances of PRIs has been submitted to the XIth Finance Commission by this Ministry.

**Initiatives taken by the Ministry**

A Conference of the Chief Ministers on Panchayati Raj was held on 2nd August, 1997 at Vigyan Bhavan, New Delhi, under the chairmanship of Prime Minister to review the functioning of the Panchayati Raj Institutions where the outstanding issues like devolution of powers/ functions and responsibilities upon PRIs, setting up District Planning Committees; implementation of the reports of the State Finance Commissions, linkage of DRDAs with Zilla Parishads, training to Panchayati Raj elected representatives/ functionaries were discussed in great detail. The Conference also called upon the concerned 8 States to enact the required State Legislation on the Provisions of the Panchayat (Extension to the Scheduled Areas) Act, 1996 before 23rd December, 1997.

Based on the detailed discussions, the Conference recommended setting up of two Committees - (a) the Committee of the Panchayat and the Tribal Development Ministers of the 8 States covered under Schedule V of the Constitution under the Chairmanship of Minister for Rural -Areas and Employment to examine and to give their recommendations to enact the State legislation in consonance with the Central Act, 1996 before the cut off date i.e. 23rd December, 1997; and (b) the Committee of the Chief Ministers under the Chairmanship of Prime Minister to examine the issues regarding the devolution of powers, functions and responsibilities upon Panchayati Raj Institutes (PRIs) and to recommend measures to streamline the Panchayati Raj system.

The Committee of Panchayat and Tribal Development Ministers of the Schedule V Sates and the Committee of Chief Ministers under the Chairmanship of the Prime Minister have since submitted their reports which have been circulated to the States for appropriate action. The important recommendations of the Committee of Chief Ministers were:

- Leave selection of beneficiaries to Gram Sabha.
- Waive requirement of Technical sanction for works upto Rs. 10,000.
- Innovate to provide adequate manpower support to the Gram Panchayats.
- Delegate total control over such manpower to Gram Panchayats.
- Zilla Parishad Chairpersons be made the Chairpersons of DRDAs.
- Provide reasonable opportunity of hearing to the PRIs before suspension/dismissal.
- Gram Panchayat President to be accountable solely to Gram Sabha.
- Expeditious constitution of District Planning Committees.

In order to ensure that Panchayati Raj Institutions function as instruments of local government, it is important that their functional and financial autonomy is guaranteed and transparency in their functioning is ensured. This has to be accomplished in most of the States. The role of the Gram Sabha is, perhaps, the most important in ensuring the success of Panchayati Raj Institutions at the village level. The role of local people in conducting social audit and fixing responsibility on panchayat functionaries will be effectively ensured with Gram Sabha becoming active. It is essential that the village community perceives meetings of the Gram Sabha as useful. The most important factor for that is the empowerment of the Gram Sabha.

An important factor for the success of the Panchayat! Raj system is the need for transparency in the functioning of these bodies. Panchayats being closer to the people, their right to information and accessibility to the panchayats must be ensured. This issue was discussed in the Chief Ministers Conference held on 2nd August, 1997 and the Committee of Chief Ministers as well. The Ministry has written to the States. The Hon'bie Prime Minister too, in his letter to the Chief Ministers, has urged that all relevant information on development schemes taken up by the Panchayat along with the budget for them should be displayed prominently in the Panchayat Office. Relevant records should be made available for inspection by members of the public. Photocopies of documents such as muster rolls, vouchers, estimates etc. can be made available to the public on payment of a nominal fee. Technical manuals may be prepared for execution of various works at the Panchayat level so that transparency can be ensured.

The Ministry of Rural Areas and Employment convened a Conference of State Ministers of Rural Development and Panchayati Raj on May 13, 1998. This meeting was inaugurated by the Prime Minister. The resolutions adopted in the Conference held on 13.5.98 are - (I) a Task Force for studying the structure and functioning of the Panchayats should be set up; (ii) provisions of 73rd Amendment Act and Central Act 40 will be complied with; (iii) Gram Sabhas should be convened on a single predetermined day every quarter and (iv) care should be taken to respect the autonomy and independence of each tier of PRIs and to build up capability of the village level Panchayats. In pursuance of the resolution, a Task Force has been constituted under the Chairmanship of Minister of State (independent Charge), Ministry of Rural Areas and Employment to study the structure and functioning of PRIs. The State Governments have been requested to ensure that the Gram Sabha Meetings are convened once in each quarter preferably on -26th January-Republic Day; Ist May-Labour Day; 15th August-independence Day and 2nd October-Gandhi Jayanti.

The Ministry intends to introduce a bill for amending Article 243-M of the Constitution to exempt Arunachal Pradesh from the requirement of providing for Scheduled Castes reservation. This will provide a legal and Constitutional basis for Panchayati Raj Institutions in Arunachal Pradesh in accordance with the sociopolitical ethos of the State.

**Issues arising out of implementation of Act 40 of 1996**

The provisions Of the Panchayats (Extension to the Scheduled Areas) Act, 1996 has come into force on 24th December, 1996. This Act extends Panchayats to the tribal areas of eight States of India namely, Andhra Pradesh, Bihar, Gujarat, Himachal Pradesh, Maharashtra, Madhya Pradesh, Orissa and Rajasthan, which intends to enable tribal society to assume control over their own destiny to preserve and conserve their traditional rights over natural resources. The State Governments were required to enact their legislation in accordance with the Provisions of Act before the expiry of one year i.e. 23rd December, 1997.

All States barring Bihar and Rajasthan have enacted State Legislation to give effect to the provisions contained in Act 40, 1996.

However, there are certain problems, both with certain Central laws and State legislations as have been passed in pursuance of Act 40 of 1996. Certain crucial issues arise:

- Definition of Minor Forest Produce - the Indian Forest Act, 1927 defines timber as including within its definition, bamboo as well as cane. The Ministry of Environment and Forests define Minor Forest

Produce to exclude bamboo and cane. While doing so, they have decided to adopt the definition of timber as given in the Indian Forest Act, 1927. In most States, tribals have been traditionally depending on bamboo and cane for their livelihood. However, for the last so many years, Forest Corporations and Forest Departments have prevented tribals from access to bamboo and cane while at the same time giving these to private industry at highly concessional rates. In many cases, tribals have been driven to desperation on account of this policy of State Forest Departments. It is felt that the definition of timber in the Central Act, 1927 is neither scientific nor equitable. It is a colonial definition and goes against the spirit of the provisions of Act 40 of 1996.

- There are also issues arising from the interpretation by the Ministry of Environment and Forests of the intention of Parliament regarding vesting of ownership of Minor Forest Produce in Gram Sabhas. The proposals made by the Ministry of Environment and Forests interpret the intention of Parliament as giving not ownership per se, but making available to the Gram Sabhas, residual profits of State Forest Corporations/Federations. This necessarily means that according to the Ministry of Environment and Forests, State Forest Corporations/Federations will continue to trade in Minor Forest Produce and if there is any surplus, that surplus will be given to the Gram Sabhas. This Ministry has already taken up these issues with the Ministry of Environment and Forests.
- The continued application of the Minor Forest Produce (Trade Nationalisation) Acts of the States of Maharashtra and Gujarat contravene the provision of Act 40, 1996 in that, powers of control

over Minor Forest Produce vested in Gram Sabha is curtailed.

**Training of PRI members**

As a result of the elections of Panchayats in all the States, there are about 3.4 million elected representatives at all levels of Panchayats. Out of this, an overwhelming majority is new entrants, particularly from the weaker sections of the society, i.e., Scheduled Castes, Scheduled Tribes and women (33%). The Constitution having placed enormous responsibility on the Gram Panchayats to formulate and execute various programmes of economic development and social justice, elected representatives will have to acquire the required skill and given appropriate orientation. The success of the Panchayati Raj system hinges largely on the extent to which their capabilities are built to perform these functions and responsibilities. Thus, a time-bound and systematic training programme to provide orientation of the elected representatives on a very large scale is considered to be the most important prerequisite for the success of the PRIs. The States/UT governments are required to work out systematic and comprehensive training programmes for the entire Ninth Five Year Plan (1997-98 to 2002-03) to train PRIs and to generate awareness among the masses at the grassroots, level and to strengthen the Gram Sabha. The Ministry extends limited financial assistance to the States in their effort to train and create awareness among the PRI elected members and functionaries. The development functionaries working under the PRI framework are required to undergo a certificate course. The Indira Gandhi National Open University (IGNOU) has been entrusted with the task of preparation of the syllabus for the certificate course. The SIRDs/State Governments are being requested to conduct these courses. IGNOU is also involved in the Distance Education Programme. For IEC activities this ministry mainly provides funds for publication of "Panchayat Unnati" to the National Institute of Rural Development (NIRD).

The Central outlay for training during the Eighth Plan was Rs. 8.80 crores, During 1998-99, Rs. 3 crores were provided. An amount of Rs.3 crores has been proposed for 1999-2000.

The Ministry has also been providing financial assistance through the Council for Advancement of People's Action and Rural Technology (CAPART) to Non-Governmental Organisations with proven track record for conducting training and awareness generation programmes on Panchayati Raj.

The Research Advisory Committee headed by the Secretary (Rural Development) also approves proposals on research and studies related to Panchayati Raj received from the voluntary organisations/institutions. This Ministry has commissioned some reputed NGOs/ Institutions to conduct a number of research and evaluation studies.

### National social assistance programme

The National Social Assistance Programme (NSAP) which came into effect from 15th August 1995 represents a significant step towards the fulfilment of the Directive Principles in Article 41 and 42 of the Constitution. It introduces a National Policy for social assistance benefit to poor households in the case of old age, death of primary breadwinner and maternity. The Programme has three components, namely:-

1. National Old Age Pension Scheme (NOAPS)
2. National Family Benefit Scheme (NFBS)
3. National Maternity Benefit Scheme (NMBS)

These schemes were modified in 1998 based on the feedback received from the State Governments. The salient features of these schemes in their present modified form are given below:

**National old age pension scheme**

Under this Scheme, Central assistance is available as per the following criteria:

- Age of the applicant (male or female) is 65 years or more.
- The applicant is a destitute in the sense of having little or no regular means of subsistence from his/ her own sources of income or through financial support from family members or other sources.
- The amount of old age pension is Rs. 75 per month for the purpose of claiming Central assistance.

**National family benefit scheme**

Central assistance is available under this Scheme for a lump sum family benefit for households below the poverty line on the death of the primary breadwinner in the bereaved family subject to the following conditions:

- The 'primary breadwinner' is the member of the household, male or female whose earnings contribute substantially to the total household income.
- The death of such a primary breadwinner occurs while he or she is more than 18 years of age and less than 65 years of age.
- The bereaved household qualifies as one below the poverty line according to the criteria prescribed by the Government of India.
- The amount of benefit available is Rs. 10,000 in the case of death of the primary breadwinner irrespective of the cause of death - natural or accidental.

- The family benefit is paid to such surviving member of the household of deceased who, after local enquiry, is determined to be the head of the household.

**National maternity benefit scheme**

Under this scheme, maternity benefit is provided as a lump sum cash assistance to women of households below the poverty line, subject to the following conditions:-

- The maternity benefit is restricted to pregnant women for up to the first two live births provided they are of 19 years of age and above.
- The beneficiary belongs to a household below the poverty line as per criteria prescribed by the Government of India.
- The amount of the benefit is Rs. 5
- While the benefit should disbursed 8-12 weeks prior to delivery, in case of delay the benefit may be disbursed even after the child is born.

Under the modified Guidelines the State Government would be free to adopt any mode of disbursement of benefits, namely, cash, Money Order, Bank Account of beneficiaries in the Post Office Saving Bank/Commercial Bank. The benefit under NOAPS could be disbursed in not more than two instalments in a year. In case of cash disbursement, the payment shall be made in public meetings preferably of Gram Sabha in villages and in neighbourhood/mohalla committee meetings in towns.

**Objectives of the programme**

The NSAP is a 100% Centrally Sponsored Programme. The NSAP aims at ensuring minimum national standards in providing social assistance benefits to poor households. These are in addition to the benefits that the States are currently providing or might provide in future.

The intention in providing 100 per cent Central assistance is to ensure that social protection to the beneficiaries everywhere in the country is uniformly available without interruption. Accordingly, it should be ensured that Central assistance does not displace States' own expenditure in this respect and States/UTs may expand their own coverage of social assistance independently wherever they wish to do so.

The NSAP provides opportunities for linking social assistance packages to schemes for poverty alleviation and provision of basic needs. Specifically, old age pension can be linked to medical care and other benefits for the old and the poor. Integrated Rural Development Programme/Nehru Rozgar Yojana assistance may be provided in addition to the family benefit for the families of poor households who suffer the loss of the breadwinner. Maternity assistance can be linked to maternal and child care.

**Implementation of the programme**

The NSAP is implemented in the States/UTs through Panchayats and Municipalities. The Panchayats and Municipalities are encouraged to involve voluntary agencies to the extent possible in taking the benefits to the poor households for whom they are intended. The States/UTs have already taken various steps to appropriately implement the programme.

The implementation of the NSAP during the first year of its introduction was slow as States had to overcome several hurdles, both institutional and procedural. The institutional arrangements involved identification of Nodal Departments at the State/UT level, district-wise distribution of targets, constitution of State and District Level Committees, opening separate Bank Accounts at the district level to receive Central grants etc. The procedural aspects involved evolving procedures for issuing sanctions, audit and accounting mechanisms etc. To ensure proper implementation during the following year i.e. 1996-97 the concerned State Level Authorities were kept in constant touch and the performance of the programme was monitored regularly.

During 1997-98, a series of meetings was held at various levels with State Government Officials to review the progress of implementation of schemes and some of these States have since shown improvement in the implementation. The Central Advisory Committee under the Chairmanship of Smt. Nirmala Buch met on 15th July 1997 to review the implementation of the NSAP Schemes during the year.

Since the beginning of the year 1998-99, special efforts have been made to ensure that the implementation of the Schemes under NSAP improves substantially. Accordingly, the Nodal Secretaries of the States were invited in batches to New Delhi on 20th to 22nd April 1998 for discussion and also to work out strategies for efficient implementation of the Schemes in their respective States/UTs. The process continued for the whole year and the last batch of Nodal Secretaries was called for discussion on NMBS on 15th January 1999. An All India Review Meeting and Workshop of NSAP Secretaries was held at Yashada, Pune during November 1998. Two Studies have been commissioned to assess the performance of the Scheme in various States. Out of these two, the Final Report of the Study carried out by ORG in eight States of the country has been submitted. Another Evaluation Study involving the two States (Rajasthan and Uttar Pradesh) is in progress. The ORG Study suggests, inter-alia, effective targetting of beneficiaries under NSAP.

**Numerical ceiling, qualifying financial entitlement and Budget provision**

The Numerical Ceiling and Qualifying Financial Entitlement (QFE) for the NSAP Schemes for a State/ LIT is originally fixed as per the procedure laid down in the Guidelines. The actual allocation to the States in the subsequent years is however, dependent on the performance they show in the foregoing year. The districts are also given 4% of their QFEs as Administrative charges for meeting expenses towards Money Order Commission and Publicity etc. The Nodal Department of the States/UTs are also given I % of their QFEs for publicity and such other measures for the effective implementation of the programme. During 1998-99, an amount of Rs. 700 crores, has been provided as Budgetary allocation for NSAP which is likely to be fully utilised. About 55.56 lakh people including 24.37 lakh women, have been benefited so far during 1998-99.

**Release of fund during the year 1998-99**

As stated above, the Budget provision for NSAP during 1998-99 is Rs. 700 crores. The Scheme- wise allocation out of this Budget provision and the amount released to the district implementing agencies so far (1-2-99) is given below:

*(Rs. in crores)*

| *Scheme* | *Allocation* | *Release* |
|---|---|---|
| NOAPS | 450.29 | 351.05 |
| NFBS | 177.09 | 130.87 |
| NMBS | 70.00 | 41.36 |
| Total | 692.73 | 523.27 |

**Rajiv Gandhi national drinking water mission**

Provision of safe drinking water in the rural areas is the responsibility of the States. Funds are being provided for provision of the facility in the State budgets right from the First Five Year Plan period. The Accelerated Rural Water Supply Programme (ARWSP) was introduced in 1972-73 by the Government of India (GOI), to assist the States and Union Territories to accelerate the pace of coverage of drinking water supply. To ensure maximum inflow of scientific and technical input into the rural water supply sector to improve the performance, cost effectiveness of the on-going programmes and ensure adequate supply of safe drinking water, the entire programme was given a Mission approach. The Technology Mission on drinking water and related water management was launched in 1986. It was also called the National Drinking Water Mission (NDWM) and was one of the five Societal Missions launched by the Government of India. The NDWM was renamed Rajiv Gandhi National Drinking Water Mission (RGNDWM) in 1991.

It was realised that the objective of supplying safe water would not be achieved unless the sanitary aspects of water and the issue of sanitation are addressed together. The Centrally Sponsored Rural Sanitation Programme (CRSP) was launched in 1986 with the overall objective of improving the quality of life of the rural people

It is envisaged that the two programmes, the ARWSP and the CRSP, implemented simultaneously would help break the vicious circle of disease, morbidity and poor health, resulting from water borne diseases and insanitary conditions.

**Accelerated rural water supply programme**

The Accelerated Rural Water Supply Programme (ARWSP) aims at providing safe and adequate drinking water facilities to the rural population by supplementing the efforts made by the State Governments/UTs under the State Sector Minimum Needs Programme (MNP).

Keeping in view the different kinds of problems arising while providing potable water in the rural areas, 56 Mini-Missions (pilot projects) were identified covering all States/ UTs. These pilot projects helped to evolve models that are replicable and can be incorporated in the on-going programmes.

**Norms**

The provision of drinking water facilities in the problem villages is based on the following norms:

- 40 litres of safe drinking water per capita per day (Ipcd) for human beings.
- 30 Ipcd additionally for cattle in the Desert
- Development Programme (DDP) areas.
- One hand pump or stand post for every 250 persons.
- The water source should exist within the habitation or within a distance of 1.6 km. in the plains and within 100 metres elevation difference in the hills.
- Drinking water is defined as safe if it is free from bacteria contamination, chemical contamination viz. fluoride, iron, arsenic, nitrate, brackishness in excess or beyond permissible limits.

**Priorities**

Viewing the objective of providing safe drinking water facility in all the villages, there is need for a certain order of priority which is as follows:

- To cover the "Not Covered" (NC) habitations.
- To fully cover the "Partially Covered" (PC) habitations getting less than 10 Ipcd.
- To cover all habitations having water quality problems.
- To supply water to all habitations with per capita supply of less than 40 Ipcd at the rate of 40 Ipcd.

- To provide water supply facilities for the scheduled castes (SC), scheduled tribes (ST) and the landless agricultural labourers.
- To provide safe drinking water in every rural primary school.

Once the task of providing every village with at least one source of safe drinking water is completed, the enhancement and expansion process may be initiated to provide adequate drinking water. The above mentioned norms can then be liberalised so as to now cover:

- Villages that do not have an assured source of safe drinking water within a distance of 0.5 km. (as against 1.6 km.).
- To enhance per capita rate of supply (as against the 40 Ipcd rate).
- Adopting the above norms would mean providing one source for every 150 persons (as against one source for every 250 persons).

**ARWSP allocation criteria**

The allocations are subject to matching provision by States under their MNP. The criteria for allocation of funds is as given below:

| *Components* | *Weightage (%)* |
|---|---|
| 1. Rural Population | 35 |
| 2. Rural Area | 20 |
| 3. Incidence of poverty | 20 |
| 4. No. of problem villages spilled over from Sixth Plan, States/UTs covered under DPAP, HADP, DDP and special category hill States in terms of: | |
| (a) Rural Population | 12.5 |
| (b) Rural area | 12.5 |
| Total | **100** |

States/UTs have to earmark 25% as minimum outlay for SCs and 10% as minimum outlay for STs, for taking up water supply schemes exclusively for them. The ARWSP guidelines state that at the time of scheme formulation, the coverage of SC/ST should be given first preference so as to ensure equal access to water supply facilities.

**Physical and financial progress**

The status of coverage of habitations with drinking water facilities as on 1.4.98 is as under:

| | | |
|---|---|---|
| Not Covered | : | 56269 |
| Partially Covered | : | 313473 |
| Fully Covered | : | 1060921 |
| Total | : | 1430663 |

The total habitations (NC and PC) targeted to be covered in 1998-99 are 105902.

Statewise allocation of fund/releases under ARWSP and State sector MNP are given at Annexure (XXIII to XXV). Statewise habitation coverage details are given at Annexure XXVI.

**Policy initiative**

The expenditure Finance Committee (EFC) in its meeting held on the 11th of November, 1998 has considered and approved the proposal to revamp the Accelerated Rural Water Supply Programme.

The proposal to institutionalise community-based, demand driven Rural Water Supply Programme with cost sharing by the communities aims at gradually replacing the current Government driven centrally monitored non-people participating Rural Water Supply Programme.

The proposal also envisages and earmarks 20% of the annual outlay to be given to those State Governments who undertake community-based Rural Water Supply Programmes by:

- Adopting the demand driven approach based on empowerment of villagers to ensure their full participation in the project, through a decision-making role in the choice of key design and management arrangements.
- 10% of capital cost and 100% O & M cost to be borne by users.
- The share of States, which do not introduce the reforms, will be given to other States willing to implement the reform measures.

The revised policy will be taken up for implementation after it is approved by the cabinet.

**Community participation In RWS programme**

As a follow up to the recommendations of the National Workshop on 0 & M held on the 25th -27th September, 1996 and the National Workshop on Water Quality Monitoring and Surveillance (WQM&S) held on the 7th - 9th August, 1997 five regional workshops were organised at:

| | | |
|---|---|---|
| Jaipur | - | 18th - 19th August, 98 |
| Bangalore | - | 26th - 27th October 98 |
| Chandigarh | - | 26th - 27th November, 98 |
| Guwahati | - | 3rd - 4th December, 98 |
| Calcutta 4th | - | 5th February, 99 |

At these workshops, the Action Plans incorporating the ideas envisaged in the new policy initiative indicated above, for institutionalising community participation in the capital cost sharing, O&M and WQM&S have been finalised for selected pilot districts in each State/UT of the respective region. Detailed project reports (DPRs), based on the Action Plans finalised, are being prepared by the States/UTs. It is envisaged that the experience gained from these pilot projects will enable replication in the remaining districts of the respective States/UTs.

**R.W S. sector supportive activities/programmes**

*Submissions*

The Sub-Missions were initiated with the objective of providing safe drinking water facilities in the water quality affected habitations. The details are as under:

**Control of brackishness**

Excess brackishness causes the problem of taste and has laxative effects. Control measures include either providing alternate sources free from brackishness or supply of water with total dissolved solids within permissible limit of 1500 ppm (parts per million) by treating brackish water with the help of treatment processes like reverse osmosis, electro dialysis etc. For treating brackish water, 194 desalination plants were approved by the RGNDWM and 150 plants have been commissioned.

**Eradication of guineaworm**

Guineaworm is a water-borne disease caused by dracunculiasis medinensis. Efforts to control this disease were started in early eighties. It is a good example of how the coordinated efforts of organisations like National Institute of Communicable Diseases (NICD), RGNDWM, International organisations like WHO, UNICEF, and State Health & PHE departments could attack and eradicate an otherwise difficult problem. India has approached the International Commission for Certification of dracunculiasis medinensis eradication.

**Removal of excess iron**

Excess iron in the drinking water is prevalent in the

northeastern States. Consumption of water with excess iron causes constipation accompanied by other physiological disorders. Control measures include providing alternate sources free from iron or treating iron contaminated water (to within permissible limit I ppm) with the help of iron removal plants. For treating iron contaminated water, 16415 plants were approved and 9355 plants have already been commissioned.

**Control of fluorosis**

Excess fluoride in drinking water causes dental and skeletal fluorosis. The problem is prevalent in 150 districts of 16 States of the country, including Delhi. Control measures include providing alternate sources free from fluoride or treating fluoride contaminated water (to within permissible limit 1.5 ppm) with the help of treatment processes such as Nalgonda technique or activated alumina process. So far 499 plants (fill and draw type and handpump attached type) have been approved by the Mission of which 427 plants have been installed up to December, 1998.

**Control of arsenic**

Contamination of ground water with arsenic was first noticed in 8 districts of West Bengal, in the early 80s. The first attempt to tackle the problem was made by the Government of India in 1988 by sanctioning an investigation project. Thereafter, the Government of India has sanctioned several R&D projects as well as field oriented projects in the arsenic affected areas. Four water supply projects costing Rs. 349.09 crores have been approved for control of arsenic/providing alternate safe drinking water sources in West Bengal. Rs. 3080 lakh have been released during 1998-99.

**Ensuring sustainability**

This is an important Sub-Mission for the success of water

supply schemes, on a long-term basis. CGWB and NGRI have been engaged in the programme since the inception of the Mission. With the introduction of scientific methodologies for scientific source finding, the success rate of wells has gone up considerably. Under the water conservation measures, funds worth Rs. 30.75 crores were approved against which Rs.. 25.90 crores have been released and the expenditure reported so far is Rs. 20.67 crores.

**Water quality surveillance**

For testing of the water quality and for water quality surveillance, 411 laboratories have been approved and 300 have been established up to December, 1998. It is proposed to provide one laboratory in each district of the country. Twenty-two mobile laboratories have also been provided to various states.

**Decentralisation of technical clearance of schemes**

In December 1994, the Central Government delegated full powers to the States/Union Territories to give technical and administrative clearance to schemes under ARWSP, subject to the same per capita cost ceilings as under Minimum Needs Programme (MNP). The powers for sanctioning and executing Submission projects were also delegated to the States with effect from Ist April, 1998.

**Human resource development**

Sustainable management of rural water supply and sanitation needs not only the engineering systems but also community participation and empowerment, together with adequately trained professional and sensitized planners, administrators and decision-makers. To build up a human resource base of appropriately trained personnel to serve the needs of the rural water supply and sanitation sector, the National Human Resource Development Programme (NHRDP) was launched in 1994. The major objectives of the NHRDP are (a) to train at least one beneficiary, especially women, at the grassroots level in each village of the country, (b) improve the productivity of sector professionals through specialised courses and (c) to introduce rural orientation in technical education sector coupled with publication of manuals on rural water supply and rural sanitation.

The implementation of the NHRDP involves:

- Creating a resource pool of trainers for training grass-root level trainees in the villages through the Indian Training Network (ITN).
- Establishing Human Resource Development (HRD) Cells in all the States to undertake HRD activities in the State, based on trainer assessment.
- Networking with NGOs, Teachers' Training Institute, community polytechnics, training institutes/organisations etc.
- Conducting specialised courses and experience sharing workshops for sector professionals, in India and abroad.
- Evolving courses, for introduction at diploma and degree levels, to introduce rural orientation and appropriate technologies and practices.

HRD Cells are functioning in 24 States. Up to 1997-98, a sum of Rs. 23.00 crores had been released to the States, for HRD activities. An amount of Rs. 103 lakhs has been released for the programme during 1998-99.

Four workshops have been held so far for operationalising grassroots level Training Programmes. Four multimedia packages, focusing on four focal themes given below, have been prepared by the Technical Teachers' Training Institute for conducting Grassroots Level Training Programmes.

- Operation and Maintenance (O&M) of handpumps.
- Construction of sanitary toilets and other rural sanitation facilities. Motivation for community support mobilisation.
- Health education and hygiene promotion.

Under the programme for development of capability of in-house training instructors, the course on Ground Water Development which was being conducted in United Kingdom through the Overseas Development Agency (ODA) assistance has now been fully transferred to the Gujarat Jai Sewa Training Institute, Ahmedabad, one of the seven key institutions selected under the ITN.

**Foreign training programme**

Two State Government officers were nominated by this Ministry for a short term training (4th - 23rd May, 1998) on Monitoring and Effectiveness, for improving community based Water Supply and Sanitation Projects, at IRC, the Hague, Netherlands.

**Research and development**

It was realised that the objective of providing necessary scientific and technological inputs required to improve the performance, cost effectiveness and management practices of the on-going programmes would not be achieved without the Research and Development (R&D) input and support. A series of R&D initiatives have therefore been taken to provide the necessary scientific and technological inputs into the Mission programmes. The following activities have already been carried out:

- Formulation of the policy guidelines for R&D support.
- Identification of priority areas for R&D support.
- Establishment of an R&D cell in the Mission.
- Formation of Research Advisory Committee (RAC)

with Secretary (RD) as Chairman and eminent scientists and others members to oversee the R&D activities.

- Establishment of Documentation and Information Centre (DIC) for R&D related activities.
- Networking with large number of universities, institutions, organisations and the concerned, State departments for identifying and solving required research problems.
- 95 projects have been sanctioned involving more than 40 organisations across the country. An amount of Rs 43.88 lakh has been released for R&D activities during 1998-99.

**Documentation and information centre**

A lot of valuable data and information is being generated under the sector related R&D projects being carried out by Universities, R&D organisations, and NGOs. A number of field level activities that are in progress add to the available information base by their findings. There are also a number of developing countries that are engaged in R&D activities leading towards low cost appropriate rural technologies for rural environment.

The need for dissemination of and access to information on drinking water and sanitation globally was recognised and the Mission entrusted the responsibility of conceiving, establishing and maintaining a Documentation and Information Centre on drinking water and sanitation to the Indian National Scientific Documentation Centre (INSDOC), a national laboratory under the Council of Scientific and Industrial Research (CSIR), Government of India.

The Documentation and Information Centre at the Mission was inaugurated by the Minister of State for Rural Areas and Employment (IC), Shri Babagouda Patil, on the 17th of July, 1998.

It is planned to put the information resources of the centre on the Web. Information products are also planned on CD ROMs for the benefit of those who do not have Internet Web access facility.

**Information, education and communication**

The awareness creation campaign programme of the Mission, based on its Information, Education and Communication (IEC) strategy, is being implemented in the selected pilot districts of 20 States, at a total approved cost of Rs 2411.70 lakhs (on a 50:50 cost sharing between the Government of India and the State Governments), to be released in two instalments. The main objective of the campaign programme is to inculcate hygiene sense and bring about a change in the concept/attitude of the people towards water and sanitation. The implementation stage of the programme in the States is at different levels.

The States of Andhra Pradesh, Kerala, Tamil Nadu and Uttar Pradesh have taken the lead in implementing the programme activities. In fact, Uttar Pradesh launched the campaign in the district of Kanpur Dehat in November, 1998 and the launch in the other three districts is scheduled in January-February, 1999.

The IEC, activities to be undertaken at the National level, as envisaged in the guidelines, are being carried out. Slogans/messages related to water and sanitation have been printed on post cards and inland letter cards in Hindi, English and ten other regional languages. The Doordarshan is telecasting spots relating to sanitation (hand washing and latrine construction). Funds have been allocated to the States to meet the expenditure towards broadcast charges of similar films/spots related to water and sanitation. The information regarding rural water supply and sanitation is also disseminated through bi-weekly radio programmes sponsored by this Ministry -

'Chalo Gaon ki Ore' and 'Gram Vikas Ki Ore'. Discussions regarding the prospect of using the railways (tickets) as a medium for propagating messages/slogans related to the sector are at a advanced stage with the Northern Railway (first phase).

**Monitoring and evaluation**

The implementation of the programmes in the States is being monitored and evaluated at the National level. The Monitoring and Evaluation (M&E) focuses on the following aspects:

- Coverage of the Not Covered (NC) habitations -status, Partially or Fully Covered (PC/FC).
- Full Coverage of PC villages.
- Population coverage, category-wise i.e. SC, ST and general.
- Defunct status of schemes (hand pumps/piped water supply etc.).
- O&M status (physical & financial).
- Extent of community participation in O&M, capital cost sharing, planning and implementation of schemes.
- Issues and problems being faced by the community and the implementing agency.

Periodic studies are carried out by Non-Government agencies to evaluate the schemes and give an unbiased assessment of the implementation/coverage status. A monitoring and evaluation study of the RWS Schemes (including sanitation) in selected districts of 13 States was carried out by seven organisations. The final reports are under submission.

**Externally aided projects**

The Integrated Rural Water Supply and Sanitation (RWS&S) Project in Maharashtra supported by the World

Bank has been completed during the year 1998-99. The World Bank aided RWS&S Project in Uttar Pradesh and Karnataka is progressing satisfactorily. Fresh RWS&S project proposals from Tamil Nadu, Madhya Pradesh, Kerala and Andhra Pradesh, incorporating the features stated in the Generic Project Concept Document (GPCD) issued by the World Bank were received and these proposals have been forwarded to the World Bank by the Department of Economic Affairs, for possible funding.

**Management information system/computerisation**

The Management Information System (MIS) is extremely important for planning, effective monitoring of the implementation of the various components of the programme. It also facilitates the availability of data not only to the Central and State Governments and people's representatives, but also to the users. A quick to and fro flow of information between the Mission and the States (including formations up to the Division and Subdivision level) is proposed to be established by using the state of the art Information Technology (IT). It will be ensured that public has access to habitation-wise data through NIC and there is effective communication system using NICNET.

The MIS project consists of Selection of hardware, Selection of operating system, Preparation of Software Requirement Specifications (SRS) Document, and Development of Customised Application Software.

Hardware for the project and vendor for the supply of the same for whole country has been finalised. A multi-user operating system has also been procured. The SRS defining the organisational objectives and priorities, user needs and establishing linkages within various organisations in all States/UTs have been taken up. The selection of application software is under process.

**Rural sanitation**

The Centrally sponsored Rural Sanitation Programme (CRSP) was launched in the year 1986 with the objective of improving the quality of life of the rural people and to provide privacy and dignity to the women. The concept of sanitation includes safe disposal of solid and liquid waste including human excreta, personal, domestic and environmental hygiene. The Central funds allocated under the CRSP supplement the state sources made available under the State Sector MNP.

**Objectives**

- Accelerate coverage of rural population, specially among households below poverty line (BPL), with sanitation facilities, complementing the efforts in Rural Water Supply.
- Generate felt need through awareness creation and health education involving Voluntary Organisations (VOs) and Panchayati Raj Institutions (PRIs).
- Eradicate manual scavenging by converting all existing dry latrines into low cost sanitary latrines.
- Encourage cost effective and appropriate technologies to support other objectives.

**Programme components**

- Construction of individual sanitary latrines for households below poverty line with subsidy (80%) where demand exists.
- Encourage other households to buy facilities through markets, —including sanitary marts.
- Assist in setting up of sanitary, marts.
- Launch intensive awareness campaigns in selected areas.
- Establish sanitary complexes exclusively for women.
- Encourage locally suitable and acceptable models of latrines.

- Promote total sanitation of village through construction of drains, soakage pits for liquid and solid waste disposal.

**Brief details of each component**

***Construction of individual household latrines***

Construction of individual household latrines by persons below poverty line may be supported in cluster of 20 or more in a village.

The unit cost of construction should be limited to Rs. 2500 of which 80% could be paid as subsidy to the selected beneficiaries below the poverty line. In case the unit cost exceeds Rs. 2500, the additional cost should be borne by the beneficiaries or specific approval of the Government of India may be obtained before execution. Out of the total annual funds a minimum 20% should be earmarked for paying subsidy to the individual households from SCs and STs below the poverty line where the percentage of SC/ST population to the total population below poverty line is less than 20%. Where the SC/ST population below poverty line is more than 20% of the total population below poverty line earmarking should be enhanced at least to match the percentage of SC/ST population.

**Technological options**

The Mission has already circulated the report of the Expert Committee, which has recommended a wide range of (27 Nos.) Technical Options, with cost estimates, keeping in view the concept of vertical upgradation, varying soil and hydrogeological conditions and acceptability and affordability of the beneficiaries.

In order to explore for additional models and to supplement the information provided in the report of the National Expert Committee on Technological Options for the implementation of the rural sanitation programme in the country, a committee has been constituted under the Chairmanship of the Mission Director. The committee will suggest additional models/technologies to supplement the information provided in the Handbook on Technological Options, with special emphasis to waterlogged / rocky areas and the islands.

**Village sanitation complexes for women**

Though public latrines have not proved to be very successful in the past, in view of the difficulties experienced by rural women in some areas, where individual household latrines are not feasible, village sanitary complexes exclusively for women could be attempted, on a pilot basis. Upto 10% of the annual funds can be utilised to provide public latrines in selected villages during the plan period, where the panchayats/ charitable trusts/NGOs offer to construct and maintain village complexes exclusively for the use of women.

**Rural sanitary marts**

United Nations International Children's Fund (UNICEF) have successfully demonstrated the validity of the concept of sanitary marts by implementing the scheme through voluntary organisations in Uttar Pradesh and the Ramakrishna Mission in Midnapur district, West Bengal. Rural Sanitary Marts (RSMs) are outlets dealing with materials required for construction of latrines and other sanitary facilities. Besides, it also keeps the designs of various low cost sanitary facilities showing estimated costs and the list of trained masons. Rural Sanitary Marts also serve as service centres. UNICEF provides assistance of Rs 50,000 for each Mart with turnover of Rs 2 lakhs per annum. Managerial subsidy is provided upto Rs 18,000 per annum for a period of two years. One time assistance upto Rs 12,000 is provided for publicity etc.

Where UNICEF assistance is not available for setting up RSMs, the State Governments/UT Administrations can set up Rural Sanitary Marts with assistance from the Central Government through reputed Voluntary Organisations/Panchayati Raj Institution in difficult areas where proper marketing facilities for sanitary components do not exist. Such voluntary organisations should be carefully selected, based on the assessment of their ability to carry out the task.

**Total sanitation of village**

Other Sanitation facilities such as drains, soakpits, solid and liquid waste disposals etc. should be taken up as far as possible under Jawahar Rozgar Yojana or any other programme for civic amenities in the Panchayat. Where this is not feasible due to other priorities and non-availability of adequate financial resources, the facilities can be taken up under CRSP.

**Campaign for creation of felt need**

While Government machinery for publicity may be useful to some extent, a well orchestrated programme of publicity, health, education and creation of required facilities only can make any change in the attitude of the people. Support of the reputed local voluntary organisations, autonomous institutions, social, political and religious organisations who carry conviction with the people can be enlisted in creating the felt need. These organisations should be selected for their reputation for good and adequate infrastructure already available with them.

**Model village**

Assistance is also given to States to develop model villages under the programme. A model village is covered with facilities like sanitary latrines, garbage pits, soakage pits, drains, paved lanes, sanitary latrines in village institutions (school, health centre, panchayat ghar, aanganwadi), smokeless chullahs, clean tanks, ponds and surroundings, sanitary wells and safe drinking water sources (handpumps, stand posts) with platforms for bathing and washing and drains.

So far, the States of Andhra Pradesh, Bihar, Assam, Karnataka, Kerala, Tamil Nadu, Madhya Pradesh, Maharashtra, Orissa, Rajasthan and Uttar Pradesh have taken up the model village scheme.

**Extent of subsidy**

The extent of subsidy from Central/State Governments and contribution from persons below poverty line/ panchayat for various components of the Programme are as follows:

| *Item* | *Subsidy Centre* | *State* | *Contribution by User Panchayat* |
|---|---|---|---|
| **Construction of sanitary latrines and conversions of dry latrines for individual households below poverty** line | 40% | 40% | 20% |
| **Village complex for women** | 35% | 35% | 30% |
| Drains and other sanitation facilities (as far as possible, to be met out of JRY and other funds) | 25% | 25% | 50% |
| Awareness campaigns, health education, demand creation, etc. | Upto 10% of annual allocation | | Nil |
| Administrative cost | Upto 3% of annual allocation | | Nil |

For sanitary marts, the assistance will be limited to an interest free-loan as revolving fund of Rs. 50,000 per mart for the purpose, which would be repayable at the end of three years. Adequate funds for this purpose can be provided from the funds released to the States/UTs depending upon the actual need.

**CRSP allocation criteria**

Funds available under the Annual Plan are allocated to the States/UTs in accordance with the following:

- 50% weightage given to incidence of poverty in the State/UT.
- 40% weightage given to rural population.
- 10% weightage given to recognised hill States and hilly areas on the basis of their population.

Statewise physical progress is given at Annexure-XXVII. Statewise allocation of funds/ releases under CRSP and State Sector MNP are given at Annexure XXVIII to XXX

**The second national rural sanitation seminar**

The second National Seminar on Rural Sanitation was held on the 9th - 10th July, 1998 at Vigyan Bhavan, New Delhi. The Seminar, which was inaugurated by Shri Babagouda Patil, Minister of State (IC) for Rural Areas and Employment, was attended by the representatives of the Central Ministries, State Governments, UN Organisations, NGOs, bilateral agencies. The Seminar sought to assess the current status of sanitation in India, identify major thrust areas, explore new interventions and suggest appropriate strategies. The recommendations of this seminar have been incorporated in the new strategy being planned by the Mission.

**Policy initiative**

The Expenditure Finance Committee (EFC) in its meeting held on the 23rd December, 1998 considered and approved the following proposals for modifying the programme.

- Raise sanitation coverage to at least 50% by Ninth plan.
- Emphasis on school sanitation.
- Total Sanitation Campaigns (TSC) in selected districts with 50% allocation during first year.
- Balance 50% for existing "allocation-based" programme.
- Progressively phasing out "allocation- based" programme.
- Subsidy for RSM and Production Centres-to be used as "seed money", linkage with IRDP, PMRY & institutional finances.

**Land reforms**

The National Government, since independence has been continuing to play its advisory and co-ordinating role in the field of land reforms as the subject is under exclusive legislative and administrative jurisdiction of the States as per Entry No. 18 of the List II (State List) of the VIIth Schedule of our Constitution. Even then agrarian reforms remained as a central issue of our National Agenda for rural reconstruction ensuring social justice to actual tillers as well as landless rural poor and thus for creating sustainable base for the overall growth of industrial and tertiary sector of our economy. Generating greater access to land by the landless rural poor is also considered as an important programme for poverty alleviation in the rural sector. The Land Reforms (LR) Division has been, since the First Plan Period, playing a crucial role of evolving national consensus at various stages for taking up major steps towards effective land reforms which include abolition of zamindari and all intermediaries since the beginning of fifties, introduction of family ceiling from mid-fifties, reduction of ceiling limit in 1972 and monitoring the progress of distribution of ceiling surplus land as a part of the 20-Point Programme of the

Government. It organised a large number of conferences of the Revenue Ministers, Chief Ministers, and initiated amendments of the Constitution 13 times for incorporation of 277 land laws in the Ninth Schedule. The last such amendment was the 78th Amendment of the Constitution to incorporate 27 land laws in the 9th Schedule.

In addition to playing advisory and coordinating role on land reforms, the LR Division acts as administrative division of this Ministry for the purpose of administering the Land Acquisition Act including the issues covered under Entry No. 42 of the Concurrent List in addition to execution of certain Centrally Sponsored Schemes. The activities of the Division can, therefore, be divided into three major groups i.e. discharging Constitutional obligation, monitoring of land reforms measures and implementing three Centrally Sponsored Schemes as illustrated below in Part -I, Part - II and Part - III.

## PART - I

### Discharging of constitutional/legal obligations

#### *Administration of land acquisition act.*

This Ministry being the Administrative Ministry in the Union Government to administer the Central Act on Land Acquisition, any proposal relating to amendment to the said Act by the Centre has to be taken up by the Division. The aforesaid Act was last amended by this Division in 1984 and the current phase of amendment proposals to bring radical and pro-people changes has reached a culmination point and the Land Acquisition (Amendment) Bill, 1998 has been referred by the Cabinet to the Group of Ministers.

***Examination of central and state legislations on acquisition and requisition of properties***

"Acquisition and Requisition of Property" is a subject enlisted in Entry No. 42 of the Concurrent List vide VII Schedule of the Constitution. As per Allocation of Business Rules-1961 it is allocated to this Ministry. The Division has to examine and concur all proposals pertaining to the State Governments for amendments of their Land Acquisition Act, 1894 as required under Clause (2) of Article 254 of the Constitution. All State legislative proposals covering any enactment on the subject of acquisition and requisition of property or any other state legislation having a bearing upon the acquisition and requisition of land, has to be examined by the Division for the purpose of according Presidential Assent to such legislations as required under Article 200 (in case of Bills) or under proviso to Article 213(1) of the Constitution (in case of Ordinances).

***Examination of other land laws***

This Ministry being the Nodal Ministry in the Union Government as regards to implementation of land reform programmes, all proposals for introduction of land reform legislations or amendments initiated by the States/UTs are referred to it for examination and comments particularly in the light of their conformity with the National Land Reforms Policy. The Division processes all progressive land legislations for incorporating them in the 9th Schedule of the Constitution to protect them being challenged in any Court of law on the ground of violation of fundamental rights (with special reference to Article 3 1 A and 31 Q and moves the Parliament for amendment of the Constitution for the aforesaid purpose. The Constitution of India has been amended 13 times so far to incorporate 277 land legislations in the 9th Schedule of the Constitution.

When President's Rule is imposed upon a State, this Ministry is required to discharge the responsibility of laying Ordinances in Parliament or enacting President's Act as and when powers of the State Legislature are conferred on the President by the Parliament under Article 357(1) In addition, any Central Ministry, whoever proposes to make legislation having bearing upon acquisition/requisition of land seeks comments/ observations from this Nodal Ministry. During the year under report, 6 Central legislations and 27 State legislations were examined.

***Acting as administrative ministry for RR planning and monitoring at the central level***

As per the direction of the Cabinet Secretariat, LR Division, on behalf of this Ministry, has been acting as Administrative Division for drafting/formulating the National Policy, Packages and Guidelines on Resettlement and Rehabilitation since 1992. During the current financial year the efforts of the Division have reached a culmination point and the NPRR -1998 is under the final stage of examination by the Cabinet. For providing statutory backing to the proposed National Policy Packages and Guidelines, this Division has initiated necessary amendments of the Land Acquisition Act. It has also initiated steps to prepare a National Level RR Data Base and to create necessary secretarial set up to support the proposed National Level Implementation and Monitoring Board to be constituted to overview the RR activities in this country.

## PART - II

**Monitoring of land reforms activities**

To play an effective coordinating and advisory role in the matters of various land reform activities taken up by the States/UTs, the LR Division specially monitors distribution of ceiling surplus land, government wasteland, bhoodan land, conferment of ownership rights to the tenants, prevention of alienation and restoration of tribal land, consolidation of holdings and other miscellaneous issues. A short resume of the latest position on each of the aforesaid issues in the national perspective is placed below:-

**Distribution of ceiling surplus land**

As per point no. 5A of the 20-Point Programme of the Government of India, the Land Reforms Division fixes annual target for actual distribution of ceiling surplus land and brings out quarterly progress report collecting QPRs from the States.

Since inception of the ceiling laws on agricultural holdings, according to reports received upto the 30th September, 1998, the total quantum of land declared surplus in the entire country was 73.74 lakh acres, out of which about 65.11 lakh acres have been taken possession of and a total area of 53.05 lakh acres have been distributed to 55.37 lakh beneficiaries, of whom around 36% belong to the Scheduled Castes and around 14% belong to the Scheduled Tribes. The Statewise break-up of declared surplus, possession taken, ceiling-surplus land distributed and number of beneficiaries (cumulative upto 30.09.98) is given in Annexure-XXXI.

During the current financial year there has not been a substantial change in the figures of disposal and achievement on the four issues mentioned below. However, the cumulative position of implementation of the ceiling laws as regards to area declared surplus, area taken possession, area distributed and number of beneficiaries during the last two decades is indicated below to have a comparison with the latest figure as may be seen in table.

*(Lakh Acres)*

| *Pre-revised and revised ceiling laws* | *As on 31.3.80* | *As on 31.3.85* | *As on 31.3.90* | *As on 31.3.95* | *As on 30.9.98* |
|---|---|---|---|---|---|
| Area declared surplus | 69.13 | 72.07 | 72.25 | 74.10 | 73.74 |
| Area taken possession | 48.50 | 56.98 | 62.12 | 65.42 | 65.11 |
| Area distributed | 35.53 | 42.64 | 46.47 | 51.46 | 53.05 |
| No. of beneficiaries | 24.75 | 32.90 | 43.60 | 49.94 | 55.37 |

It is evident from the above data that there is a large gap between the annual targets and actual achievements. Unfortunately such gaps are increasing every year, While the implementation of present ceiling laws is undoubtedly tardy, it is unfortunate that an environment is sought to be created lately for giving exemption from ceiling laws to industry and large farmers. Some State Governments have already given relaxation without seeking Government of India's permission. The Government of India is, however, not in favour of any relaxation in the existing ceiling laws.

**Distribution of government Wasteland and Bhoodan land**

In addition to the distribution of 53.05 lakh acres of ceiling surplus land, figures collected from the States/ UTs show that an area of 147.44 lakh acres of Government Wastelands have also been distributed amongst landless rural poor. However, the quantum of land reported by the States as distributed during 1998-99 till December 1998 is 2.48 lakh acres. The Statewise position of distribution of Government wasteland is given in Annexure-XXXII.

Similarly, the State Governments are requested to send the latest figure both showing the cumulative figure as well as current year's figure pertaining to distribution of Bhoodan land. The Statewise latest position as regards to distribution of Bhoodan land, as per revised reports received till December, 98 is given in Annexure-XXXIII.

The Annual Conference of the Revenue Ministers held on 17th September, 1998 deliberated upon various issues connected with the implementation of the land reform programmes and the States were impressed upon to take new initiatives including special drives, to hasten the process of the aforesaid land reforms measures.

**Conferment of ownership rights to the tenants**

Legislative provisions have been made in extensive areas of the country providing for conferment of ownership rights on tenants or allowing cultivating tenants to acquire ownership rights on payment of a reasonable compensation to the landlords. Some of the States have acquired ownership of land from the landowners and have transferred it to the tenants who have to pay a certain amount of premium to the State. Sub-tenancies are generally prohibited except in certain cases viz. widows, members of armed forces, minors, unmarried women, persons suffering from disabilities etc.

The programme for conferment of ownership rights to the tenants or otherwise protecting the rights of the tenants/sharecroppers from eviction-at-will is not getting adequate attention from the State machineries. The States are not giving specific figure on the number of tenants who have been conferred ownership rights on the tenanted land separately from those who have been only recorded to prevent eviction at will. Such separated figures could not be obtained.

However, 124.22 lakh tenants have their rights protected over an area of 156.31 lakh acres. Cumulative figure showing the total number of tenants and sharecroppers received ownership rights or protection from eviction-at-will in connection with land held by them under personal cultivation.

**Prevention of alienation and restoration of alienated tribal land**

Article 46 of the Constitution enjoins an obligation upon the States to promote the interests of the Scheduled Castes and Scheduled Tribes and to protect them from social injustice and all forms of exploitation.

The State Governments have accepted the policy of prohibiting the transfer of land from tribals to non-tribals and for the restoration of the alienated land to the tribals. The States with large tribal population have enacted laws prohibiting alienation of tribal land and for restoration of alienated land. The legal provisions are however, generally applicable to the tribals living within the Scheduled and notified areas. Though some results have been forthcoming in the efforts undertaken by different States for restoration of tribal lands, the task still remains unfulfilled.

As per reports received from 11 States on the aforesaid subject 4.65 lakh cases of tribal land alienation have been registered so far covering 9.18 lakh acres of land, of which 2.02 lakh cases have been disposed of in favour of the tribals covering a total area of 5.31 lakh acres of alienated land but only 4.61 lakh acres of land have been physically restored to the tribals.

With a view to prepare a draft model law on tribal land alienation, during 1998-99 steps were continued for the preparation of State-specific status papers after which a consolidated view is to be taken and the model law prepared in consultation with the Ministry of Welfare and the SC/ST Commission.

**Consolidation of land holding programme**

Consolidation of Agricultural Holdings forms an integral part of land reforms policy and Five Year Plans have accordingly been laying stress on the importance of its implementation. This operation is considered necessary for planned development of villages and achieving efficiency and economy in agriculture. In pursuance of this strategy, a number of States have enacted legislation for carrying out consolidation of holdings. However, it appears that the programme of consolidation of agricultural land holdings has virtually stopped all over the country except in the State of Uttar Pradesh, where annually about 900 to 1000 villages are being covered under the programme. So far an area of 1583.45 lakh acres or 640.81 lakh hectares have been consolidated in the country.

## PART - III

### Implementation of centrally sponsored schemes

***Central sector scheme for financial assistance to institutions/ agencies for agrarian studies***

The aforesaid Central Sector Scheme was introduced in the year 1972-73. Under the scheme financial assistance is provided to various institutions/agencies for conducting agrarian studies on important aspects of land reform measures to have a concurrent evaluation of the impact of various land reform legislations in the entire country.

During the Eighth Five Year Plan a total amount of Rs. 92.76 lakh have been utilised for conducting agrarian studies through 45 institutions/organisations/ subject-matter specialists covering various aspects like evaluation study on allotment of ceiling surplus land, impact of tenancy reforms, problem of tribal land alienation, gender discrimination in land laws, displacement and rehabilitation of families affected by land acquisition, impact study on computerisation of land records, etc. The expenditure under the Scheme during 1997-98 was Rs. 38.84 lakh.

During the year under report, against the budgetary provision of Rs. 61.00 lakh, Rs. 58.00 lakh has already been utilized by 31.12.98 for conducting agrarian studies on various subjects including evaluation studies on the programme of Computerisation of Land Records. The number of new studies sanctioned during the year upto 31.12.1998 is as under:

| S. No. | Subject | Number of Studies sanctioned |
|---|---|---|
| 1. | Evaluation studies on the Scheme of Computerisation of Land Records | 8 |
| 2. | Conversion of Agricultural Land for Non-agricultural purposes | 5 |
| 3. | Impact of Industrialization/ Urbanization | 2 |
| 4. | Rehabilitation | 2 |
| | Total | 17 |

A Research Advisory Committee examines the proposals and based on its recommendations, decision on release of funds is taken for utilisation of the budgetary allocation.

In addition to having a concurrent evaluation on various aspects of land reforms in India by the Land Reforms Unit, now known as 'Centre for Rural Studies' of the Lal Bahadur Shastri National Academy of Administration, Mussoorie, the said Unit has brought out a number of good publications on various issues pertaining to land reforms written/edited by eminent personalities in the concerned field. During the financial year 1998-99 funds to the tune of Rs. 25 lakhs were provided to the Academy which have been fully utilized by the Academy under the programmes/schemes/ activities suggested by the Ministry.

**Central sector scheme for computerisation of land records**

During 1988-89, pilot projects for computerisation of land

records were taken up as a sub scheme of agrarian studies and upto 1991-92 a total amount of Rs. 5.02 crores was released to cover 24 districts under the programme in various States.

During the Eighth Plan period the budgetary provision for both agrarian studies and computerisation of land records was Rs 65.00 crores, out of which funds for computerisation were separated from the total allocation, providing Rs. 48 crores for the computerisation programme exclusively. Out of the aforesaid amount, the expenditure under the scheme was Rs. 59.42 crores on financing a total number of 323 projects in various States/UTs.

During 1997-98 against the allocation of Rs. 20 crores, under the Programme funds to the tune of Rs. 20.19 crores were released to the States/UTs to cover additional 177 new project districts in addition to providing second /third/fourth/final instalments for the on-going projects and for operationalisation of the Programme in 470 Tehsils /Blocks. Thus by 1997-98, 500 Districts and 470 Tehsils in the country were covered under the Programme. The number of Districts covered under the Scheme also include Districts which have been bifurcated by creating new Districts by the States.

With a view to develop an 'on-line' Land Management System in the Country, in addition to computerisation of land records, it was decided to take up computerisation/digitization of the existing cadastral maps. Accordingly, during 1998-99 the Budget Provision under the Scheme was increased by Rs. 10 crores from Rs. 20 crores during 1997-98 to Rs. 30 crores. Out of this budget provision, upto 31.12.1998 funds to the tune of Rs. 12.84 crores have been released to the States by covering 28 new Districts under the Scheme and by operationalization of the programme in 275 Tehsils/

Talukas/Mandals. In addition, 4 pilot projects on digitization of existing cadastral maps have also been sanctioned. The balance funds are proposed to be provided to the States by operationalization of the Scheme in more number of Tehsils and by sanctioning more pilot projects on digitization of cadastral survey maps.

In spite of correspondence, field visits and National level Conference held in connection with speedy and effective implementation of the programme of Computerisation of Land Records, the physical and financial progress reported by the States are not satisfactory. The reasons forwarded by the States include late delivery/installation of hardwares by the NIC, delay in constructing computer rooms at district/ tehsil / headquarters, deficiency in training input and lack of necessary infrastructure at tehsil/block/mandal levels. However, the States have been urged to take up appropriate and corrective steps to improve upon the process of implementation of the programme.

To have an evaluation of the programme of Computerisation of Land Records, eight studies have been entrusted to eight reputed Non-Governmental Organisations during the year. The results of the studies are expected to help in initiating effective steps for better implementation of the programme.

The Statewise position of total number of projects sanctioned and funds released is given in Annexure XXXVII.

Centrally Sponsored Scheme for Strengthening of Revenue Administration and Updating of Land Records (SRA&ULR)

This scheme was first approved by the Cabinet during 1987-88 for States of Bihar and Orissa. In the year,

1989-90 the scheme was extended to other States and funds were released to various States during 1989-90, 1990-91 and 1991-92. The expenditure under the Scheme up to 1991-92 was Rs. 36.63 crores towards Central Share.

The Eighth Plan provision for the Scheme was Rs 175.00 crores. However, the expenditure under the scheme was Rs. 98.23 crores. The main reason for this lower level of expenditure has been that the State Governments have not been able to provide their matching share in time which results in accumulation of unspent balances with them towards Central Share and non-release of further funds to them. During the year 1997-98, against the budget provision of Rs. 18.80 crores, the expenditure under the Scheme was Rs. 18.83 crores.

During the financial year 1998-99, keeping in view the increased requirement of funds under the Computerisation of Land Records Programme and that the overall allocation under the Land Reform Schemes remaining the same, the budget provision under this Scheme was reduced from Rs. 18.80 crores to Rs. 8.80 crores which has almost been utilized by providing funds to the States for strengthening their revenue administration and updating of land records by way of induction of modern technology/ equipment in the field of survey and settlement, strengthening of training infrastructure of the Revenue, Survey and Settlement staff, creation of facilities for maintenance and storage of land records, purchase of basic office equipments for the offices of Revenue/ Settlement Department at the lower levels etc.

The States/UTs have been advised to expedite expenditure, submit utilisation reports as well as seek funds on schemes having higher priorities and also to enhance State budgetary provision to avail more financial assistance under the scheme. The States have also been requested to take up resurvey and settlement operations by preparing necessary schemes and programmes to adopt new technology in the field of survey, settlement, updation/reproduction of maps and revenue records which include use of Photogrammetric System, Global Positioning System (GPS), Total Station, use of Scanner and Digitizers for preservation, updation and reproduction of cadastral maps etc.

During the last few years, the Programme Division has allocated major amount of funds under this Scheme for development of infrastructures for revenue administration as well as to meet training need of the revenue officials. Some States have, with such financial assistance, developed State-level, regional level and Held level training institutes or have upgraded the same. Further, some States have constructed record rooms for proper storage of land records.

**Other activities during the financial year**

***Conference of revenue ministers and secretaries of the state governments***

The conference was organised in Vigyan Bhavan on 17th September, 1998 to monitor the progress and suggest effective measures for time-bound implementation of the programme of computerisation of land records including digitization of cadastral maps. In addition, the other components of the Land Reform Policy viz. distribution of ceiling surplus land, updation of land records etc. were also discussed in the Conference. The Conference laid stress on further intensifying the programme for distribution of ceiling surplus land, Bhoodan land and Government wastelands inter-alia by gearing up the revenue machinery, by preparing action plans and by undertaking special drives for completing the distribution process of the ceiling surplus land, Bhoodan land and

Government wasteland which are free from all encumbrances. The Conference also emphasized the need for launching a special drive for restoration of alienated tribal land and involvement of Panchayati Raj Institutions and other non-governmental organisation in the process. While considering the status of revenue administration and land records, the Conference recommended the need for time-bound action plans for taking up survey and settlement operations, adoption of modern technology in this field and computerisation of the land record system including digitization of cadastral maps. These recommendations are being vigorously implemented with the assistance and cooperation of the State Governments.

***Publication and circulation of policy papers***

Policy Paper on the following subjects were prepared, published and circulated to the concerned Ministries/ Departments of the Government of India and the State Governments for obtaining their views so that suitable further action could be taken for finalizing the policies:

- Women and Land.
- Land Acquisition
- Resettlement and Rehabilitation of displaced persons.
- Conversion of Agricultural Land for Non-Agricultural Purposes.
- Tenancy Reforms

***Conferences/workshops on resettlement and rehabilitation***

To have a national and international perspective of Land Acquisition and Rehabilitation, the following meetings/ workshops were organised/financed during the year:

- An international workshop on 'Displacement and Rehabilitation in India - Future Perspectives', held from I st to 3rd June, 1998 at the Lal Bahadur

Shastri National Academy of Administration, Mussoorie was financed.

- A workshop of NGOs on Land Acquisition and Rehabilitation, held on 11th November, 1998 at the Indian Social Institute, Lodhi Road, New Delhi, was financed.
- A workshop on Land Acquisition and Rehabilitation was organised on 21 st December, 1998, at SCOPE Complex, New Delhi.

In addition to what has-been said above, the division has many other miscellaneous activities including conducting action-researches, workshops, studies through National Institute of Rural Development, Hyderabad and Lal Bahadur Shastri National Academy of Administration, Mussoorie. It also runs the Centre For Rural Studies at Mussoorie.

**Rural roads**

Rural Roads are defined as those roads, which connect villages. They constitute Other District Roads (ODRs) and Village Roads in the hierarchy of the system of roads. The ODRs are feeder roads serving the rural areas where agriculture is the predominant occupation, providing them with outlets to urban market centres. These roads also play a significant role in opening up backward areas and accelerating socioeconomic development. The systematic development of these roads received fillip during the Fifth Plan when construction of these roads was made a component of the Minimum Needs Programme.

During the Fifth Plan, the programme envisaged connection of villages with a population of 1500 and above with all-weather roads. Against this, the Sixth Plan laid down the target that all villages with a population of 1500 and above and 50% of villages with population between 1000 and 1500 should be connected with all-weather roads by 1990. In respect of villages in hilly, coastal, tribal and desert areas, separate norms and targets were adopted. The Minimum Needs Programme on rural roads was continued during the Seventh Plan also. The total expenditure on rural roads under the Minimum Needs Programme from the Fifth to Seventh Plan was Rs. 2976,39 crores. The number of villages estimated to have been connected upto 1991-92 is indicated below:

| *Village Category No. of* | *Total villages villages* | *No. of connected connected* | *Balance to be* |
|---|---|---|---|
| With Population 1500 and above | 71623 | 64633 | 6990 |
| With population between 1000- 1500 | 58229 | 41966 | 16263 |
| With population less than 1000 | 459465 | 167789 | 291676 |

The Eighth Plan envisages linking of all villages with a population of 1000 and above with all-weather roads. There are about 1.3 lakh such villages. It is estimated that about 86% of such villages have been connected with all-weather roads by the end of the plan.

The MNP outlay for Rural Roads during the Eighth Plan was Rs. 3066 crores. Against this, the expenditure incurred during the period was Rs. 2679.83 crores.

Apart from the MNP outlay, funds were also available for construction of rural roads under jawahar Rozgar Yojana (JRY). Works having a wage to material ratio of 60:40 are taken up under this Scheme. Though no specific earmarking of JRY funds is made for rural roads, a substantial part of JRY outlay has been spent for rural road works in the past.

**Targets and requirement of funds during the ninth five year plan**

The Working Group on Roads for the Ninth Five Year

Plan has estimated that an amount of Rs. 14,040 crores would be required for construction of rural roads to achieve the target of covering 85% of villages with a population above 1500 (1991 census basis). Of this, Rs. 4410 crores would be required for construction of 49,000 kms of roads in villages with population of 1000 and above, Rs. 9,000 crores for construction of about one lakh km. of additional roads in villages with less than 1000 to ensure connectivity of 85% of village population and Rs. 6.30 crores for black topping as mentioned above. However, the Working Group has proposed only an outlay of Rs. 10,540 crores for the Ninth Plan recommending a smaller outlay for villages with less than 1000 population.

**Roads in special problem areas**

The scheme, "Roads in Special Problem Areas" is centrally sponsored and its implementation is limited only to the dacoity infested areas of the States of Uttar Pradesh, Madhya Pradesh and Rajasthan. The scheme is being implemented from 1985-86 onward and the Government of India and State Governments share the cost of the works in the ratio of 50:50.

In February 1992, the progress of the works sanctioned under the scheme was reviewed. It was found that the progress in respect to this programme was very slow and the States are not evincing adequate interest in it. The implementation of programmes is done by the Public Works Department of the State Governments, whose response to this programme was lukewarm. It was also observed that the original objective of improving communication facilities in dacoity prone districts has become less significant as the problem of dacoity has been practically eliminated.

In view of this, the State Governments have been

requested to complete only the ongoing works and no new/additional works should be taken up. Therefore, from the first year of the Eighth Plan i.e., 1992-93, the funds available each year are being released to the States to meet the central liability for ongoing works depending on their progress.

The Budget outlay for 1997-98 was Rs. 2 crores and for 1998-99, Rs. 1.5 crores. An outlay of Rs. 1.50 crores has been proposed for 1999-2000.

### Agricultural marketing

Agricultural Marketing is a process which starts with a decision to produce a saleable farm product and involves all aspects of market structure or system, both functional and institutional, based on technical and economic consideration. Though agricultural marketing is a State subject, the Government of India has an important role to play in laying down general policy framework, framing of quality standards, conducting survey and research studies and in providing guidance, technical and financial support to the State Governments. The Central Government is aided and advised by two organisations under its control, namely, the Directorate of Marketing and Inspection (DMI) and the National Institute of Agricultural Marketing (NIAM), Jaipur. The organisational structure and the objectives of these organisations are given below:

### Directorate of marketing and inspection

It is an attached office of the Ministry and is headed by the Agricultural Marketing Adviser to the Government of India. The organisation set up of the DMI is as under: -

| | | |
|---|---|---|
| Head Office | : | Faridabad |
| Branch Head Office | : | Nagpur |

| | | |
|---|---|---|
| Regional Office | : | Chennai, Delhi, Guntur, and Mumbai |
| Central Agmark Laboratory | : | Nagpur |

Besides, there are 57 sub-offices and 22 Regional Agmark Laboratories spread all over the country as per details given below: -

| *Region* | *Sub-office units* | *Regional Agmark Laboratories* |
|---|---|---|
| Northern region | 13 | 5 |
| Western region | 15 | 4 |
| Eastern region | 04 | 4 |
| Southern region | 14 | 8 |
| South central region | 11 | 1 |
| Total | 57 | 22 |

The main functions of the Directorate of Marketing and Inspection are:

- Rendering advice on Statutory Regulation, Development and management of agricultural produce markets to the States/Union Territories;
- Promotion of grading and standardisation of agricultural and allied products under the Agricultural Produce (Grading & Marking) Act, 1937;
- Market Research, Survey and Planning;
- Training of personnel in agricultural marketing; and
- Administration of Cold Storage Order, 1980 (except regulatory functions) and Meat Food Products Order, 1973.

**National institute of agricultural marketing**

The Institute started functioning at Jaipur (Rajasthan) with effect from 8th August 1988. It is an autonomous body under the administrative control of the Ministry of

Rural Areas and Employment, and is registered as a society with 30 members in the General Body. The Minister-in-charge of Ministry of Rural Areas and Employment is the President of the General Body. Ail the executive and financial powers of the Institute are vested in the Executive Committee subject to the directions of the Government of India and General Body. Director General is the Chief Executive of the Institute. The main objectives of the Institute are as follows:

- To augment the agricultural marketing infrastructure of the country through programmes of teaching, research and consultancy services;
- To design and conduct training courses appropriate to the specific identified needs of the personnel and enterprises and institutions that they serve;
- To undertake research to demonstrate and replicate better management techniques in the field of agricultural marketing;
- To provide consultancy services for formulating investment projects and for problem solving advice; and
- To offer educational programmes in agricultural marketing for supplementing the existing facilities.

The Institute has constructed a new office building complex at Jaipur and the Institute has shifted to the new office complex on 2nd April 1997.

**Regulation and management of agricultural produce marketing**

The DMI, as a central advisory organisation, has been providing technical assistance and advice to the States in framing suitable market legislation. For this purpose, the DMI has framed a "Model Act" which not only provides guidelines for framing of legislation but also intends to bring about uniformity in State legislations. Due to constant endeavour of DMI, all States and UTs except

Manipur, Kerala, Andaman & Nicobar Island, Lakshadweep and Dadra & Nagar Haveli have enacted legislation. The Jammu & Kashmir Assembly has passed the Bill on Market Regulation in its State. The DMI is pursuing with remaining States/UTs for enactment of necessary legislation. Out of 7245 wholesale assembling markets in the country, 7062 markets have been brought under the ambit of regulation as on 3 1 st March 1998.

**Market research, survey and planning**

The DMI is presently conducting 20 market surveys for various commodities and the reports are likely to be brought out soon. Four studies relating to the planning of wholesale markets for fruits and vegetables are also at various stages of completion. Marketing Planning and Design Centre (MPDC) of DMI prepares State Master Plan for the development of Agricultural Produce Markets and imparts training to the personnel of State Governments/Marketing Boards for the preparation of State Master Plan. Draft of the Master Plan for Market Development in Mizoram State is almost complete. So far, DMI has brought out 325 reports on market surveys for various agricultural and allied commodities.

The NIAM has also taken up the formulation of State Master Plans for the Development of agricultural produce markets for Goa, Himachal Pradesh, Andhra Pradesh, Jammu and Kashmir and Sikkim. Further, the Institute has taken up case studies on post-harvest management of various commodities and formulation of integrated action plan for promotion of handlooms and handicrafts in Varanasi and Nadia Districts in collaboration with the Institute of Rural Management, Anand during the year 1997-98. Apart from this, NIAM has taken up Research Projects on the Action Plan for Horticulture Produce Marketing and an all India Research Study on Cost and spread of margins in vegetables - A case of Tomato. The NIAM has also taken up case studies on the following subjects: -

- Study of Chilli production, procurement and marketing in Tonk District of Rajasthan.
- Problem areas in the development of spices in Rajasthan.
- Marketing practices and problems of fruits and vegetable growers in Jammu & Kashmir.
- Study of oilseed production of Rajasthan.
- Spatial distribution of markets in Southern Jaipur.
- Organisational and functional pattern of Chaksu market.

Besides this, studies are undertaken under the Scheme of Research Grants and a total of 35 research studies are going on. Under this scheme, an amount of Rs. 72.19 lakhs has been released to various Research Institutions/Universities throughout the country.

A scheme for estimation of marketable surplus and post-harvest losses in foodgrain was launched by the Ministry during the year 1995-96 in 100 selected districts of 25 States, An amount of Rs. 3.43 crores has been released to Designated State Agencies for conducting the field survey under the scheme.

**Training**

The NIAM has conducted six training programmes on various aspects of agricultural marketing during the year 1997-98. During 1998-99, the DMI imparted training to 169 personnel from States/UTs, cooperative societies, Marketing Boards etc. in different courses upto 3 1 st December, 1998.

**Grading and standardisation**

The Agricultural Produce (Grading & Marking) Act, 1937

empowers the Central Government to fix quality standards, known as 'AGMARK' standards and to prescribe terms and conditions for using the seal of 'AGMARK'. So far, grade standards have been notified for 159 agricultural and allied commodities. During the year 1997-98, new grade standards have been formulated for five commodities viz. Caraway seeds, Vermicelli, Macaroni and Spaghetti, Cloves, Mace and Large Cardamom.

As a result of special efforts initiated to increase grading under 'AGMARK', 271 new packers have been enrolled during 1998-99 up to September, 1998.

**Cold storage order and meat food products order**

The Cold Storage Order, 4980 which was uniformly applicable throughout the country except in the States of Haryana, Punjab, Uttar Pradesh and West Bengal. It was promulgated under Section 3 of Essential Commodities Act, 1955 to ensure hygienic and proper refrigeration conditions in the cold storages all over the country. This has been repealed with effect from 27th May, 1997 with a view to remove the controls laid down in the said Order in the areas of licensing, price control and requisitioning of cold storage space etc. and allow functioning of free market mechanism for demand based growth of cold storage industry in the country free from all kinds of administrative interference.

The objective of the Meat Food Products Order, 1973 is to ensure quality control and hygienic manufacturing conditions of meat food products for domestic consumption and the Order is applicable all over the country. A total of 128 licenses have been issued to the manufacturers operating under the Order upto December, 1997. Necessary amendments are being proposed to be made in the Order to streamline the implementation of the Order in a broad based manner, keeping in view the interests of the manufacturers and license holders in the meat food products industry.

**Publicity and extension**

The DMI participated in 'AGMARK' exhibitions during 1998-99 at Bangalore in the India International Trade Fair, 1998 and AHARA-98 at New Delhi. As part of its programme to create awareness about quality, the DMI has conducted 210 programmes in different schools/colleges from April, 1998 to September, 1998. Talks on 'AGMARK' were also organised by AIR, Hyderabad during the year 1997-98.

**Revenue**

During 1998-99, a total revenue of Rs. 4.10 crores was realized upto December, 1998 on account of grading charges etc.

**High power committee on agricultural marketing**

A High Power Committee on Agricultural Marketing was constituted in January, 1992 under the chairmanship of Shri Shankarlal Guru, former chairman of Council of State Agricultural Marketing Boards (COSAMB), New Delhi to review the present State Market Acts and working of various agricultural marketing bodies and to recommend appropriate measures for streamlining and strengthening the set up for marketing of agricultural produce. The High Power Committee in their report has submitted 81 recommendations to the Government, out of which 58 recommendations have been accepted and 21 recommendations rejected. The accepted recommendations have been communicated to the State Governments/UT Administrations for implementation. Further, the recommendations have been discussed in the first meeting of Ministers-in-charge of Agricultural Marketing of all States/UTs held on 30th January, 1997 at

New Delhi. The States/UTs have been directed to implement the recommendations of the High Power Committee as early as possible.

**Distribution of Rashtriya Krishi Vipnan Puraskar, 1995**

Nominations for "RASHTRIYA KRISHI VIPNAN PURASKAR, 1998" have been invited from individuals/ Directorate of Agricultural Marketing in State/UTs and State Agricultural Marketing Boards, which have done exemplary work in the field of Agricultural Marketing between 1.1.97 to 31.12.97.

**Transfer of the subject of agricultural marketing**

The Subject of Agricultural Marketing has been transferred to the Department of Agriculture and Cooperation, Ministry of Agriculture, Government of India with effect from 19th December, 1998 vide Cabinet Secretariat Notification No. 1/22/1/98-Cab. dt. 19.12.98.

**Training**

Training is one of the tested tools for performance improvement as well as upgradation of knowledge and skills of the personnel. Organizational motivation and moral, as reflected in the attitudes and administrative culture, are rendered relevant and sharply focused through effective training programmes. Training has thus constantly gained an important position in Rural Development activities in the various poverty alleviation programmes which calls for an efficient and motivated stream of Government as well as Non-government functionaries. This is a very challenging task. As training, research and development are inextricably linked, continuing education of both policy makers and programme implementers, is imperative. Towards facilitating this, the National Institute of Rural Development (NIRD), an apex Training and Research

Institute was set up in 1965 to impart training to the rural development functionaries as well as Panchayati Raj Institutions through classroom interaction and field work. Thereafter, 25 State Institutes of Rural Development (SIRD) and 87 Extension Training Centres (ETCs) were set up in the country for intensifying training related activities.

In consonance with the National Training Policy (1996), these Training Institutes have made a variety of programmes including participatory methods of training with a view to not only imparting skills to the trainees but also enlisting participation of people, action groups and local institutions like the panchayats. In addition, extensive support has been provided to a number of Training and Research Institutions dealing with issues related to rural development.

Training has been started for ministerial staff also. During the year 1998-99, training on Responsive Administration for the Section Office rs/ Private Secretaries, Assistants and Personal Assistants of this Ministry was conducted. More than 200 personnel from these categories were imparted training. Similarly, about 150 officers and officials of the Ministry were also deputed for computer training programmes with various reputed computer training institutes as a part of their HRD activity under the Career Management Scheme.

**National institute of rural development**

The National Institute of Rural Development (NIRD) is the country's apex body for training, research, action research, consultancy and documentation functions in the Rural Development Sector. NIRD is an autonomous organization under the aegis of Ministry of Rural Area and Employment situated at Hyderabad. It also has a regional centre at Guwahati to cater to the special needs of the north eastern region.

The NIRD's vision is to focus in the coming years on the policies and programmes that benefit the rural poor, strive to energise the democratic decentralisation process, improve the operation and efficiency of rural development personnel, promote transfer of technology and its social laboratories and technology park and create environmental awareness.

The objectives of NIRD are to organize training programmes, conferences, seminars and workshops for senior level development managers, elected representatives, bankers, NGOs and others; undertake, aid, promote and coordinate research on its own and through other agencies; study various aspects of the Panchayati Raj Institutions and Rural Development programmes across the States; analyse and propose solutions to problems in planning and implementation of the programmes of Rural Development and disseminate information through periodicals, reports and other publication.

NIRD works as a 'think-tank' for the Ministry of Rural Areas and Employment and also acts as a storehouse of information on rural development to assist the Ministry in policy formulation. There are sixteen Centres in the Institute with about 100 well-qualified faculty members, specialized in various subjects with national and international exposure and experience. Each Centre of the Institute looks after specific programmes of the Ministry on which groups work on a tenure basis in the respective programme areas.

The Institute has a well-equipped computer centre with facilities of Local Areas Network (LAN), Internet, E-Mail, NICNET, Multimedia, etc. NIRD thus aims to share its resources with other training institutions and bring about improvements in training activities. It has a well-organized and growing library with a large collection of books, periodical clippings and other literature on rural development and allied subjects. It provides audiovisual inputs to the training programmes being conducted. Research activities of the Institute cover a wide range of issues relating to Rural Development. The main aim of research studies is to enhance understanding of the changing rural socioeconomic scenario and identify major constraints in the proper implementation of various development programmes and schemes. During the period from April to December 1998, about 22 research studies have been completed.

Training is a major activity of the Institute. NIRD trains senior officers, development functionaries, representatives of NGOs etc. The training efforts of the Institute are intended to create knowledge-based development of skills and understanding of the various dimensions of rural development. During the period from April to December, 1998, the Institute has conducted 85 training programmes including NERC, Guwahati and, in total, 2207 participants have been trained, of which 322 are women participants.

Consultancy is another important activity of the NIRD. Consultancy services offered by the Institute include specific custom made training programmes, evaluation studies, baseline studies, feasibility studies, impact assessment studies etc. The clientele for consultancy services comprise the Ministries of Government of India, the State Governments and the Public Sector Undertakings on the one side and the International Organizations like CIRDAP, EEC, UNDP, WHO, WEP, World Bank, ILO, SAARC Countries, UNIFEM, UNICEF, AARRO, Ford Foundation, Konrad Adeneur Foundation on the other.

As a part of the outreach programmes, the Institute launched District Link Officers (DLOs), Ministry Link

Officers (MLOs) and Programme Link Officers (PLOs) Schemes. These schemes aim at improving the faculty members/institute's understanding of District, Ministry and programme related developments.

NIRD is a leading publisher of Rural Development literature in India. A pioneering achievement of the Institute is the preparation and distribution of a monthly newsletter 'Panchayat Unnati' in 12 languages, including English which is sent to over 2.5 lakh gram panchayats all over the country.

The Institute made sustained efforts to upgrade information handling capacities by (a) installing Local Area Network (LAN), (b) INTERNET connectivity (c) developing data base consisting of books, journals, articles, etc. and has also set up a Computerized Library and Information Clearing House (CLIC) in the Centre of Rural Documentation.

NIRD celebrated its foundation day on November 5-6, 1998.

The Institute had been allocated Rs. 5.00 crores and Rs. 5.66 crores under Plan and Non-plan respectively during 1998-99.

**State institute of rural development**

The Centrally Sponsored Scheme for strengthening/ establishment of State Institute of Rural Development (SIRD) was considered vital for human resources development. This scheme was taken up for implementation during the Sixth Five Year Plan. The Scheme was continued during Seventh and Eighth Plan to revitalise training infrastructure so as to train the rural development functionaries and implement the programme more effectively. With this in view, it was decided to set up/strengthen one apex training Institute at State level in each State.

There are 25 SIRDs set up under this scheme in 25 States which include 8 Composite Institutes in Gujarat, Himachal Pradesh, Jammu and Kashmir, Karnataka, Maharashtra, Manipur, Rajasthan and Tripura. Out of the 25 SIRDs, 23 SIRDs have become operational either in their own building or in rented buildings.

The SIRDs in Goa and Mizoram are yet to be operationalised. The SIRDs have the requisite linkages with NIRD and ETCs so as to function in a hierarchy to serve the vital role of imparting training to the rural development functionaries. The scheme is being monitored constantly at the various levels in order to chalk out requisite strategy/plan for further strengthening and removing constraints in the functioning of the SIRDs. A system of regional consultations has been introduced between the Ministry, the NIRD and the State Governments. In these consultations, emphasis is laid on improving the content and quality of training programmes.

After the enactment of the 73rd Constitutional Amendment Act, it has been decided to strengthen existing training infrastructure both at the State level as well as district level to meet the training requirements of elected Panchayati Raj functionaries and officials in the near future. The financial assistance by Government of India to SIRDs is 100% for non-recurring expenditure and 50% for recurring expenditure. The scheme is, however, demand driven in nature. Special emphasis is being given for recruitment of core faculty members in SIRDs. 100% funding support is available to cover expenditure on procuring the services of five core faculty members for each SIRD.

Keeping in view the modernisation and skill/ development, it has been decided to extend NICNET connectivity to all the SIRDs to improve their functioning. NICNET connectivity has been provided to 14 SIRDs and to NIRD, Hyderabad, NERC- NIRD, Guwahati and CAPART, New Delhi. Four SIRDs and NIRD, Hyderabad and NERC- NIRD, Guwahati have been provided with multimedia equipments.

Despite fairly impressive gains, serious lacunae with regard to the tenure of the Head of SIRDs continue to persist. In the Annual Colloquium of Secretaries of Rural Development and Directors of SIRDs which was held at NIRD, Hyderabad on 15-16 May, 1998 it was discussed that the tenure of the Heads of SIRDs plays a crucial role in the functioning of the Institute. It was noticed that some SIRDs do not have a regular Director and in some SIRDs, Directors have been frequently transferred. The general feeling was that continuity and stability in tenure are essential prerequisites for smooth and efficient working of these Institutes. Accordingly, it has been decided that the State Governments should fulfil one of the three following conditions to make them eligible for getting non-recurring grants from Government of India under this scheme.

(i) The present Director should have been on the post for at least one year at the time of sending the proposals for central assistance by the State Governments to the Government of India; or

(ii) The previous incumbent should have been there as Director, SIRD for at least two years; or

(iii) The average tenure of last three Directors should have been at least two years.

The Plan outlay for the year 1998-99 for this scheme is Rs. 3.25 crores.

**Extension training centres**

The scheme of strengthening/establishment of Extension

Training Centres (ETCs) for imparting training to village/block level development functionaries was taken up during the Seventh Five Year Plan for implementation.

The ETCs are expected to provide necessary training inputs for raising the professional competence of the village and block level functionaries. So far, 87 ETCs have been established/upgraded with central assistance. Considering the increase in the number of development functionaries and rural organisations and the rejuvenation of the Panchayati Raj system, the role of ETCs has acquired added importance.

With the enactment of the constitutional 73rd Amendment Act, 1992 relating to the setting up of the Panchayati Raj Institutions, the need for training for Rural Development/ Panchayati Raj functionaries has increased tremendously. The Extension Training Centres are the only training set up to reach down to the village level. Keeping all these in view, it has been decided to strengthen training infrastructure in the existing Extension Training Centres. For this purpose, central assistance is 100% for non-recurring expenditure and the recurring expenditure is provided to a maximum ceiling of Rs. 5.00 lakhs per annum per ETC. However, the scheme is demand driven in nature. The Plan Outlay of this scheme for the year 1998-99 is Rs. 3.00 crores.

**Organisation of training courses, seminars and workshops**

A Central Sector Plan scheme for providing financial assistance for organizing training courses, seminars, workshops etc. on the subjects relevant to rural development has been in operation since the Sixth Five Year Plan.

With the increasing thrust on target oriented programmes in the rural development and identification of specific issues in rural development seminars, workshops and training programmes on various topics became critical for policy formulation and improving delivery system for rural development. In the absence of a substantive network of State Level Training Institutes it was necessary to make ad-hoc arrangement for training of rural development functionaries in the Government as well as in local bodies and non-governmental organisations.

The training programmes, seminars and workshops under this scheme are conducted through NIRD, SIRD and other reputed Institutes, departments of Universities etc., on selected topics.

The Plan outlay for the year 1998-99 is Rs. 0. 50 crores. Out of which Rs. 30 lakhs are for the scheme of Organisation of Training Courses, Seminars and Workshops (OTC) and Rs. 20 lakhs are for the Career Management activities of the employees of this Ministry.

**Council for advancement of people's action and rural technology**

The voluntary sector plays an important role in development particularly with reference to the programmes aimed at the rural poor and for improving the quality of life in rural areas. The Ministry of Rural Areas and Employment has been earmarking funds for the voluntary sector not only in the nationally planned programmes but also for mobilizing and motivating people's participation. With a view to encouraging, promoting and assisting voluntary action in rural development and with focus on injecting new technological inputs for the enhancement of rural prosperity, the Government of India, in September 1986, set up the Council for Advancement of People's Action and Rural Technology (CAPART), a registered society under the aegis of the Ministry of Rural Areas and Employment by merging two autonomous bodies, namely People's Action for Development India (PADI) and Council for Advancement of Rural Technology (CART). The Cabinet Minister / Minister of State (IC) incharge of the Ministry of Rural Areas and Employment is the President of the General Body of CAPART. The General Body comprises officials of the Ministry of Rural Areas and Employment, eminent social activists, experts in different fields in rural development and representatives of voluntary agencies. The General Body lays down the broad policy framework within which projects under various schemes are sanctioned. The Executive Committee, which is also headed by the Cabinet Minister/Minister of State (IC) incharge of the Ministry of Rural Areas and Employment, formulates the policy parameters and guidelines for the functioning of CAPART. The Secretary, Department of Rural Development is the vice-chairman of the Executive Committee of CAPART, The Secretary, Department of Rural Employment and Poverty Alleviation has been appointed as second Vice-Chairman in the year 1998-99. The Director General, who is in the rank of Additional Secretary, is the Chief Executive of CAPART.

**Decentralisation**

As a prelude to the preparation of the Ninth Plan, the government had initiated a dialogue with the Voluntary Organisations (VOs) by forming a Working Group to formulate a viable strategy to involve them in a big way. CAPART has taken the initiative of mobilizing the efforts of VOs by decentralizing its activities for a more purposeful functioning. In order to be close to the VOs in the field, CAPART had decentralized its functioning by constituting six Regional Committees in 1994 at Jaipur, Lucknow, Bhubaneswar, Guwahati, Ahmedabad and Hyderabad. During the financial year 1997-98, two more Regional Committee offices were opened at Patna and

Chandigarh. Thus, CAPART has at present 8 Regional Committee offices. They cater to the different regions in the country. They are headed by eminent persons from the voluntary sector. The Regional Committees sanction all projects up to Rs. 10 lakhs.

**People's participation**

For ensuring the success of water supply schemes or rehabilitation of degraded lands or any capacity building project, strong people's groups with enhanced management capacities are required. Hence, the Government has issued guidelines on people's participation, stressing inter-alia that the participation should include the notions of contributing, influencing, sharing or redistributing power and of controlling resources, benefits, knowledge and skills to be gained through beneficiary involvement in decision making. Participation is a voluntary process by which people, including the disadvantaged (in income, gender, caste or education) influence or control the decisions that affect them. It has also been emphasized that the three outcomes of participation - learning, empowerment and a vibrant organisation, need to be measured through observable indicators, which will vary from project to project. Each project must develop clearly observable indicators on people's participation, so as to judge whether they are on track or not. Such indicators should then be given to monitors and evaluators, who have to do mid-course evaluation and impact assessment. Accordingly, CAPART has constituted National Standing Committees on different subject matters for sanction of projects including one on Monitoring and Evaluation at the Headquarters. These committees predominantly comprise eminent subject matter specialists and representatives drawn from the voluntary sector. In this manner, CAPART is trying to make its functioning more participatory and transparent.

- Transparency in CAPART's Working
- Regional and National Standing Committees on different subject matters formed with a larger participation of VOs to sanction projects
- VOs are involved in monitoring process.
- Particulars of project sanctioned to be exhibited at the project site made mandatory.
- Community resource network formed for dissemination of information among VOs.
- CAPART news incorporates project sanctions.

**CAPART's sssistance**

While CAPART seeks to associate the voluntary sector in several schemes that are part of planned development and are being implemented on national basis, it also supports several innovative projects keeping in view the needs of specific areas. The main thrust of these programmes is on employment generation, houses for shelterless, conservation of water, enhancement of income and development of community assets. While CAPART receives most of its funds from the Ministry of Rural Areas and Employment, it also channelises some funds to VOs from funding agencies like DANIDA, SDC, etc. Efforts are also being made to mobilize international donations both from multilateral agencies and other international donors. A beginning has been made in this direction.

CAPART provides assistance to VOs under different programmes like Indira Awaas Yojana, Watershed Management, Social Forestry, Link Road in hilly areas, Promotion of Voluntary Action in Rural Development, Development of Women and Children in Rural Areas, Organisation of Beneficiaries, Central Rural Sanitation Programme, Drinking water under the Technology Mission on Accelerated Rural Water Supply Programme and Advancement of Rural Technology. Since 1995, CAPART is also providing assistance for talking up capacity building and rehabilitation programme for persons with disability. 3% of the allocations made under different programmes to CAPART are being set aside to fund this programme. It has also been decided to give preference in the coverage to disabled beneficiaries under all the programmes.

**Policy guidelines**

A revised set of guidelines on the functioning of CAPART has been issued on 20.01.99 so that genuine and committed Voluntary Organisations are brought into the fold of CAPART in its efforts towards rural development. The guiding principle "fund every VO, if there is nothing against it" for funding by CAPART has been sought to be changed to "fund only those carefully selected ones who have done or have the potential of doing outstanding work in empowerment and welfare of the disadvantaged".

Collaboration between the Government and the Voluntary Organisation, whenever it works always yields both qualitative and quantitative results. It is the endeavour of the Government that CAPART should make all-out efforts to help growth of collaboration between the Government and the VOs.

CAPART will add the following qualifications to the existing eligibility criteria: -

- The VO must have proven experience in social mobilization of the rural community for development projects and in improving the capability of the rural people in ensuring that development funds from Government and other sources are well spent without leakage;

- Generation of awareness among them regarding social and economic development;
- Projects by the VO must have been implemented through people's participation preferably through their role in control over funds; and
- The VO's projects in the past must have led to empowerment of any of the following: the socio-economically disadvantaged groups, viz. SC, ST, people below the poverty line, women, people living in remote areas, involuntarily displaced due to development projects, people who are suffering because of any particular policy of Government, people with physical disability and bonded labourers, etc.

With the new emphasis on innovation and participation, the quality of outcomes and impact is required to be judged objectively and regularly. CAPART shall therefore, develop verifiable indicators for effectiveness of these additional eligibility criteria.

CAPART will work out a system for continuous monitoring and grading as well as upgrading/ downgrading of VOs based on their performance after completion of each project along with grading of VOs on the basis of organizational profiles. This would enable VOs constantly to strive to improve their performance.

Towards acting as a think tank, CAPART would provide a forum for experts / VOs and others associated with rural development to present concepts, discuss issues and even review CAPART's policies at the regional, national and / or international level.

Whereas on the one hand, CAPART will play a pro-active role in identifying and supporting VOs with good track record, it is equally important for CAPART to take stringent action against those VOs which have misutilised CAPART's funds.

**Performance of CAPART since inception up to 31.12.98**

| | | |
|---|---|---|
| No. of projects sanctioned | - | 18126 |
| Amount sanctioned | - | Rs. 495.20 crores |
| Amount released | - | Rs. 368.86 crores |

The scheme of Young Professionals (YPs) started in 1988 continued with some modifications with a view to strengthen the VOs and the DRDAs in which their services were made available. Since the inception of the scheme, CAPART has so far selected about 205 YPs and out of which about 65 are women. The scheme evoked positive response from the selected professionals and several of them evinced interest in continuing to work in rural areas after the tenure of two years with CAPART. The organisations floated by them gets a preferential treatment in the sanction of projects. In this way, CAPART could also reach under-served and unrecalled areas of this country.

**Promotional role**

CAPART has a significant role in promoting a variety of activities of transfer of technology, people's participation, development of marketing for products of rural enterprises, generating awareness among rural masses for bringing about attitudinal changes towards persons with disability to contribute in the field of rural development and promotion of other developmental activities and delivery systems in non-governmental sector.

Examples of such activities are:-

- Establishment of regional resource centers for training and propagation of appropriate technologies throughout the country.
- Facilitating large-scale production and marketing of proven technologies by the voluntary sector by propagation and dissemination of proven technologies appropriate to the rural areas.

- Provision of marketing support and services to the beneficiaries of the IRDP/DWCRA programmes. This effort has resulted in the organisation of popular "Gram Shree Melas " throughout the country. Till 31 st December 1998, CAPART has organised 127 Gram Shree Melas throughout the country involving a sales turnover of Rs. 20 crores.
- Organisations of seminars/workshops to provide an opportunity for direct interaction between beneficiaries and professionals; providing support for establishing marketing outlets; creating linkages with established outlets/institutions, buyers for continuous marketing facilities, etc.
- Funding training Programmes for grassroots level VOs.
- Dissemination of information through communication resources network. The network is in the business of distribution of material and information in their area of specialization.
- Production of audiovisual material and broadcasting through All India Radio in local languages.
- Information technology is being upgraded with the help of National Informatics Center both to deal with the decentralized set up and disseminate information to the VOs on various aspects of rural development.

**Promotion of voluntary action scheme**

Keeping in view the new thrust given to the functioning of CAPART, the guidelines of the scheme on Promotion of Voluntary Action have been revised. The revised guidelines of the scheme seek to integrate rural developmental activities through experimental and innovative efforts which can be replicated. To increase people's participation, it has also been provided that the projects normally will be assisted up to a maximum of 95% of total cost. Contribution of 5% or more would be expected from other sources like banks' loans, Government subsides and assistance, sponsoring organization's contribution and contribution of beneficiaries. Thus CAPART would now be able to fund any innovative, experimental and composite project under this scheme.

**Housing development**

Housing programme encourages not only economic activities but also generates employment opportunities and creates a solid base for healthy and hygienic living. CAPART has been providing funds to VOs for construction of houses with infrastructure such as roads, soakpits, other common facilities and individual sanitation units to the targeted population consisting of SCs/STs/ freed bonded labourers and other socially and economically weaker sections of the society through Indira Awaas Yojana.

**Watershed management**

In a major attempt to tackle the ecological crisis and to conserve water to bring about all round development with the Government announcement of Integrated Watershed Conservation and Development Programme, CAPART, too, took it up to associate VOs in a big way. It had formulated its own guidelines and created a separate division to sanction projects. During the year under report, the division organised State level orientation workshops to make VOs aware of the requirements, developed formats for different stages for circulation among VOs and also devised formats for capacity building. A subcommittee for setting up training institutes formulated the training content.

**Advancement of rural technology**

The broad mandate was to coordinate all efforts for Advancement of Technology relevant for rural areas. The thrust under this programme is to promote and support efforts for transfer of technology to the rural areas. The technologies which benefits a larger spectrum of people in rural areas are supported and the major fields are as follows:

- Construction/Housing technologies
- Water conservation
- Village Industries
- Primary sector fields
- Food Processing
- Herbal medicine
- Energy
- Bio-mass utilization
- Handicrafts

Regional Resource Centres are created to test technologies feasible for specific geographical area, make modifications where necessary and initiate the process of transfer of viable technologies through demonstration, training and manufacture. CAPART has so far supported 14 VOs to establish Regional Resource Centers involving an assistance of Rs. 5. 12 crores and plans are on the anvil to create more centers under the Ninth Plan.

**Employment and income generation**

CAPART has played a significant role in creating employment and income generation among the rural poor, through its schemes like, Promotion of Voluntary Action in Rural Development, DWCRA and IRDR. The schemes are structured so as to provide permanent source of income to target beneficiaries. The financial assistance is provided by CAPART for building infrastructure, training, assets creation, production and marketing. Under Promotion of Voluntary Action Scheme, innovative projects are encouraged as per the needs and requirements of the area. For landless labourers and persons with no employment, Jawahar Rozgar Yojana provides partial employment through such activities as house building, road construction in hilly areas, social forestry, etc.

**Drinking water and environmental sanitation**

For improving the quality of life, safe drinking water and rural sanitation programmes are taken up by CAPART. The schemes called ARWSP and CRSP respectively provide financial assistance to VOs for taking up sinking of tubewells and construction of individual family latrines in rural areas through the mobilization of local resources and contributions of enlisted beneficiaries. Both the programmes are popular with the VOs throughout the country.

**Awareness generation programme**

Organisation of beneficiaries is given due importance by CAPART. The objective of the scheme Organisation of Beneficiaries (OB) is to create awareness among the rural poor, organise them into groups and strengthen their bargaining capabilities. The guidelines of the scheme have recently been revised to provide support to community / groups consisting of poor people who wish to organise or have organised themselves either on their own or due to efforts of a Voluntary Organisation for a cause which is sufficiently just or serious and to sustain their campaign/struggle for their betterment of economic status or social power. It has been clarified that OB was not merely a training scheme and definitely not a scheme for providing funds to organise meetings where government functionaries are invited just once to inform beneficiaries about government schemes, subsidies or projects. It is a scheme about people's struggle against injustice and should result in increased confidence of the people to fight corruption and misuse of authority. Financial assistance under the scheme is provided for mobilization of beneficiaries, organising them into groups, holding awareness generation camps and to monitor follow up programmes so that real benefits of development programmes reach them.

Another programme for consolidation of benefits of awareness is the training of social animators so as to create change agents in rural areas. It is expected that by such efforts, development programmes will be more effective and speedy in the thrust areas. Under this, CAPART is also providing financial assistance to VOs to take up motivation programme for the benefit of elected members of the Gram Panchayats. The entire programme is mainly dealt at the Regional Committee level as a quantum of assistance provided falls within the financial ceiling of Rs. 10 lakhs.

# 4

# Special Component Plan and Tribal Development Planning

The Ministry of Rural Areas and Employment is implementing various programmes for providing avenues for employment to most disadvantaged sections of the society through special employment generation programmes and for improvement in quality of life in rural areas. The Ministry has provided for specific guidelines in the programmes being implemented to ensure adequate flow of resources to the Scheduled Castes and Scheduled Tribes.

**Jawahar Rozgar Yojana**

Jawahar rozgar yojana (JRY) is a centrally sponsored scheme being implemented throughout the country. The objectives of JRY are :

- Generation of additional gainful employment for the unemployed and under employed in the rural areas;
- Creation of sustained employment by strengthening the rural economic infrastructure and also assets in favour of the rural poor for their direct and continuing benefits and overall improvement in the quality of life in rural areas. While people below the poverty line constitute the target group under the JRY, preference is given to the SCs, STs and freed

bonded labourers. Funds provided under the Yojana are distributed among the three tiers of Panchayati Raj Institutions i.e., Village Panchayats, Intermediate level Panchayats and DRDAs/Zilla Parishads in the ratio of 70:15:15 respectively.

The implementing agencies are required to spend 22.5% of their respective funds for the benefit of SC and ST. Also 30% of the employment opportunities are reserved for women and 3% of the funds are earmarked for physically handicapped persons. While the actual flow of funds to SCs, STs is not separately available, the share of SCs and STs in employment generation in terms of lakh mandays during 1997-98 and 1998-99 is indicated below:

*(lakh mandays)*

| *Year* | *Total Achievement* | *SCs* | *STs* |
|---|---|---|---|
| 1997-98 | 3925.97 | 1402.96 (35.74) | 743.53 (18.94) |
| 1998-99* | 2069.64 | 753.21 (36.39) | 372.87 (18.02) |

* Provisional

(Figures in brackets indicate % to total)

**Employment assurance scheme**

The basic objective of the Employment Assurance Scheme (EAS) is to provide gainful employment during the lean agricultural season in manual work to all able adults in rural areas who are in need and are desirous of work but cannot find it, either on farm or on other allied operations or on the ongoing normal plan/non-plan works during such period. Since the target group under the scheme comprises all the rural poor, there is no separate earmarking of funds for SCs and STs. However, the interest of the SCs and STs, who are generally landless and sustain mostly on wage employment, is specially taken care of by virtue of the fact that the EAS is being implemented in all the blocks of the country.

Under this scheme, benefits to SCs, STs in employment generation in terms of lakh mandays during 1997-98 and 1998-99 is given below:

*(lakh mandays)*

| *Year* | *Total* | *SCs* | *STs* |
|---|---|---|---|
| 1997-98 | 4717.74 | 1507.56 (31.96) | 1019.08 (21.60) |
| 1998-99* | 2466.00 | 831.38 (33.71) | 92.06 (19.95) |

* Provisional

(Figures in brackets indicate percentage to total)

**Million wells scheme**

The objective of million wells schemes (MWS) is to provide assistance free of cost to poor, small and marginal farmers belonging to Scheduled Castes/ Scheduled Tribes and freed bonded labourers for construction of irrigation sources and land development. From 1993-94 onwards, MWS has been extended to include poor, small and marginal farmers belonging to non-SC, ST category who are below the poverty line and are listed in the IRDP register of the village also. However, financial assistance provided to non-SC, ST poor, small and marginal farmers under this scheme should not exceed one third of the total funds utilized in any year. The physical and financial progress during 1997-99 and 1999-99 is indicated below :

(Rs. in crores)

| *Year* | *Wells constructed* | | *Expenditure incurred* | |
|---|---|---|---|---|
| | *SC/ST* | *Others* | *SC/ST* | *Others* |
| 1997-98 | 71530 (70.30) | 30224 | 331.61 (67.30) | 161.17 |
| 1998-99* | 33849 | 15452 | 149.21 (64.94) | 76.08 |

*Provisional

(Figures in brackets indicate percentage to total)

**Indira Awaas Yojana**

The Government of India is implementing Indira Awaas

Yojana (IAY) with the objective of providing dwelling units free of cost to the members of SCs/STs and freed bonded labourers below the poverty line in rural areas. Now its scope has been extended to cover non-Scheduled Castes, Scheduled Tribes rural poor, subject to the condition that the benefits of the scheme should not exceed 40% of total IAY allocation. Funds under the scheme allocated to the States/UTs are distributed to the districts in proportion to the SC, ST population in the district. The physical and financial progress during 1997-98 and 1998-99 is indicated below :

(Rs. in crores)

| *Year* | *House constructed* | | *Expenditure incurred* | |
|---|---|---|---|---|
| | *SC/ST* | *Others* | *SC/ST* | *Others* |
| 1997-98 | 548136 | 213341 | 1144.89 | 453.21 |
| 1998-99* | 251200 | 99283 | 533.76 | 229.98 |

*Provisional

**Integrated rural development programme**

The main objective of Integrated Rural Development Programme (IRDP) is to create employment opportunities for self-employment in rural areas for families living below poverty line so that they can generate additional income to enable them to cross the poverty line on a sustained basis. It is stipulated that 50% of the total coverage should be of SC, ST families.

Under IRDP during 1997-98, out of total actual expenditure (subsidy) of Rs. 1109.54 crores, Rs. 300.43 crores were for SC, ST families. During the period, the physical coverage of SC, ST in terms of number of families assisted under IRDP, SITRA, TRYSEM and DWCRA was 46.40%, 13%, 47. 10% and 4.90% respectively. During 1998-99, under IRDP, upto November 1998, the coverage of SC, ST families has been around 44.88% of the total.

**Accelerated rural water supply programme**

The objective of the scheme is to provide sources of safe drinking water to the rural poor. The guidelines for implementation -of the scheme provide that the States/ UTs have to earmark and utilize a minimum of 25% of the annual outlay for drinking water supply to SCs and another minimum of 10% for STs. The first source of drinking water has to be provided in the SC, ST localities. Coverage of SC, ST habitations should be given first preference.

**Central rural sanitation programme**

This is a programme to provide sanitary latrines to the rural poor. The guidelines provide that a minimum of 20% of annual funds should be earmarked for paying subsidy to SC and ST households below the poverty line where the percentage of SC, ST population is less than 20%. Where the SC, ST population below poverty line is more than 20% of total population below poverty line, earmarking should be enhanced at least to match the percentage of SC/ST population.

## Empowerment of women

Women's empowerment is critical to the process of the development of the community. Bringing women into the mainstream of development has been a major concern of the government since independence. Yet, despite significant steps taken by the government, the participation of women in all spheres of life varies in the context of differences in the social, economic, cultural and regional factors. It is being increasingly realised that the goal of poverty alleviation cannot be achieved without the full and active participation of women who constitute a large section of the work force in the country. In order to empower women and bring them into the mainstream, an enabling environment with requisite policies and programmes, institutional mechanisms at various levels and adequate financial resources has been created. The Ministry of Rural Areas and Employment has special components for women in all its programmes and a certain amount of funds is earmarked as 'women's component' to ensure a flow of adequate resources for women.

By virtue of the provisions of the Constitutional (73rd Amendment) Act 1992, a substantial number of women have been enabled to take direct part in the process of self-governance through the panchayats. Women now play an active role in the decision-making process relating to programmes which have direct relevance to the rural poor such as Development of Women and Children in Rural Areas (DWCRA). Women are members of watershed committees which plan and implement watershed development projects. Women are active participants in the self-help groups and user groups. They also take on the responsibility of operation and maintenance of the assets created. The Ministry also accords importance to awareness generation and dissemination of information among women. Considering the important role envisaged for women in the new Panchayati Raj set up, the Ministry has decided to provide financial assistance through CAPART to non-governmental organisations with a proven track record for conducting training and awareness generation programmes on Panchayati Raj.

The Ministry has several schemes for providing better opportunities to women in rural India.

The programme of DWCRA was started in 1982-83 on a pilot basis in 50 districts, as a sub-scheme of the Integrated Rural Development Programme (IRDP), which has now been extended to all districts of the country. It is an exclusive programme of its kind which aims at empowering poor rural women through economic means. It seeks to encourage collective action in the form of group activities. Through such social and economic empowerment, the programme seeks to improve the access of rural women to health, education, safe drinking water, sanitation, nutrition etc., and to bring about an enhancement in the quality of life and general well being of women and children. Further, by encouraging the habit of thrift and credit, it aims at making poor women self-reliant. Through assistance from the Government in the form of Revolving Fund, it seeks to integrate women in the economy by providing additional opportunities for self-employment. Under DWCRA, 10-15 women form groups, for taking up economic activities suited to their skill, aptitude and local conditions. A Revolving Fund amounting to Rs. 25,000 is given to each group to meet its working capital requirements etc.

About 2,49,000 groups of women have been formed with membership of about 39 lakh women since inception of the programme in 1982-83. During the year 1998-99 about 22,921 groups have been formed so far benefiting about 3 lakhs women. Recently, there has been greater emphasis on empowering women by imparting knowledge, information and training. The Community Based Convergent Services Programme and the Information, Education and Communication component under DWCRA seek to sensitise women regarding their needs, and to help them prioritize and articulate these effectively and fulfil them by utilizing existing facilities and provisions under various Government programmes in a better way. DWCRA Programme is linked to IRDP for credit and Training of Rural Youth for Self-Employment (TRYSEM) for training.

Under IRDP, assistance is given to the rural poor through Government subsidy and bank credit to help them take up income generating activities. 40% of total assistance under IRDP is reserved for women. Coverage of women has been rising under the programme from a mere 10% of total beneficiaries in 1985-86 to 34.4% in 1998-99. Under the Scheme for TRYSEM, it has been laid down that 40% of the trainees must be women. About 46,400 women have been covered under TRYSEM during April to November, 1998.

Jawahar Rozgar Yojana (JRY) aims at providing additional gainful employment for the rural unemployed and under employed. Thirty per cent of the employment opportunities are reserved for women. Of the total employment generated under JRY, the share of women has been 533.84 lakh persondays till November, 1998. Under Employment Assurance Scheme 639.46 lakh persondays of employment have been generated during April to November, 1998.

Under the Indira Awaas Yojana (IAY), there is a provision for giving houses free of cost to the rural poor. Under this programme, priority is given to widows and unmarried women. It has also been laid down that IAY houses shall be allotted in the name of the women members of the household or in the joint names of husband and wife.

The National Social Assistance Programme (NSAP) which came into effect from 15th August 1995, represents a significant step towards introducing a national policy for social assistance benefits to households below the poverty line, with a major focus on women. The National Maternity Benefit Scheme (NMBS) is exclusively aimed at assisting expectant mothers financially by providing them Rs. 500 each for the first two live births. Under the National Old Age Pension Scheme (NOAPS), women as well as men can avail of old age pension if they are 65 years of age or above and have little or no regular means of subsistence from their own sources of income or through financial support from family members or other sources. Central assistance is Rs. 75 per month under the NOAPS. Women are also the beneficiaries under the National Family Benefit Scheme (NFBS). Under this scheme, Central assistance of Rs. 10,000 in the case of death of the primary breadwinner due to natural or accidental causes, is available to the bereaved family living below the poverty line.

The Central Rural Sanitation Programme (CRSP) provides for construction of sanitary latrines for rural households. This essential step towards clean living also ensures privacy to women. Separate bathing and washing places are also provided for women. Up to 10% of the annual funds can be utilised to provide public latrines in selected villages during the plan period, where the panchayats/charitable trusts/non-governmental organisations offer to construct and maintain village complexes exclusively for use by women.

Training is being given to women to enable them to play an active role in using and maintaining handpumps for supply of drinking water. They are represented in village level committees and are actively involved in selection of sites for handpumps and other sources. CAPART provides funds to voluntary agencies working for rural women's welfare. CAPART also works to promote rural technology that makes work easier and quicker for women in their households and outdoor activities.

Quality Control through grading and marking of agricultural products is of great benefit to women consumers. The quality certification scheme 'Agmark' has resulted in increased quality awareness among the consumers. Consumer organisations with women representatives have been empowered to inspect Agmark products and draw samples for testing.

The States have been asked to issue joint pattas where ceiling surplus land is distributed, to landless poor families. This will significantly improve women's access to land.

The Ministry recognises the need to have an institutional mechanism for reviewing the content and scope of the on-going programmes meant for enhancing the level and quality of participation by women. A Committee has been constituted in the Ministry under the chairmanship of the Additional Secretary and Financial Advisor to advise on matters pertaining to women in Rural Development. This Committee would help in monitoring the implementation of the women's component and also identify areas/schemes for special intervention to increase the flow of benefits to women in Rural Development. There is a proposal to create a women's cell in each District Rural Development Agency to look after women's components under various schemes.

Steps are being taken for convergence of various programmes for women at the grassroots. The Ministry is working towards intra-departmental convergence of services available under various programmes. At the same time, it is exploring mechanisms to synergise with other ministries and departments, specially the Department of Women and Child Development, which implements programmes like Rashtriya Mahila Kosh, Integrated Child Development Scheme etc.

**Communication and media support**

Media can be a powerful advocate in the whole spectrum of development. Effective communication assumes more significance in the context of programmes of this Ministry which aim at improving the socioeconomic conditions of nearly one-third of the population living below the poverty line in rural areas, spread over a wide geograhical area and marked by pronounced regional, linguistic and cultural diversity. For the success of the programmes of Poverty Alleviation and Rural Development, there is increased need of people's participation in the implementation of these programmes. The lack of awareness about the various programmes/ schemes has been felt to be one of the stumbling blocks in achieving people's participation in the development process. Media plays a vital role in creating awareness, mobilising people and making the development participatory through advocacy and by transferring knowledge, skills and techniques to the people.

During the year 1998-99, the Ministry continued in its endeavour to disseminate information through the available modes of communication such as Print Media, Electronic Media, Outdoor Media, Field Level Communication Campaigns, Interpersonal Communication and Traditional Media to the following three broad categories of people.

- Beneficiaries/intended beneficiaries of the Programmes.
- Opinion makers
- General public

While the Media Division of the Ministry of Rural Areas and Employment has the overall responsibility of planning major IEC activities and media campaigns, the implementation has been largely carried out by the Media Units of the Ministry of Information and Broadcasting and national, state and district level institutions.

**Standing committee**

A Standing Committee on Media constituted in this Ministry approves and oversees implementation of the action plan for media activities. It periodically monitors the various media activities and gives policy directions for mid course corrections.

**Advisory committee on media**

An advisory committee on media comprising eminent journalists and media persons has been constituted in the Ministry to evolve a cohesive communication plan, taking advantage of the rapid expansion of mass media channels. The Committee has the following terms of reference :

- To review and assess the impact of various media and other activities undertaken for creating awareness and to suggest corrective measures to make them more effective.
- To advise the Ministry on appropriate media strategy to be adopted so that the objective of involvement of beneficiaries and participation of the community in the implementation of the programmes/schemes of the Ministry could be realised.
- To identify 'thrust areas' in respect of media and communication efforts of the Ministry and suggest an action plan for undertaking the proposed media activities.

The Committee meets periodically to deliberate on various issues under its terms of reference.

**Print media**

The Ministry through regular interaction with the Press Information Bureau (PIB) sensitized the media personnel on development issues so that the policies of the Ministry are highlighted in the media. Press Conferences and other media events of the Ministry were covered extensively in the print and electronic media. To enable the media personnel to understand the rural development issues and problems and to encourage their participation in the development process, Press Tours to rural development projects at different places in the country as well as individual visits by journalists were organised through the PIB.

The Ministry also issued several advertisements in national as well as regional press on various themes relating to the programmes of the Ministry through Directorate of Advertising and Visual Publicity (DAVP). On the occasion of 2nd October, 1998 a full page advertisement depicting various development initiatives and achievement under different programmes of the Ministry was released in Hindi, English and regional languages all over the country in newspapers and magazines. Press advertisement on National Social Assistance Programme and its three components i.e., National Old Age Pension Scheme, National Maternity Benefit Scheme and National Family Benefit Scheme was also issued to enable people to avail of assistance under the schemes.

Leaflets on different programmes of the Ministry in Hindi and regional languages were printed and distributed up to the Block Level all over the country. Booklets and folders containing information on all the programmes and schemes of the Ministry are also brought out to disseminate information to the people. Conscious efforts were made to improve the quality of communication through the medium of the printed word.

The Ministry brought out a wall Calendar for the year 1999, depicting major schemes of the Ministry which was distributed up to the Panchayats. Desk Calendars were also brought out during the year.

The Ministry continued to extend financial assistance to Publication Division of the Ministry of Information and Broadcasting and National Institute of

Rural Development (NIRD) for the publication of monthly journals namely 'Kurukshetra' and 'Panchayat Unnati'.

'Kurukshetra' is a 40 year old monthly which is published in Hindi and English. The-journal carries authentic, analytical and research based material on various issues and themes relating to rural development and poverty alleviation. During the year, efforts were made to further improve the content, presentation and reach of the journal in consultation with the Publication Division.

'Panchayat Unnati', a monthly newsletter is brought out by NIRD on behalf of this Ministry with the objective of disseminating information to the grassroots level functionaries. The newsletter published in Hindi, English and major regional languages is mailed free of cost to the Panchayats all over the country. The circulation of 'Panchayat Unnati' is 2.5 lakh copies per month.

The Communication Cell of the Ministry continued to bring out guidelines, manuals, evaluation reports and essential documents such as the Annual Report. Guidelines on Indira Awaas Yojana were printed for distribution to programme functionaries and intended beneficiaries.

**Electronic media**

To tap the potential and outreach of radio as a means of mass communication in the rural areas, the Ministry continued to sponsor two weekly radio programmes 'Gaon Vikas Ki Ore' and 'Chalo Gaon Ki Ore' over 30 Commercial Broadcasting Stations (CBS) and 15 Primary Stations in the North-East region for creating awareness about different programmes/schemes of the Ministry. The sponsored programmes produced in 20 languages are broadcast twice a week on every Sunday at 2.15 P.M and every Tuesday at &P.M.

Besides the sponsored radio programmes, several radio spots of 30 second duration on NSAP were produced and broadcast over CBS and primary channels of the All India Radio.

The medium of television was also used to spread the message of the Ministry. During the year, six video spots on Panchayati Raj and NSAP were produced, besides three video spots on NSAP for the northeast. The spots were telecast over Doordarshan National Hookup and regional channels. Information was also disseminated through CCTV on six Railway Stations in Tamil Nadu and Howrah in West Bengal.

Both AIR and Doordarshan have a strong mandate and commitment to include Rural Development programmes and related issues in all Indian languages as part of their regular programming.

**Outdoor publicity**

Outdoor publicity channels such as Bus Back Panels, Wall Paintings, Kiosks, Hoardings, Cinema Slides etc. were utilized throughout the country and Computer Animation Display were used at selected places for putting across the message to the target groups. 2830 wall painting in 9 languages on various themes, 3555 bus back panel in 9 languages and 1200 hoarding in 5 languages were put up. Computerised Animation Display at Katra, Jammu and New Delhi were also organised.

**Field level communication campaigns**

Directorate of Field Publicity (DFP) and Song and Drama Division organised long intensive campaigns on themes of NSAP, Panchayati Raj, Watershed Development and EAS covering backward districts across the country. With the help of its field units, DFP organised group discussions, pubic meeting, seminars, posters exhibitions and film shows; and distributed literature to the people at the grassroots. 4970 films shows, 6233 oral communication, 2963 photo exhibitions, 944 special programmes were organised by DFP as part of the special campaigns from April to June 1998. During the months of March-June, 1999 it is proposed to mount special campaigns to highlight the themes of Panchayati Raj, IAY, IRDP EAS and NSAP. The Song and Drama Division conducted extensive communication activities at the community level using performing arts, folk media, traditional arts, mythological recitals, puppetry etc. From April to June, 1998, the Song and Drama Division presented 1481 programmes, About 1400 programmes are proposed to be held during the months of February-March 1999 on NSAP, Panchayati Raj, IAJ, IRDP and EAS.

**Exhibition**

The Ministry of Rural Areas and Employment has a permanent pavilion at Pragati Maidan, New Delhi and it participates in major trade fairs particularly those related to social development through the CAPART.

**Interpersonal contact and traditional media**

Since the target beneficiaries of programmes of this Ministry living in the rural areas tend to rely more on interpersonal contact and traditional media as a source of information, the District Rural Development Agencies (DRDAs) have also been involved in undertaking IEC activities on various Rural Development and Poverty Alleviation Programmes. For this purpose, grants-in-aid are released to the DRDAs by the Ministry.

During the year apart from the budgetary allocation of Rs. 400 lakhs available under the Communication Cell, the Media Division planned and executed media activities from the allocation of Rs. 1278 lakhs made available for IEC activities by different programme divisions of the Ministry.

**Organisation**

**Administration**

Shri Babagouda Patil took over as Minister of State (independent Charge) on 19.3.1998.

Dr. N.C. Saxena held the charge of the office of Secretary, Department of Rural Development and Department of Wastelands Development till 5.2.1999.

Dr. P.L.S. Reddy has been holding the charge of the office of Secretary, Department of Rural Employment and Poverty Alleviation since 6.11.1997.

Shri M. Shankar is the Additional Secretary and Financial Advisor in the Ministry of Rural Areas and Employment.

Shri S.B. Mohapatra is the Additional Secretary in the Department of Wastelands Development.

The posts of joint Secretary in the Ministry of Rural Areas and Employment are being held by the following officers:

1. Shri Palat Mohandas, IAS (KL:68)
2. Shri P.S. Rana, IAS (HP:70)
3. Shri Satish Chandra, IAS (UT:70)
4. Dr. J.S. Sarma, IAS (AP:71)
5. Smt. Sudha Pillai, IAS (KL:72)
6. Shri Anil Kumar, IAS (UP:73)
7. Shri Sukumar Das, IAS (WB:76)
8. Shri Kuldip Rai, CSS

Smt. Sushma Singh, IAS (BH:72) relinquished the charge of joint Secretary with effect from 30th June, 1998. Shri Hoshiar Singh, IAS (MP:76) was repatriated to his State prematurely with effect from 3rd July, 1998 on his request.

The following are the Economic Advisers in the Ministry:

1) Dr. V.N. Mishra, IES
2) Dr. P.V. Thomas, IES

**Attached/subordinate offices and autonomous bodies**

In the Directorate of Marketing and Inspection, an attached office under this Ministry, Shri M.K. Mandal continued to hold the post of Agricultural Marketing Adviser to the Government of India from 21.3.1997. However, the following subjects have been transferred from the Ministry of Rural Areas and Employment to the Ministry of Agriculture vide Cabinet Secretariat Notification No. 1/22/1/98-Cab. Dated the 19th December, 1998:

1. Setting up of agricultural markets in rural areas
2. The Agricultural Produce (Grading and Marking) Act, 1937 (1 of 1937)

The Ministry has three autonomous bodies under its administrative control. These are:

1. National Institute of Rural Development, Rajendranagar, Hyderabad.
2. Council for Advancement of People's Action and Rural Technology (CAPART), India Habitat Centre, Lodi Road, New Delhi.
3. National Institute of Agricultural Marketing, Kota Road, Bambala (Near Sanganer), Jaipur.

Shri R.C. Choudhary is the Director General, National Institute of Rural Development, Hyderabad. Shri P. Vanamali continued as Deputy Director General in NIRD till 12th January, 1999.

Shri N. Ramji handed over charge of the office of Director General of Council for Advancement of People's

Action and Rural Technology (CAPART) to Shri Rangan Dutta on 7th December, 1998. Shri Ashok Thakur and Shri K.K. Bangar continued as Deputy Director General in CAPART. Shri R.K. Anand continued as Director (Chief Vigilance Officer) in CAPART.

Shri T.R. Verma continued as Director General in National Institute of Agriculture Marketing (NIAM). Shri R.P. Meena continued as Director (A&F) in NIAM.

**Grievance redressal machinery**

The Deputy Secretary/Director in-charge of Administration in this Ministry functions as Director of Staff Grievances and joint Secretary in-charge of Administration wing as Director of Grievances. Anyone having any grievance may directly approach them. In addition, Under Secretary in-charge of Administration has been nominated to examine the grievances column of the newspapers for picking up related case for taking quick action and also for publicising the action taken. However, the functioning of the Ministry of Rural Areas and Employment is such that there is no direct interface with the public as a result the public grievances are not much.

Monitoring of public grievances redressal has been computerised in this Ministry with the help of the NIC. Officers from different divisions of this Ministry have been imparted training and are actively involved in coordinating the data entry of information in the computer in respect of grievances pertaining to their respective divisions and to that extent grievance redressal is decentralised. The consolidated information is transmitted to the Department of Administrative Reforms and Public Grievances by NIC, every month.

Staff grievances are also dealt with promptly as and when they are brought to the notice of the concerned authorities. The suggestions received from the staff side are considered and implemented through the meetings of the Office Council, held under the JCM scheme. Staff grievances of general nature are also discussed in the meeting of senior officers held every month.

Facilitation counter is also functioning at Gate No. 6 of Krishi Bhavan, where the headquarters of the Ministry is located.

**O&M activity in the ministry**

The Internal Work Study Unit (IWSU) of the Ministry examines the proposals relating to organisational structure, fixation of staff strength, besides conducting organisational/simplification/work measurement studies. It also oversees matters relating to Organisations and Methods, administrative reforms, delegation of powers and records management.

During 1998-99, a study regarding restructuring of cadre of chemists in the Laboratory Wing of DMI was undertaken with a view to reorganising the laboratories for upgrading their status and performance and to improve upon the promotional prospects. A critical study was also undertaken to assess the manpower requirements in Cold Storage Division in the Directorate of Marketing and Inspection after repeal of Cold Storage Order. Work Measurement Studies of GC Section in Administration Wing and NSAP Wing have also been initiated.

An annual programme of O&M and administrative inspection of sections/desks was drawn and closely followed up with a view to ensuring that the provisions laid down in the Manual of Office Procedure and other instructions are followed scrupulously. A special drive was undertaken in the year to review and weed out the old records.

**Progressive use of Hindi during 1998-99**

Hindi Division of the Ministry has the nodal responsibility for effective implementation of the Official Language Act and Rules made thereunder. Efforts were made to increase the use of Hindi in the Ministry as well as its Attached/Subordinate Offices/ Institutes during the period under report. A Departmental Official Language Implementation Committee has been constituted under the chairmanship of Joint Secretary (Administration) which held its meetings regularly during the period under review. In the meetings suggestions were made to increase the use of Hindi and to remove the difficulties in the use of Hindi. Letters received in Hindi were replied in Hindi. Provisions of Section 3(3) of the Official Language Act, 1963 were complied with fully. During the year, General Orders, Circulars, Notifications, Cabinet notes on various programmes and papers laid on the tables of both the Houses of Parliament were issued bilingually in Hindi and English. Beside, some important documents such as Annual Reports, Performance Budget of the Ministry, matter pertaining to Consultative Committee Meetings, papers on Jawahar Rozgar Yojana, Panchayati Raj, IRDR and agenda and minutes of various conferences etc. were also issued bilingually in Hindi and English.

To encourage the officers and employees of the Ministry to use Hindi in their official work on a large scale, "Hindi Pakhwada" was organised from 1st September, 1998 to 15th September, 1998. "Hindi Day" was celebrated on 14th September, 1998. During this period 11 Hindi Competitions were organised and 47 prizes and certificates were given to the successful officers/employees.

As an incentive for writing original notes and drafts in Hindi a cash awards scheme is in operation in the

Ministry under which five prizes were given to the officers/employees during the period under report. All the prizes and certificates were distributed by the Minister in a function held on "Hindi Day". Some of the employees were trained in computer operation in Hindi by NIC during the period under report. Non-Hindi knowing employees were trained in Hindi. Similarly stenographers and typists were sponsored for training under the Hindi Teaching Scheme of the Government of India.

**International cooperation**

The Department of Rural Development continues to shoulder the important responsibility of a nodal Department for the two international organizations viz., Centre of Integrated Rural Development for Asia and the Pacific (CIRDAP) and the Afro-Asian Rural Reconstruction Organization (AARRO).

Currently CIRDAP is implementing 15 projects in various member countries relating to research, training, information and communication. These projects are at different stages of completion. Further, 12 projects concerning various facets of rural development are in the pipeline.

In addition CIRDAP also conducts various training courses, seminars and workshops on different aspects of Rural Development viz., Environment and Rural Development, Participatory Planning and Management, Micro-Enterprises and Micro Finance Programmes for Poverty Eradication, Participatory Monitoring and Evaluation, Disaster Management, Geographic Database Support to Population Activities, Project Formulation and Analysis for Rural Development, Watershed Development Programme with Special Focus on Drought Prone Areas, Capacity Building of Rural Development Functionaries for various Anti-Poverty Programmes etc.

CIRDAP continues to extend its expertise and technical know-how in conducting various programmes.

Similarly AARRO conducted a number of training programmes and workshops in different member countries on various subjects viz., Land and Water Management, Integrated Rural Development, Rural Women Entrepreneurship, People's Participation in Rural Development, Agrarian Reforms etc. AARRO also plans to conduct training programmes and workshops on different subjects like Agricultural Services, Cotton Production Technology, Vegetable Production, Fish Culture Development, Poultry Production and Health, Rural Development and Poverty Eradication, Integrating Gender Issues in Rural Development Projects etc.

Sh. Babagouda Patil, Minister of State (independent Charge) for Rural Areas and Employment, visited Philippines, Vietnam and Thailand from 26 June to 2nd July 1998, South Africa from 11 - 19 October 1998 and Israel from 30th October to 4th November 1998. The visits of the MOS (IC) aimed at, inter-alia, studying successfully implemented rural drinking water programmes, sharing experience/information on various rural development and poverty alleviation programmes/projects and discussing matters relating to agriculture and allied aspects.

Dr. P L S Reddy, Secretary (RE&PA) visited Bangkok from 14-18 September 98 to attend first session of the ESCAP Committee on Socio-Economic Measures in Rural and Urban Areas.

He also accompanied, MOS (IC) on his visit to Israel during the period 30th October to 4th November 1998 to discuss agricultural and allied matters.

Sh. M Shankar, Additional Secretary and Financial Adviser visited Ghana from 14-16 April 1998 to attend

45th Session of the Executive Committee meeting of AARRO. He also visited Switzerland from 23-25 September 1998 to attend the workshop on Logistics for Population Poverty Environment.

In addition Sh. Palat Mohandas, Sh. Satish Chandra, Smt. Sudha Pillai, Dr. J. S. Sarma, Sh. Anil Kumar and Sh. Sukumar Das, joint Secretaries visited Switzerland, Uganda, Japan, UK, Bangladesh, Malaysia and Bangkok in connection with various Meetings, Conferences and Workshops etc.

Delegates from Tanzania and Vietnam visited India to share experience/information and study various aspects of rural development programmes being implemented in the country.

Department for international Development (DFID), UK and the Ministry of Rural Areas and Employment held a series of meetings to identify areas of cooperation concerning different facets of rural development. The discussion during the meetings centred around how best the Ministry's programmes could be carried out to get the best value of money spent. Follow up actions on the recommendations/ decisions made during the meetings have already been initiated.

**National fund for rural development**

With a view to encourage individuals, corporate and non-corporate bodies to participate in the national effort for rural development, the National Fund for Rural Development (NFRD) was established in February, 1984. The Fund is managed by a Committee under the Chairmanship of the Prime Minister.

The donations made by all categories of taxpayers to the NFRD are deductible while computing taxable income under Sections 35 CCA and 80 GGA of the Income-Tax Act, 1961.

The NFRD projects can be executed through an implementing agency having the legal status of:

(a) An irrevocable public charitable trust registered under the Income Tax Act, 1961, or

(b) A society registered under the Societies Registration Act, 1860 or under any law corresponding to that Act in Force in any part of India, or

(c) A company incorporated under Section 25 of the Companies Act, 1956, or

(d) A Corporation established by or under a Central/State Act concerned with development of rural areas.

The donors while making donations may recommend their preference for the area or locality and the rural development programmes for which the donations may be utilised as also the implementing agency through which the programme may be undertaken and implemented. The recommendations, if any, of the donors are given due consideration to the extent deemed appropriate by the Government/Management Committee of the Fund.

During the year 1998-99 (up to 31.01.99) an amount of Rs. 50 lakhs has been received.

# 5

# Wastelands Development

### National wastelands development board

National Wastelands Development Board (NWDB) was established in 1985, under the Ministry of Environment and Forests, mainly to tackle the problem of degradation of lands, restoration of ecology and to meet the growing demand of fuel-wood and fodder at the national level. During Seventh Five Year Plan, the strategy adopted by National Wastelands Development Board was more on tree planting activities. In the year 1992, the Department of Wastelands Development under the Ministry of Rural Development (now Ministry of Rural Areas and Employment) was created and National Wastelands Development Board was placed under the Department. The Board was reconstituted in August 1992 and was made responsible for development of wastelands in non-forest areas, checking land degradation, putting such wastelands in the country into sustainable use and increasing bio-mass availability specially fuel-wood and fodder. After the composition of the 12th Lok Sabha, the National Wastelands Development Board has been reconstituted. The composition, role and functions of the NWDB are given in Annexure-XL.

So far the Board has met five times and the last meeting was held on 13th May 1997 under the Chairmanship of Minister for Rural Areas and

Employment. The sixth meeting is likely to be held shortly.

**Review of plan scheme 1989-99**

The National Wastelands Development Board (NWDB) was required to adopt a Mission Approach for enlisting people's participation, harnessing science and technology for planning and implementation of wastelands development.

The Department of Wastelands Development is implementing the following Schemes/Programmes for achieving its objectives :

I. Integrated Wastelands Development Project (IWDP) Scheme
II. Support to NGOs/VAs (Grants-in-Aid) Scheme
III. Technology Development, Extension and Training (TDET) Scheme
IV. Investment Promotional Scheme (IPS)
V. Wastelands Development Task Force (WDTF)

**Integrated wastelands development project scheme**

***Background***

This is a flagship scheme of the Department. This scheme has been under implementation since 1989-90, and has come to this Department along with the National Wastelands Development Board in July, 1992. From 1st April 1995, the scheme is being implemented on watershed basis under the new Guidelines for Watershed Development.

**Objectives**

The basic objective of this scheme is to take up integrated wastelands development based on village/ micro-watershed plans. These plans are prepared after taking into consideration the land capability, site condition and local needs of the people.

The scheme also helps in generation of employment in rural areas besides enhancing people's participation in the wastelands development programmes at all stages. This leads to equitable sharing of benefits and sustainable development.

**Activities**

The major activities taken up under the scheme are:

- In situ soil and moisture conservation measures like terracing, bunding, trenching, vegetative barriers etc.
- Planting and sowing of multipurpose trees, shrubs, grasses, legumes and pasture land development.
- Encouraging natural regeneration.
- Promotion of agro-forestry and horticulture.
- Wood substitution and fuel-wood conservation measures.
- Measures needed to disseminate technology.
- Training and extension and creating greater degree of awareness among the participants.
- Encouraging people's participation.

**Common guidelines for watershed development**

The Ministry of Rural Development (as it was known then) had set up a Technical Committee under the Chairmanship of Dr. C.H. Hanumantha Rao to go into the working of Drought Prone Areas Programme (DPAP) and Desert Development Programme (DDP). As a part of its recommendations, the Committee recommended that all area development schemes should be implemented on the basis of watershed approach. Based on recommendations of this Committee the Ministry, after wide ranging discussions with the State Governments, professionals, research institutions and NGOs finalised the Common Guidelines for Watershed Development. It was also decided that the "Integrated Wastelands Development Project" Scheme would be implemented on the basis of these Guidelines from April 1, 1995. The Common Watershed Guidelines envisage the bottom up approach whereby the User Groups/Self Help Groups themselves would decide their work programme which is to be integrated at the District level.

The strength of the guidelines lies in the decentralisation of decision-making process by involving local Panchayati Raj Institutions and people at grassroots level. It is an effort on part of the Government to remove the block that have delayed the process through which people's organisations for watershed management evolve and mature. In fact, the initiatives taken by the Department of Wastelands Development aim at establishing a system under which village people can actually involve themselves in planning, implementation and monitoring of Watershed Development Programme. In the preparation of the Watershed Development Plan, User Groups and other people directly depending on the watershed have to be actively involved. Another strength of these guidelines lies in the flexible approach followed in the method of release of funds, the area to be covered in each watershed as well as choice of components. Besides this the new guidelines also attempt to make the projects sustainable by establishing watershed development fund and involving people in deciding usufructs sharing mechanism on equitable basis. The funding under these guidelines is at the rate of Rs. 4000 per hectare.

Up to 31.12.98, 232 projects (128 under old guidelines and 104 under new guidelines) have been sanctioned under the scheme. During the Eighth Plan, an amount of Rs. 216 crores was released for development of about 3 lakh ha. of wastelands. During 1997-98, an amount of Rs. 74.50 crores was allocated in B.E. which was reduced to Rs. 50 crores at R.E. stage. During 1998-99, an allocation of Rs. 82.10 crores have been earmarked for development of 1.37 lakh ha. of wastelands.

**Physical and financial achievements**

Physical and Financial Achievements under IWDP Scheme are as follows:-

| *Year* | *Physical Target* | *(in ha.) Achievements** | *Financial Target* | *(In crores) Achievements*** |
|---|---|---|---|---|
| 1992-93 | 15,000 | 27,000 | 16.83 | 16.83 |
| 1993-94 | 57,956 | 50,000 | 40.72 | 44.49 |
| 1994-95 | 65,000 | 65,000 | 49.20 | 53.04 |
| 1995-96 | 58,000 | 58,000 | 49.50 | 51.00 |
| 1996-97 | 84,000 | 84,000 | 50.50 | 50.80 |
| Total 8th plan | 2,79,956 | 2,84,000 | 206.75 | 216.76 |
| 1997-98 | 1,27,000 | 90,000 | 74.50 | 53.95 |
| 1998-99 | 1,37,000 | 66,000 | 82.10 | 39.98 |

**Support to NGOs/VAs**

Under this Scheme 100% grant is provided to registered voluntary agencies, cooperatives, mahila mandals, yuva mandals and other similar organisations for undertaking work directly or indirectly, encouraging afforestation and wastelands development. Projects meant for awareness raising, appropriate technology application, training, extension and publicity are also considered under this scheme.

During the Eighth Five Year Plan, 234 projects were sanctioned in favour of voluntary agencies and a sum of Rs. 13.75 crores was released to VAs for development of about 20,000 hectares of wastelands.

All projects under the scheme are now being sanctioned by CAPART. The Department has transferred all fresh applications and ongoing projects under the scheme to CAPART except 75 cases which are being implemented by cooperatives and trusts etc. During 1998-99 an amount of Rs. 2 crores has been kept for development of 2,650 ha. of wastelands. An amount of Rs. 1 crore has been released to CAPART for implementation of the scheme.

**Technology development extension and training scheme**

***Background***

Technology support is very critical for the success of land based programme, more so in the wastelands development programme, which has been traditionally a neglected area. Realising this, it was decided to have a separate Technology Development Extension and Training Scheme in order to develop suitable technologies for the reclamation of wastelands for sustained production of food, fuel-wood, fodder etc. The Scheme was approved in February 1994 and became operational from 1994-95. The basic idea is to develop at least one agro-forestry model for each of 131 Agro-climatic Zones covering the entire country with priority for 241 Districts having more than 5% wastelands wherein wastelands have been identified and mapping completed by NRSA on 1:50,000 scale using satellite imagery data.

**Objectives**

The objectives of this Scheme include :

- Development of data base for planning and sustainable development of wastelands;
- Operationalisation of appropriate, cost effective and proven technologies for development of various

categories of wastelands specially problem lands affected by soil erosion, land degradation, salinity, alkalinity, waterlogging etc;

- Implementation of location specific pilot projects/ demonstration models including pisciculture, duckery, apiculture, domesticated animals and birds etc;
- Dissemination of research findings and appropriate technologies for promoting wastelands development;
- Evaluation of the impact, and replication of these models to larger areas; and
- Organisation of publicity, awareness campaigns, seminars/conferences, circulation of handouts/ extension materials etc.

The scheme is being implemented through ICAR, State Agricultural Universities, Government and private institutions having adequate institutional framework and organisational backup. Successful implementation of this scheme is expected to bridge the gap between the existing technologies and the need relevant to the latest situation.

Under the scheme 100 per cent central grant is admissible to implement the projects on wastelands owned by Government/Government Institutions, Public Sector Undertakings including Universities and or panchayats from which the benefits would flow to the community. In the case of projects executed on wastelands of private farmers/corporate bodies, the cost of the project is required to be shared in a 60:40 ratio between the Department of Wastelands Development and the farmer/corporate body. Activities undertaken include:

- Testing of various agro-forestry models in different agro-climatic zones of the country.
- Testing cost effective technologies for increasing productivity of waterlogged/saline/alkaline soils.
- Bridging the technological gaps in the reclamation of wastelands belonging to the Government, community and private lands.
- Promotion of agro-forestry models with neem and bamboo as the main forestry species.
- Promotion of medicinal and herbal plants to develop non-forest wastelands.
- Composite technology for water- harvesting, treatment of degraded land through vermiculture, micorhiza and bio-pesticides.
- Development of technology for Jojoba plantations, in arid and semi-arid areas through Israeli collaboration.

During the Eighth Five Year Plan, 66 projects with total investment of Rs. 828 lakhs have been sanctioned under the scheme. During 1997-98 an amount of Rs. 5.60 crores has been spent for the project implementation. An amount of Rs. 800 lakhs has been allocated under the scheme to cover 3000 ha. of area during 1998-99. So far (up to 31.12.98) an amount of Rs. 7.86 crores has been spent under the scheme.

**Investment promotional scheme**

The Scheme was launched in 1994-95 in order to stimulate involvement of the corporate sector/financial institutions etc., to pool in resources for development of non-forest wastelands.

The principal objectives of the scheme are

- To facilitate/attract/channelise/mobilise resources from financial institutions, banks, corporate bodies and individual for development of wastelands in non-forest areas belonging to Central and State Governments, Panchayats, village communities and private farmers;

- To facilitate production and flow of additional biomass including farm forestry products used as raw material for different types of industries and horticulture/commercial plantations.

Under this scheme, central promotional grant/ subsidy to the general category (individual/groups) is limited to Rs. 25 lakhs or 25% of on farm development activities whichever is less, subject to the condition that the promoters' contribution in the project shall not be less than 25% of the project cost. The quantum of subsidy in the case of small farmers is 30% and in the case of marginal farmers and SC/ST farmers it is 50% of the project cost on farm development activities. The promoters' contribution in the case of small farmers is 10% of the project cost whereas it is 'nil' in the case of marginal and SC/ST farmers. The projects promoted by Nationalised Banks, Regional Rural Banks, Land Development Banks and Cooperative Banks are eligible for promotional grants/subsidy under the scheme.

So far, only four projects have been sanctioned under the scheme during 1994-95 and 1995-96. The scheme could not be implemented during 1996-97 and 199798 as the scheme was being restructured on the advice of Standing Committee of Parliament for Urban and Rural Development to make it more popular and broad based for implementation during the Ninth Five Year Plan.

An amount of Rs. 160 lakhs has been allocated under the scheme to cover the physical target of 100 ha. during 1998-99. The physical and financial progress during 1998-99 (up to 31 December, 1998) is nil as the revised guidelines for the scheme were approved and circulated only in the month of August, 1998. 10 projects involving release of about Rs. 100 lakhs are under consideration of this Department. Efforts are being made to obtain more projects and utilise the full budgetary provision under the scheme during 1998-99.

#### Wastelands development task force

This Scheme is being implemented through ex-servicemen for development of 1200 hectares of wastelands in the ravines of Chambal in Morena district of Madhya Pradesh since 1994. The objective of the scheme is to provide disciplined force for regeneration of wastelands through afforestation including

- Insitu soil and moisture conservation;
- Plantation and its protection;
- Employment of ex-servicemen.

The Force consist of 300 ex-servicemen under the command of the Territorial Army and Group of 15 Army/Territorial Army Personnel. Up to 1997-98 the Force has developed 824 hectares of wastelands and the remaining 376 hectares will be developed during 1998-99. The scheme has been discontinued during Ninth Five Year Plan but the existing project at Morena will continue to be funded. The project is likely to be completed by 31st March, 1999.

#### Monitoring and evaluation

There is an in-built provision for monitoring of the projects sanctioned under various schemes of the Department. The projects are monitored through Quarterly Progress Reports/Half Yearly Progress Reports/Annual Reports which are submitted by nodal agencies/PIAs etc. In addition to this, the Department is ensuring regular monitoring and evaluation of the projects through a panel of experts maintained for this purpose. In addition Area Officers appointed for various States also make periodical visits to the States to review rural development programme including Wastelands Development Projects. In certain cases officers of the Department also make on the site inspections. The performance of the projects under various schemes is evaluated as follows:

**Integrated wastelands development programme**

Independent evaluators are nominated during alternate monsoon years and project implementation/ performance is monitored on the basis of concurrent evaluation. On the basis of the evaluation reports, necessary mid-term corrective measures are suggested and shortcomings, if any, are conveyed to the Project Implementing Agencies for necessary rectifications.

**Support to NGOs/VAs (Grants-in-aid)**

The implementation of the projects by voluntary agencies is regularly monitored. The projects are evaluated by independent evaluators before release of second or subsequent instalment of grants. Further assistance is provided to those voluntary agencies only who have utilised the previous instalment satisfactorily.

**Technology development extension and training scheme**

These projects are being implemented by Research Institutions, ICAR centres, reputed NGOs and universities. These projects are also evaluated by independent evaluators during alternate years.

**Monitoring and evaluation cell under state governments**

All the State Governments have been requested to constitute State Level Monitoring and Evaluation Cell under the Chairmanship of Additional Chief Secretary/ Agriculture Production Commissioner etc., for review and evaluation of various watershed development programmes in the States. The Monitoring and Evaluation Cell will carry out, from time to time, qualitative studies relating to implementation of all area development programmes and submit these to the respective divisions in the Ministry of Rural Areas and Employment. It has been decided that funds for implementation of the watershed development programme shall be released on the basis of findings of these field studies and on the recommendation of the State Monitoring and Evaluation Cell. The Cell will be permanent in nature and constituted by drawing staff from different disciplines. The Department of Wastelands Development will provide funds for hiring of consultants, technical experts and academic organisations for undertaking field studies etc.

**Other import activites**

**Review of plan schemes**

The activities of the Department and the progress made under Plan Schemes of the Department are regularly reviewed by senior officers. Additional Secretary (WD) reviews the progress under various plan schemes every fortnight at senior officers meeting. In addition, Secretary (RD and WD) reviews the working of the Department during the meeting of the Senior Officers, held from time to time.

**International cooperation**

In order to mobilize resources for development of wastelands in addition to meagre domestic resources which are inadequate, special efforts were made for procuring external aid for problem areas like rain shadow areas of Deccan Plateau, slip prone areas of Himalayas etc., for which well-formulated proposals need to be prepared. The Department has initiated steps to harness financial resources through foreign agencies and at present Five projects in different States are being implemented with the assistance of foreign donors. The details of these projects are given in Annexure-XLII.

The Department has also received a few proposals from different States for foreign assistance and these projects are under examination.

**Eswaran committee report on training**

Under the Common Guidelines for Watershed Development there is an inbuilt provision for imparting training to PIAs and others for use of participatory Other Important Activities techniques to enable the community in the preparation and approval of micro watershed plans.

During field visits it was observed that a comprehensive strategy for capacity building is still lacking and there is a pressing need for action in this area. The Government of India accordingly constituted a Committee on Training under the Chairmanship of Shri V.B. Eswaran (Retd. Secretary, Government of India) to go into all the aspects of training under the Common Guidelines for Watershed Development. The Committee has since submitted its report to the Government. The recommendations of the Committee have been accepted by the Government. The Committee has identified the various levels which are to be trained and module of training for each level. All the State Governments have been requested to identify nodal training institutions for imparting training for watershed development. A scheme for financial support to training institutions in various states is also under consideration.

**High level committee**

The recommendation of the High Level Committee on

Wastelands Development under the Chairmanship of Shri Mohan Dharia has already been accepted except recommendation relating to Creation of Department of Land Resources which is separately under consideration of the Government. The concerned Ministries/ Departments of the Central Government have been asked to take necessary action on these recommendations. The recommendations requiring action by the State Governments have been referred to them for necessary action.

**National workshop on watershed approach for managing degraded lands in India**

National Workshop on Watershed Approach for Managing Degraded Lands in India : Challenges for the 21st Century was held on 27-29 April, 1998 in Vigyan Bhawan, New Delhi. The Workshop was held with technical collaboration of Department of International Development (DFID), UK and Overseas Development Institute (ODI), London. The Workshop was attended by the representatives of Central Government/State Governments, reputed NGOs, research institutions, training institutions and foreign donor agencies. The Workshop has given useful recommendations which are under examination.

**Regional level workshop**

A regional level workshop was convened by DRDA, Madurai on 4th September, 1998. The Workshop was attended by representatives from Central Government/ State Governments, reputed NGOs and training institutions. The recommendations of the workshop have been accepted.

**Administrative setup of department of Wastelands development**

After the formation of the new Government at the

Centre, Shri Babagouda Patil took over as Minister of State (independent Charge) in the Ministry of Rural Areas and Employment on 19.03.98. Shri N.C. Saxena, Secretary (RD-WD) continued as Secretary of the Department till 5.2.1999. Shri S.B. Mohapatra, Additional Secretary (WD) and Shri Kuldip Rai, joint Secretary (A) are functioning in the Department. Machinery for redressal of public grievances has been set up in the Department and Shri Kuldip Rai, joint Secretary has been declared as Director of Grievances for redressal of public grievances.

The organisation chart of the Department of Wastelands Development is at Page No. 120.

**Progressive use of Hindi during 1998-99**

With the appointment of Assistant Director (Official Language) a separate Hindi Section has been set up in the Department. Efforts were made for effective implementation of Official Language Act and rules framed thereunder. The following steps have been taken to ensure implementation of Official Language Policy in the Department :-

(a) The Official Language Implementation Committee has been constituted in the Department under the Chairmanship of joint Secretary (Admn.)

(b) To encourage the employees of the Department to use Hindi in their official work, an incentive scheme for noting and drafting in Hindi was launched during the year. Hindi Day was celebrated on 14th September, 1998. On this occasion a message from Minister of State (IC) for Rural Areas and Employment was circulated to employees of the Department. An essay writing competition was also conducted and prizes and certificates were given to the participants. A five day Hindi Workshop was also organised in the Department. The provision of Section 3(3) of the Official Language Act 1963 was fully complied with.

(c) During the year, general orders, circulars, letters and papers required to be laid on the table of both the Houses of Parliament were issued bilingually.

**Computerization in department of Wastelands development**

*Local area network*

All the Programme Divisions in the Department have been put under Local Area Network (LAN) which is also connected with the Ministry of Rural Areas Employment located in Krishi Bhawan. Data on each Programme is now available to Monitoring Division for coordination. A home page has also been prepared indicating the detailed information regarding the programmes of the Department of Wastelands Development under the Ministry of Rural Areas and Employment and has been put on INTERNET for users world wide.

**Website for department of Wastelands**

Development A web site for the Department of Wastelands Development has since been created and can be visited on INTERNET at the web site - www.nic.in/wasteland.